"There may, somewhere out there, be better books written by real soldiers. But no one can ever have produced a more honest one than *In the Company of Heroes*." — *Fort Worth Star-Telegram*

"CWO Mike Durant's heroism should be read by every American. His riveting story epitomizes the courage and leadership of the members of our military forces, and the sacrifices they make for all of us—and the terrible impact these sacrifices have on their families. I was thrilled and moved by this book." — *Ross Perot*

"Michael Durant is a genuine hero, and a great American patriot. Miraculously, he lived to tell the story of one of the most harrowing experiences that a human being could possibly undergo. Truly he was in the company of many great heroes in that savage battle in Somalia on October, 3, 1993. But this book is about far more than one battle. It is about the kind of men and women who serve our nation; the kind of Americans who understand the price that has been paid for our freedom and liberties, and the resolve and sacrifice that are required to maintain them for the future. This is a must read."
—General Carl Stiner, U.S. Army (Ret.), coauthor of the number-one *New York Times* bestseller *Shadow Warriors: Inside the Special Forces*

"Hats off to Mike Durant's gripping first-person account of his Somalian combat and captivity. He never lost hope, and like his Night Stalker comrades, this *Black Hawk Down* pilot never quit. His inspiring true story should be required reading for all Special Operators, and anyone who wants to understand this breed of courageous, devoted warrior."
—Major John L. Plaster, U.S. Army Special Forces (Ret.), author of *SOG: The Secret Wars of America's Commandos in Vietnam*

continued . . .

"*In the Company of Heroes* is the heroic narrative of a brave and self-less soldier performing his duties the only way he knew how—with honor and respect for his country. This is a significant account of men at war, but more important, it is a personal account of duties performed in combat, of personal courage and an unbreakable will to survive. Mike Durant's story, told so well in these pages, is a must read for those who send troops to fight, those who lead them, and first and foremost, those who, like Durant, take the fight to the enemy."
—General Gordon R. Sullivan, U.S. Army (Ret.)

"The story remains taut, and the prose evokes both the chaos of combat and the anxiety of confinement . . . a revealing portrait of the human face of war." —*Publishers Weekly*

"*In the Company of Heroes* is much more than Durant's story of being a prisoner of war. While that would have made an excellent book in and of itself, Durant goes further, giving the reader insights into the rest of his military career. *In the Company of Heroes* is exceptionally written and gives the reader profound insight into the ugliest parts of war. It is a story that everyone should read and learn from—not only about war, but also about the human spirit and its willingness to survive in even the harshest of situations."
—Bookreporter.com

IN THE COMPANY OF HEROES

IN THE COMPANY OF HEROES

MICHAEL J. DURANT
CHIEF WARRANT OFFICER 4 (USA, RET.)

WITH STEVEN HARTOV

NEW AMERICAN LIBRARY

New American Library
Published by New American Library, a division of
Penguin Group (USA) Inc., 375 Hudson Street, New York, New York 10014, U.S.A.
Penguin Books,Ltd, 80 Strand, London WC2R 0RL, England
Penguin Books Australia Ltd, 250 Camberwell Road, Camberwell, Victoria 3124, Australia
Penguin Books Canada Ltd, 10 Alcorn Avenue, Toronto, Ontario, Canada M4V 3B2
Penguin Books (N.Z.) Ltd, Cnr Rosedale and Airborne Roads, Albany, Auckland 1310, New Zealand

Penguin Books Ltd, Registered Offices: 80 Strand, London WC2R 0RL, England

Published by New American Library, a division of Penguin Group (USA) Inc. This is an authorized reprint
of a hardcover edition published by G. P. Putnam's Sons. For information address G. P. Putnam's Sons, a
division of Penguin Group (USA) Inc., 375 Hudson Street, New York, NY 10014.

First New American Library Printing, May 2004
10 9 8 7 6 5 4 3 2 1

Grateful acknowledgment is made for permission to reprint the following:
Lyrics from "Hell's Bells" © 1980, J. Albert & Sons, Pty. Ltd. Used by permission.

Lyrics from "Seminole Wind" by John Anderson. Alamo Music Corp on behalf of itself and Holmes
Creek Music. All rights reserved. Used by permission.

Lyrics from "Rooster" (written by Jerry Cantrell) reprinted with permission of Buttnugget Publishing, ©
1992 Buttnugget Publishing.

Except where otherwise credited, photos have been graciously provided to the author by people on
active duty who wish to remain anonymous.

 REGISTERED TRADEMARK—MARCA REGISTRADA

New American Library ISBN: 0-451-21060-3
The Library of Congress has catalogued the hardcover edition of this title as follows:

Durant, Michael J.
   In the company of heroes / Michael J. Durant with Steven Hartov.
      p.   cm.
      1. Operation Restore Hope, 1992–1993—Personal narratives,
   American.   2. Durant, Michael J., date.   3. Black Hawk
   (Military transport helicopter).   I. Hartov, Steven.
   II. Title.
   DT407.42.D87   2003   2003043196
   967.7305'c—dc21

Designed by Brian Mulligan

Printed in the United States of America

Frontispiece: Detail of Mike Durant's marked-up kneeboard map of Mogadishu, August–October 1993

Acknowledgments

I WOULD LIKE to take this opportunity to thank Ross Perot, Al Zuckerman, my editor Doug Grad, and all the great staff at Penguin Group (USA) who helped turn the concept of this book into a reality. I'd also like to thank my writer, Steven Hartov, for producing an extremely great read, and for the laughs we had in the process. Thanks to the crew chiefs, maintainers, armament dogs, and support elements that do the work to make flying possible. Every time an aircraft lifts off, it does so as a result of your hard work and dedication. To the customers out there in the community, past and present, I appreciate having had the privilege to work with you and to say that I was once a part of such a prestigious band of brothers. To my commanders, whose leadership and professionalism served as a model for us all. To the crew of Super 64: Ray Frank, Bill Cleveland, and Tommy Field; and to Randy Shughart and Gary Gordon for sacrificing it all so that others might live. To the families of the fallen, for your graciousness and compassion throughout such a trying ordeal. Stephanie, your letter speaks volumes about the people who stand behind the soldiers that we send off to make war on our enemies; thank you for allowing me to share your thoughts. A special thanks to Gerry, Dan, Jane, Stan, Wendy, Cliff, Clay, Brian, Father Baker, Nick, Tom, and my parents for the pictures, the fact-checking, and a lifetime of unwavering support. To my family and my children for giving purpose to it all, and most of all to my wife, Lisa, for the late-night sanity checks, the encouragement, the great ideas, and the love.

The acts described in these pages appear unique in many ways, but they have been repeated throughout our proud history in the countless displays of courage and sacrifice that are the hallmarks of the American patriot. This work is dedicated to those patriots, the millions of men and women who have served this great country and those who continue to serve our nation so valiantly.

Introduction

I FIRST MET MICHAEL DURANT in April 1997, at Fort Campbell, Kentucky, when I was researching my book *Black Hawk Down*. Durant was still an active-duty pilot with the 160th Special Operations Aviation Regiment, a unit with a top-security clearance, and it had taken me more than a year to get permission to interview him.

When I arrived at Fort Campbell, I was surprised to find myself with not one, but three public affairs officers as escorts. They introduced me to Durant, a fit man with ramrod posture and a very serious manner, and then asked if we minded if they all sat in on the interview. It seems they weren't worried about a security breach; they just wanted to hear Durant tell his story.

No wonder. Durant's experience is one of the most harrowing in the history of the American military, and one of the most compelling ever told. Shot down over Mogadishu, injured in a hard crash landing, briefly rescued by two brave Delta Force operators, Gary Gordon and Randy Shughart, who died protecting him (and who were awarded posthumous Medals of Honor, the first since the Vietnam War), beset by an angry mob, stripped, and beaten, and certain of his own pending death, only to be spared, carried off into captivity, shot, publicly interrogated, and finally, after eleven days, released. The pilot's story was about being thrown into a terrible, exhausting extreme of human experience, and somehow coming back alive. We all listened spellbound.

In a calm, deliberate voice, Durant unfolded the tale. He clearly remembered every detail of the event. Given the lives that were lost around him, Shughart, Gordon, his copilot Ray Frank, his crew chiefs Bill Cleveland and Tommy Field, Durant felt compelled to get the story straight—indeed, he told me that the only reason he had agreed to talk to me was his concern that the incident be recorded correctly. In captivity he had kept notes secretly scribbled in the margins of a Bible given him by visiting members of the International Red Cross. His determination to remember his story had begun then, lying in pain on a cot in some dark quarter of Mogadishu, not knowing if he would ever see home again.

When he did get home, Durant found himself in an awkward and often painful predicament. He was celebrated as a hero, but he didn't feel like one.

"All I did was get shot down," he told me.

The real heroes were the men who died trying to save him, yet Durant was the one who got to come home and get on with his life. There were offers for books and movie deals, some of which rankled the families of those whose men didn't make it. The army considered Durant's performance under terrifying circumstances to have been a model for soldiers in captivity. Durant did a dignified and admirable job of coping with it all, of acknowledging the heartfelt admiration of his countrymen, never failing to downplay his own heroism and salute that of the men who fought to save his life. In light of it all, it's little wonder that he took such care in telling the story to me. When I went to Somalia and found the man who had supervised Durant's captivity, Abdullahi Hassan, known as "Firimbi," he confirmed Durant's story down to the smallest detail, and was filled with admiration for the American helicopter pilot.

In writing *Black Hawk Down*, I was faced with the challenge of blending hundreds of stories, and by necessity Durant's, like the others, was reduced to fairly summary form. I am very pleased that he has the opportunity in this book to tell the whole thing in his own words. Having once sat and listened to him myself, I can tell you that you are in for an adventure.

Mark Bowden
January 2003

A Note from Michael J. Durant

THERE ARE MANY REASONS why I decided to write this story. I felt compelled to do so from the beginning, yet put it off for some reason. Knowing well the pain suffered by those involved, I thought that perhaps it might be best to let it become a not-so-distant memory. I have written it at last, because so many people have asked me to do so, and more important, so that when my children are old enough to read it they will have their father's account of what happened.

This story is about loyalty, duty, honor, and love: loyalty to your comrades, your unit and your country; dedication to duty; honor in the face of extreme adversity; and love for a small boy, very far away, whose life together with his father had only just begun. It is a story about doing what you know is right in your heart, despite what others might think or say. It is about never giving up, ever, under any circumstances.

This story is, of course, all based on my perspective. Therefore, some may remember these events slightly differently. Hopefully, the discrepancies will be only minor, and if not, rest assured that no intentional deviation from the truth is in these pages.

On the morning of October 4, 1993, I swore allegiance to the truth, no matter the consequences. It is one of the most important promises made to God that I have kept.

"It is not the critic who counts, not the one who points out how the strong man stumbled, or where the doer of deeds could have done better. The credit belongs to the man who is actually in the arena; whose face is marred by the dust and sweat and blood; who strives valiantly; who errs and comes up short again and again; who knows the great enthusiasms, the great devotion and spends himself in a worthy cause; who at the best, knows in the end the triumph of high achievement; and who, at worst if he fails, at least fails while daring greatly; so that his place shall never be with those cold and timid souls who know neither victory or defeat."

THEODORE ROOSEVELT
SORBONNE, PARIS
APRIL 23, 1910

IN THE COMPANY OF HEROES

PROLOGUE

**Somalia
October 3, 1993**

IT WAS A PERFECT DAY FOR PRAYER, a bright and tranquil Sunday morning. The skies and seas were polished blue, soft winds bore silver-edged clouds, and the coastal sands gleamed white like ribbons of salt. It would have been easy to believe in some sort of heavenly power.

But for most of us in Task Force Ranger, the helicopter pilots and our crews, the eager young Rangers and squint-eyed Special Forces, the muscled armorers and whiz-kid intelligence analysts, these autumn mornings in Mogadishu all ran together. A Sabbath day felt hardly different from any other, blending into the workweek like the steamy, bleached hues of the African vista. Sure, a few guys knelt before the army chaplain with heads bowed, praying for salvation.

The rest of us prayed for another mission.

We had come here to do a job, dispatched by our government to stem the rampant corruption that was bleeding Somalia dry and decimating its people. Already a famine of Old Testament proportions had swept the country, starving more than 300,000 Somalis to death. Now a vicious warlord, Mohamed Farrah Aidid, had stormed into the power vacuum, leading a coalition of thugs called the Somali National Alliance. A sand dune buccaneer, he was pillaging our humanitarian aid and selling it off for a profit, while cold-bloodedly murdering any and all who tried to interfere and stop him.

Ours wasn't the first protective force on the ground or in the skies over Somalia. For over a year, U.S. Army troops and Special Forces, Navy SEALs, and Marines had been conducting operations here in support of United Nations relief efforts. When our unit arrived, Operation Restore Hope was already in full swing, with the men of Joint Special Operations Forces–Somalia capturing caches of small arms, destroying illicit ordnance depots, and forging alliances with friendly indigenous forces. Our comrades had felt that their efforts were at last turning the tables on starvation and allowing the Somalis free access to the U.N. relief provisions.

But back in June, Aidid's gunmen had suddenly ambushed and slaughtered twenty-four Pakistani soldiers assigned to UNOSOM, United Nations Operations–Somalia. American AC-130 gunships were sent in, blasting Aidid's weapons-storage facilities, SNA tank compounds, and even his personal propaganda station, "Radio Mogadishu." The warlord himself was driven underground, yet the effect of the interdiction turned out to be somewhat like stomping a boot on a hornet's nest. SNA attacks swelled against U.S. and U.N. personnel and installations, and Secretary of Defense Les Aspin ordered deployment of our Joint Special Operations Task Force. The JSOTF was a quick-reaction outfit composed of U.S. Army Rangers, Special Forces, Special Ops helicopters, Air Force special tactics personnel, and Navy SEALs. It was code-named "Task Force Ranger," and our mission was to capture Mohamed Aidid and all of his key henchmen and turn them over to UNOSOM forces.

To most of us, the job seemed pretty straightforward and simple.

Mogadishu was Tombstone, and we were Wyatt Earp. We were going to clean up the town.

I ran that morning, as I did on most mornings. After my standard breakfast of grapefruit slices and oatmeal, I got out there with a bunch of guys from our 160th Special Operations Aviation Regiment (Airborne)—the U.S. Army's only special ops aviation unit that handles "high-risk" missions—and we jogged the three miles around the Mogadishu Airport perimeter. The intense summer swelter had receded, so it was an easy run. Most of us wore training shorts and T-shirts, but there wasn't much more than a chain-link fence separating us from the Somalis, so someone always slung a fully loaded MP-5 submachine gun over a shoulder, its stock banging against his spine as we loped.

Once we were outside the Task Force Ranger compound, a fenced-in area of battered old hangars, mobile barracks trailers, and sandbag emplacements, the airfield seemed to host a convention of international troops. The Russian pilots who flew relief missions for the U.N. were all out-of-shape vodka drinkers who grinned and waved as we passed, looking us over as if relieved that the Cold War had never gone hot. The Italian *carbinieri* lounged back in their easy chairs and smirked from beneath their sunglasses, while the French paratroopers raised their noses, as if we personally had desecrated Paris with McDonald's franchises.

Already the sun was hard and slicing through the morning haze, a humid, steady breeze coming in off the nearby Indian Ocean. One thing for sure, I was going to go home in great physical condition and with a suntan to envy. I was hoping to run the Marine Corps marathon in Washington, D.C., as I'd done the year before. My wife had come up to watch that one and brought along our baby boy, Joey. I had swelled with pride when I crossed the finish line, even though it took me days to recover. This year, chances were slim that we'd be out of the "Mog"—like the *Mog* in Mogadishu—in time for the race, but I wanted to be ready for it, just in case.

There was another purpose for PT, of course—to stay physically tuned up and ready. You never knew when a two-hour mission would turn into ten or more. Guys played volleyball out on the compound asphalt or lifted weights in the makeshift gym, because it was always a "hurry up and wait" situation and you had to keep active. You might be doing nothing for hours, or even days, and then all of a sudden you'd be "jumping through your ass" to go out and fly a mission.

After my run and a quick shower, I pulled on my desert flight coveralls and settled down in the shade of a small tree, just outside the crumbling building that held the JOC—the Joint Operations Center. As Flight Lead and a Standardization Instructor Pilot, I was planning an aerial gunnery training mission for the next day. Somewhat like the old "squadron leaders" of earlier airpower days, I was responsible for keeping my element razor sharp. That consisted of four Blackhawk assault helicopters, escorted by one SAR (Search and Rescue) bird and two AH-6 Little Bird gunships. Most of our Blackhawks were new aircraft, the latest Sikorsky model; twin engine MH-60Ls with myriad special mission equipment upgrades. Under the right conditions, they were capable of speeds up to 193 knots and a service ceiling in excess of 20,000 feet. But with our load of eighteen Rangers and four crewmen on board, the best we could do was about 160 knots. The Blackhawk had become the workhorse of Army aviation, with the capability to haul 9,000 pounds of external payload on the cargo hook or an equivalent amount of cargo inside. It could be set up for a wide variety of missions, and in Somalia, we were configured to carry the maximum number of troops. But we could also be called upon to fly our Blackhawks in an attack helicopter profile, using them as gun platforms, so that was why we needed to train. We could change configurations in a matter of minutes, so for gunnery practice, we'd be going out the next day with a pair of the MH-60Ls, each armed with a 19-shot 2.75-inch rocket pod, a wing-mounted 30mm M-230 chain gun, and two 7.62mm window-mounted miniguns, all fixed forward. We would select a remote and desolate range

area, set out some old tires as targets, and practice running fire, honing those skills that can deteriorate even in combat conditions.

I was a Chief Warrant Officer–3, but as Flight Lead I sometimes
felt more like a logistics manager: conducting the briefing, writing
the operations orders, setting up ranges, attending to safety issues, getting clearances from commanders, making sure the ammo was laid
on and the crews ready. I never saw it as mundane and I truly enjoyed
it, and it was all necessary prep work for the biggest thrill ride of a
lifetime: aerial gunnery. We were finalizing our plan when I caught
the flash of a human form rushing by and heard the slap of boot soles
and an urgent warning.

"Possible mission developing downtown."

I raised my chin, and I think it was the first time that I really
smelled Somalia. I hadn't taken in much of that before, but there it
was: the heavy stench of fetid garbage, mixed with the nostril-flaring
fumes of JP-4 jet fuel. We were right on the ocean, the wind usually
blowing from the southwest, carrying the brine of the sea. Coffee was
constantly brewing in the JOC, and it blended with the cold con-
coctions from the mess hall, floating above a thin layer of urine and
feces fog from the Porta Potties. There were no sewage facilities, so
shower water puddled on the ground, stagnating in the sun. There
were men who showered rarely, or to little effect, carrying a halo of
dried sweat like the infamous Pigpen of "Peanuts" comic strip fame.
Our Task Force members were fitness freaks, so few of them smoked,
but most chewed tobacco of some kind and the compound was
stained with stinking clots of brown juice, like puddles of blood after
a pitched battle.

I didn't smoke or chew or drink, but I did have a bottle of Jack
Daniel's whiskey stowed in my rucksack, to be swigged in celebration
when we finally captured Mohamed Aidid. I didn't know then that
I'd never get a chance to crack it open.

Inside the JOC, Brigadier General Bill Garrison, the commander
of Task Force Ranger, paced as the leaders of his "cells" assembled.

He was a man who engendered great respect and he looked like something out of a Hollywood movie, with his bristle-steel hair, pilot's Ray-Bans, and a cigar clenched in his teeth that he rarely lit. Element leaders hustled in from volleyball, their bunks, or the latrine. Cliff Wolcott was there, a 160th CWO like me and Flight Lead of the assault force. I represented the blocking force of four Blackhawks assigned to carry a company of Rangers, who were commanded by Captain Mike Steele. My own 160th battalion commander was there too, Lieutenant Colonel Tom Matthews, as well as the commander of the exfiltration ground element, Lieutenant Colonel Danny McKnight. The mission was profiled as a "snatch and grab," and the point men of the assault would be the special operators. They weren't just Special Forces, they were Delta, and there is no other military unit in the world as highly trained, and with an attitude to match it. Just working with them swelled the chests of the younger Rangers, who often sneered, "We're just the road guards for Delta." But they sneered it with great pride.

The mission profile wasn't new. We'd practiced it more times than I could count and had already executed it six times inside the city, three at night and three by daylight. We hadn't encountered much resistance, just some inaccurate small-arms fire and a few Rocket-Propelled Grenade rounds, but no aircraft had been damaged and no ground troops seriously injured. It was like a well-rehearsed ballet of zipping helos and lightning infantry. First, Little Bird gunships would take out any heavy weapons at the target. Next, Wolcott's assault flight would take in the Delta operators to make the snatch. Just behind them, I would bring in my Rangers as the blocking force, and then the entire Task Force would withdraw with its shocked and blindfolded prisoners. The only factors that differed with each of these missions were the target details: Who, Where, and When.

Today, the targets were two of Mohamed Aidid's "top tier" lieutenants, Omar Salad and Abdi "Qeybdid" Hassan Awale, major players in the warlord's Habr Gidr clan. An indigenous intel asset had fingered them inside a building in the "Black Sea," the roughest part of town just next to the Bakara Market, and already a P3 Navy Orion surveillance plane was high overhead, its cameras focusing on the target area. The large video monitors in the JOC flickered with images of the Olympic Hotel and Hawlwadig Road. The area teemed with people, rusty bicycles, and battered old cars hissing steam from overheated radiators, or abandoned and stripped down to the frames. It made me think of a flea market, inside an auto wreck yard, inside a suburban slum.

For a second, something crawled up my stomach. The men and birds of our 160th SOAR(A) had been nicknamed "The Night Stalkers," because utter darkness was the environment in which we thrived. The technology of night-vision equipment had become so advanced that we could fly, assault, insert, and withdraw, seeing all without being seen, until it was way too late for the opposition to react. We owned the night, as if it was broad daylight. But this *was* broad daylight, and although we'd successfully executed six previous missions, we had lost the element of surprise.

In the bustling JOC the mission was developing very rapidly. We couldn't wait to see if our targets would just hang around, drinking tea and bullshitting about women and the weather. We couldn't hope to have a CIA asset wander into the target building, snap a covert photo of the party, and hustle back out with a one hundred percent confirm. We had to go on information and belief. And faith.

But in a special ops environment, no element leader can afford to be shy about offering solutions or raising dilemmas. I was a combat "vampire" who loved the night, but I held my peace about the risks of a daylight op, because there was no other option. Yet a number of other officers quickly voiced issues, to a background score of distant helo turbines whining up and desert combat boots thumping across the tarmac like heavy hail.

"Sir?" someone said to General Garrison. "I've got some exfil issues."

"What's on your mind?"

"Okay, air exfiltration is not an option, so we're forced to use the ground convoy. But I think we might wrap it up long before the vehicles are in position."

"We'll be there when you're ready," said Colonel McKnight. His lightly armored Humvees and five-ton trucks were already assembled to move to a rendezvous point near the Olympic Hotel. I wondered if the hotel had had a single client this year, or ever.

"But the place is nasty with Skinnies today," someone else said, using the nickname for hostile Somalis. "We might get boxed in on the return."

"Exfil by air's a negative," another pilot stated firmly. The plan called for the helos to hover at about thirty feet, uncoil fast ropes, and let the D-boys and Rangers slide down like firemen on slick poles. But there was nowhere to then land our choppers and pick them up. "We could do a rooftop extraction, but like we saw on the last mission, hovering up there like sitting ducks makes us very vulnerable to the RPG gunners."

"And there's an antenna tower on the target building." An SF officer jabbed at a video monitor with his gloved finger. "We'd have to blow it before the helos come back in, and it'll take time."

"Don't sweat it, boys," McKnight said to his Ranger officers. "Your convoy will be there."

"And if it's not," Garrison grinned around his cigar stub, "the helos will come in and pull your asses out like they always do."

And that was it. We had been in there for all of ten minutes. Garrison gave the order to load the helicopters. An intel officer had already "burned" enough copies of the aerial recon photos to pass around, and we snatched up our gear and pushed out the door. We still had no final launch order, but my gut told me the mission was "go." I didn't even take the time to sprint back to my bunk for my kneeboard, which contained a mission packet with all the standard procedures relevant to the op. I had decided that a quick crew briefing was more important than getting my kneeboard, and I didn't have time to do both. Besides, my copilot, Ray Frank, had his for certain, and we were never more than an arm's length apart. It didn't matter. I knew this thing by heart.

For the second time that day, I ran, and I was far from alone. More than a hundred men ran with me—Rangers, Delta operators, chopper pilots—charging half a klick across the tarmac to a flat dirt apron where our helos were parked just off the main runway. More than a score of coal-black aircraft hulked there in the sun, their rotors still immobile, but auxiliary power units building to a controlled scream, providing juice to get the radios and critical systems up and running. Four of them were AH-6 Little Bird gunships, not much larger than fat Ford Explorers, but lethal in a street fight. And four more were fixed with steel slat benches jutting out from their airframes, on which the assaulters would perch like insane circus acrobats. There were eight Blackhawks, including Wolcott's pair for hauling more SF operators, my four for the Ranger blocking element, a Search and Rescue bird, and the C2 Command and Control bird, containing Colonel Matthews and SF Colonel Harrel and a stuffing of commo gear. The wind of my sprint was in my hair, and our charge reminded me of something out of *Apocalypse Now*. *I love the smell of jet fuel in the morning . . .*

The only things I carried were my MP-5 submachine gun, the intel photos, and an M-9 pistol strapped to my leg in a holster on my "bat belt." Everything else was already in my helo, Super Six-Four, sitting there fully armed and mission-ready as always. All the systems would be up, radios working, miniguns loaded, preflight checks all done. That was why I loved flying with Ray and my crew chiefs, Tommy Field and Bill Cleveland, so damned much. Everything was always perfect.

Tommy, in his late twenties, had a race car back in his garage in Lisbon, Maine, and he treated "his helicopter" no differently from that hot rod. The wheels were always slick with Armor All, the windshield washed after every mission. There wasn't a drop of oil on that thing. And Bill, a bit older than Tommy, I called "My Squire." When I showed up he'd have my black survival vest already in his hands, the ceramic, bulletproof "chicken plate" tucked into the chest pocket, holding it up for my arms like some medieval footman. No one worked harder than these men. They often flew missions with us from dark to dawn, and when we pilots were already snug in our racks, they were still out there turning wrenches, cleaning, repairing, topping off fluids, and filling out maintenance reports. With these guys, you didn't even have to preflight the bird. All you had left to do was hop in and hit the start buttons. I had known them for almost five years.

I stood outside my helo, and while Bill geared me up I handed out the intel photos and briefed the other pilots and crews real quick. I looked in their eyes to make sure they understood everything and didn't have any questions. They nodded and took off like ducks scattering from a gunshot.

Captain Steele, company commander of Bravo Company, 3rd Battalion of the 75th Ranger Regiment, was already herding eighteen of his men into our bird. He was a huge man, probably 280 pounds of solid muscle, and had been a lineman for the Georgia Bulldogs. Not long ago, a whole squad of his Rangers had held him down and used two of their thickest plastic prisoner cuffs to hog-tie him. He had simply snapped them in half. His fire support officer, Lieutenant Jim Lechner, was with him, and their RTO bristled with radio gear and antennae, and the rest hauled M-16A2s, CAR-15s, Squad Automatic Weapons, M-60s, ammo, IV bags, water, Kevlar vests with chicken plates, grenades and blades, and all the accoutrements of war that would take Super Six-Four to its load limits with a total of twenty-two souls aboard. They turtled into the cargo bay and tucked their legs up to make room.

I had been with this particular group of Rangers on four previous missions. We called them "The Customers," and nothing mattered more to us than keeping the customers satisfied. They were the reason for our existence, and we never forgot that.

I hopped into Super Six-Four, settled into the right seat, and harnessed up. The doors had been removed, because they provided no ballistic protection anyway and when the dust kicked up you could see better if you could just look down. Ray was already in the left seat and ready to go, just waiting for me before the blades turned. He was in his upper forties, gray haired, calm and with the easy smile of a veteran. We'd worked together for so long that we hardly needed to speak anymore. I handed him the intel photo and jabbed my finger at the target building, just north of the Olympic Hotel. He looked at the four landing zones our flight would go into and strapped it to his kneeboard. Ray was still super sharp, but he was ready to retire. This was going to be his last deployment.

I pulled on my black SPH-4 helmet, tapped the smoked visor down, pushed the mike boom right up to my lips, and plugged into the commo net. The big blades above were spinning faster and faster, flashing shadows over the canopy like strobe lights reflecting off a disco ball. Dervishes of dust kicked up and spun away from the cockpit. I spotted General Garrison, head bent into the grit spatter and moving from chopper to chopper, apparently wishing good fortunes. I hadn't seen him do that before, and wondered if he shared the only concern I had. It wasn't for us helo crews, but for the men who'd be exfiltrating by ground in the lightly armored vehicles. We really needed armored personnel carriers and tanks to guarantee their safe passage, but the request for them had been denied by the "powers that be" back in Washington. There wasn't much chatter in my headphones, just occasional commo checks and updates from the JOC. And then the various elements, or "Chalks," started to call in their ready status, one by one, from front to back of the formation, using the prearranged code word, a woman's name.

"Barber Five-One is *Lucy.*"

"Barber Five-Two is *Lucy.*"

"Super Six-One is *Lucy*. . . . Star Four-One is *Lucy*."

"Star Four-Two . . . Star Four-Three . . . Star Four-Four . . . Super Six-Two . . ."

I keyed the mike on my cyclic. "Super Six-Four is *Lucy*."

And so it went, on down to Colonel Matthews in Super Six-Three, the C2 chopper at the back.

"Roger, understand the flight is *Lucy*."

Now we waited for that one name we needed to hear, "Irene," the signal that the mission was Go. It was game time, what we'd trained and prepared for. It was also that twilight of nervous energy when the true personalities of individuals popped up. Some guys tripped all over themselves, some settled into the studied calmness of brain surgeons. Most of us were a little keyed-up, but it sure helped to have been in similar situations before.

I thought I was a pretty darn good pilot. Experience had given me that conviction. I had been to "Prime Chance," the secret antimining operations in the Gulf back in '88. I'd flown "Just Cause" in Panama in '89 and "Desert Storm" in '91. And now, Somalia. I was on top of my game. I wasn't arrogant, but there probably weren't too many people who could fly a Blackhawk or shoot as well as I could at that time of my life.

The run to the city was right there; we'd lift off and be over target within minutes. It would be real quick, and we didn't have a lot of time to think about it. It was only three miles to the Olympic Hotel.

There was no time to ponder fate, sit down, have a cup of coffee, write a goodbye letter home. I never wrote one anyway, never had one stowed in my gear. I never told one of my buddies what to say to my folks, "if." I didn't think about my wife, or my son, or home. I wasn't especially religious. I didn't pray. I was totally focused on the mission. The only time those kinds of thoughts encroached on me was when things were slow, and they weren't slow today. I never thought about what might happen if I got killed. I didn't think I *could* be killed. There was an expression for that kind of helo jock denial: *Big Sky, little bullet.*

I had been in the army for twelve years, and I had become just about all that I could be. I was still young, yet far from green, a thirty-two-year-old, battle-tested helo pilot. Cocky, maybe, but my reflexes and instincts were at their peak, a man who could meld with a multiton machine and bend it to his will. I was a Flight Lead, and when I spoke and flexed my wrists and worked my Blackhawk's controls, a cavalry of America's finest warriors would follow me to battle. I perched there at the razor tip of my country's spearhead, while behind me an armada of armored men and deadly weapons waited for the word. I felt no fear, only faith that I could do the job. Invincible.

The code word to launch crackled in my ear, and I grinned and keyed my mike as I lifted off.

"Fuckin' *Irene.*"

I AM NOT A MAN WHO BELIEVES IN OMENS, but there were sharks in the water. The formation rose up through its own enormous cloud of rotorwash dust, briefly swinging in an arc out over the sea, and I glanced down at the azure waves, sparkling in the sunlight like a sea of diamonds. And there they were, hundreds of them, slithering just below a surface that looked deceptively inviting. The sharks fed on the runoff from a camel-meat processing plant, eagerly awaiting anyone foolish enough to enter their domain. They had already ambushed and dined on a few careless members of the U.N. task force. No one swam here anymore.

I glanced down at my watch. It was midafternoon, just past 15:30. My wedding ring gleamed from my watchband, where I placed it anytime I was working. The sharp edges and hardware of military aircraft are notorious for snagging the rings of married men. I had met more than one pilot or crewman lucky to still have ten fingers after having one reattached.

The formation banked out wide to orient into the wind. With any aircraft assault, you pretty much always want to land into the wind. It increases your lift performance and helps with the noise, reducing the time the enemy can hear you coming. It cuts down on the dust cloud, blowing it back to your rear. Out in front of us I could see eight helicopters: the two Little Bird gunships, a Blackhawk, four more Little Birds with "people pods," and another Blackhawk. Clusters of legs and combat boots hung down from the cargo bays of the Blackhawks, their camo trousers whipping in the slipstream like frigate pennants. Outside the Little Bird fuselages, the "door kickers" hunkered on their benches, looking like space rangers in their black hockey helmets, headsets, goggles, and locked and cocked assault rifles affixed with all sorts of Aimpoint sights and underslung grenade launchers.

The choppers bobbed and weaved, keeping a loose formation, staying about three rotor discs apart, maybe fifty meters. We weren't the Thunderbirds, trying to look pretty; we just had to get there fast and be ready when we did. Ray and I were flying by rote, heads alternating inside and outside the cockpit, tuning radios, reviewing maps, doing our pre-assault checks, miniguns armed, shoulder harnesses locked, and all the while orienting ourselves on the city below and keeping our spot in the flight.

It wasn't even a five-minute hop and we were over the thick of the city, if you could call it that. It was more like an urban sprawl of concrete and plaster huts, corrugated roofs, frameless windows, jagged holes punched into everything. I remembered how when I'd first come into Mogadishu a month earlier aboard a C-5A, from a distance the pastel Indian Ocean and sugar cube town looked like the French Riviera. And then you got up close and the Mog's bad haircut and acne scars came into focus. Every single thing that couldn't be bolted down had been snatched up by the poverty-riddled populace. Even the telephone poles had been stripped, because the wire could be sold on the black market for its copper strands. The tallest building around was the seven-story Olympic Hotel. The leaves of the meager eucalyptus trees drooped under a thick frosting of dust.

I eased back on the airspeed to put some distance between the lead elements and my flight of four as we swept in toward the target, completely obscured now by a roiling cloud of brown dust kicked up by the six choppers putting in the assault force. All over the city, thick ribbons of black smoke were rising from clots of burning tires, the Somalis' warning signals that Americans were in the air. We had all seen these smoke signals before, but never in such volume or so early. Aidid's people were getting their shit together. *To arms, to arms, the Rangers are coming.*

The two lead Little Bird gunships zipped out of the dust cloud without firing a shot. They had found no targets, and that was a good sign. One by one, the assault birds started dropping their loads and calling it in as they banked away.

"Star Four-One is out."

"Super Six-One is out."

I kept count in my head, making sure not to progress until I heard every one of them come out. The last thing you wanted was to have a "midair." It would be bad enough getting shot down by the enemy, but it would be a dismal failure if we crashed into each other. My flight stayed with me in a loose box formation, but maintaining perfect air integrity.

I was talking internal on the intercom, keeping the "customers" situationally aware. They had things of their own to prepare and had to know how much time was left to the target. Ranger Captain Steele would be wearing a headset, listening to the radios, but within a minute of the drop he'd have to take that off and strap on his helmet. His Rangers on the door sills would be held in by a long strap, and they'd need enough warning to remove it and set up for fast roping. It was a crucial part of my job to keep them up to speed, and I couldn't let them down, not for a second. I thought of them as the most highly trained, professional soldiers in the world.

I could hear the muffled voice of Steele shouting updates to his Chalk leader, but mostly I just heard the constant whir of my own blades above and the altering tone of the engines as I worked the controls. It was a high-pitched whine, sort of like the howl of a hungry young wolf. If there was any small-arms fire already coming up at us, I didn't hear it or see it. It wasn't like what they showed in the movies, with rounds zipping by and tracers burning trails in the sky. You couldn't see small-arms tracers under the African sun, and unless something actually *thwang*ed off your cockpit you'd never know you were being shot at.

The earphones in my helmet hissed, "Star Four-Three's go-around."

One of the Little Bird pilots couldn't get into his designated landing position and had to execute a "go-around." This wasn't terrific, but it was nothing we hadn't prepared for or executed previously. I had to slow my flight even more while his Chalk endured a stomach-wrenching roller-coaster loop and came back in. The dust was unbelievable. We pulled back to a crawl, maybe only forty knots, hovering in over the rooftops. We didn't know it because of the cloud, but the RPGs were already exploding in the air around us.

Ignorance was—temporarily—bliss.

The Little Bird pilot called himself "out," rolled away, and we dipped and roared forward. We had to get our blocking force in fast, not only to keep the bad guys out of the target area but to keep any "leakers" from escaping the assault element. The only visibility I had was through the Plexiglas "chin bubble" at my feet. Ray read off the radar altimeter, describing what little he could see on his side. The Olympic was on my side and certainly the best reference point for locating the intersection I wanted. I caught a glimpse of the target building, and then it disappeared in a tornado of filth as another Blackhawk pulled up on my right to insert his blocking force. My good friend Stan was flying that helicopter, and I'd bet on him to find the right spot any day or night of the week. I brought Super Six-Four in as low as possible, to a twenty-foot hover, using a utility pole straight down through the chin bubble as a reference.

"Ropes," I called over the intercom.

My crew chiefs, Tommy and Bill, echoed me loud and the thick green hawsers were deployed. It was a well-rehearsed routine. All I had to do was keep it steady, holding the forward left box position, with Chalk Two right behind me, Chalk Three abeam me to the right, and Chalk Four right behind him. But the pilot of that last chopper, Super Six-Seven, had been flying the C2 bird until today, just up there boring holes in the sky, and this was his first encounter with the "brown monster." The dust cloud was more than a hundred feet high, and he felt his way down into it like a wader tiptoeing into cold lake water. He deployed his ropes too early, and they were only thirty feet long. A Ranger went out his door, lost his grip on the rope, and fell into oblivion. It was right then and there that the mission started to unravel, like the hem of an old sweater as you tug on one loose strand. But I didn't know any of that at the time. I was having problems of my own.

"Right rope's hung up on a wire."

It was Bill's voice in my ears, dead calm and steady, telling me we'd snagged on probably the last telephone wire still intact in Mogadishu. *Of all the damn phone poles in the city*, I thought.

"Forward, ten." Bill offered a correction as he peered down past his minigun at the snared hawser, and I carefully nudged the helo forward.

"Hooollllldd," he sang. I could tell by his tone that the rope was dangling straight and free, and I held it steady while our eighteen Rangers leaped for the lines like comic book heroes. I could hear Steele's Chalk leader barking, "*Go, Go, Go*," and the butt plates of M-16s and M-60 light machine guns scraping and banging against my floor as the troops dove into the dust storm. Within seconds, they were all gone. "Good luck, guys," I whispered as Bill and Tommy tripped the releases and the ropes fell from their mounts like limp cobras. None of us had a clue that those young Rangers were in for the fight of their lives.

"Ropes clear," Tommy announced, and I hauled the helo into a rising left bank as I keyed my mike.

"Super Six-Four is out."

And that was it. I thought it was over, at least for my element. I'd take my flight to a holding pattern, about two miles north of 21 October Road, and execute long, lazy, racetrack circles until the D-boys and Rangers came out by ground. And then we'd all head back for a raucous debrief, where we'd run through all the events and hammer each other over even the smallest mistakes. There are no perfect games.

We were out there for about thirty minutes, while the entire city skyline came around ten times. There wasn't much chatter on the nets. Folks didn't talk unless they really had something to say. On my console I could switch between frequencies and listen to the ground net, but the comms were in and out, so I paid attention to the air net. It seemed to me like nothing unusual was happening. The "principals" had already been stunned, cuffed, and blindfolded. The mission was into its consolidation phase.

But on the ground, things were decidedly unusual. That Ranger who'd fallen from Super Six-Seven was not only critically injured, but he and his Chalk were nowhere near their designated landing zone. Other ground elements had been cut loose to evacuate him, while crowds of armed Somalis, alerted by their signal fires, were quickly swarming toward the target area. The exfil convoy was starting to take heavy, murderous fire.

"We've lost a five-ton truck."

I heard that, and Ray and I glanced at each other. The ground transmissions were broken and hard to understand. We switched radios for better reception. Things were starting to heat up down there,

but we just sat there and breathed and flew around and around, waiting. I knew Cliff Wolcott and his copilot, Donovan Briley, were back
in there with Super Six-One, giving fire support from three SF shoot-
ers on board and their crew chiefs' miniguns. From what I could
gather as I squinted, straining to hear, the Somalis were coming from
every doorway and from behind every wall. But all we could do was
sit there in our safe haven, feeling helpless, while our people were
in deep shit and we knew it.

"Super Six-One is going down."

It was Cliff's voice. He was talking about himself and his own
helo. Something had hit his bird and he and Donovan were going
to crash.

I swallowed, disbelieving what I'd heard. *Super Six-One is going
down?* Cliff Wolcott and Donovan Briley were real good friends of
mine. We were all from the same platoon, and we were close. We'd
been together for a long time, traveled on the road together, partied
together. Our families knew each other very well.

I shook it off. *They'll be all right,* I decided. *They'll have to land,
maybe a hard landing or something. But the SAR bird'll fly in and pick
them up and we'll all go home.*

The possibility that Cliff and Donovan might die didn't cross my
mind. I couldn't see them from my position, so I painted it the way
I needed to see it at the moment. As it was, an RPG round had blown
off a big chunk of their bird. They started spinning out of control
while Donovan shut the engines down and Cliff tried to get the aircraft on the ground in one piece. But those damn narrow streets—
the helo smacked down on a reinforced concrete wall, pivoted, and
crashed, nose first. It furrowed into an alley, coming to rest on its right
side, just a few blocks east of the target building. In the back of the
helo, the crew chiefs and SF operators had survived it. Cliff and
Donovan were both killed on impact, but I wouldn't know that till
much, much later.

In those few seconds, everything changed. The radios, which up till now had hissed the occasional code words or updates, went crazy. Sure, we'd all prepared for the possibility of a bird going down, but the timing and location were about as bad as they could be. The ground assault element, with prisoners already in tow, was ordered to regroup at the fresh crash site. The exfil convoy suddenly had a new and even more deadly labyrinth to fight through. Air elements were being summoned for support. It was now constant chatter back and forth, the voices still steady but ominously urgent.

The survivors of Super Six-One staggered out of the wreck to find themselves immediately under assault. Only a Little Bird could slip down quickly into those narrow streets, and Karl Maier and Keith Jones rolled out of their holding pattern and zipped right down into it. Karl dropped it into an intersection between the wrecked Black-hawk and a horde of charging Somalis, buffing the ground with his skids and holding the flight controls with his knees while he opened fire outside the cockpit with his MP-5. Keith hopped out into the maelstrom, dragged two wounded D-boys back into the chopper, and they got the hell out of there. Karl flew it back to the airfield, dropped off the injured men, and came right back out to fight.

I heard the Air Mission Commander, Colonel Matthews, call the Search and Rescue bird in on Cliff and Donovan's crash site. The SAR bird is always kept in reserve with a security force on board, and it is employed only as a contingency in response to a downed heli-copter situation. That SAR mission was usually the most boring, and that's how we wanted it. If a SAR crew got involved in a real-world situation, that meant that the worst had happened.

On this mission, the worst *had* happened. We had a bird down and the survivors were surrounded.

Herb Rodriguez, my company commander, and Dan Jollota were piloting that SAR Blackhawk and they roared in close to the wreck and dropped ropes. Their Para Jumpers, medics, and security men waited only for a half-steady hover before they leaped out onto the hawsers, but three of them were still hanging there when that bird also got slammed in the fuselage by an RPG. Dan was at the controls, and anyone's first instinct would be to roll out of there, but he somehow held it steady until every man was on the ground. His rotor blades were chewed up and his helo's body was ragged with shrapnel holes, but he started limping back toward the airport, trailing turgid smoke. I heard Dan call for Crash and Rescue.

We were still holding north of the city, listening to the congested radios, trying to keep track of the situation. My three other Blackhawks were still with me in loose formation. The nets were jammed with overlapping transmissions. There were lots of decisions being made, and everyone had to stay informed.

At this point, I knew I was no longer invincible. I could feel my heart thumping in my chest. In the space of five minutes, I had gone from feeling as indestructible as an iron dragon to fragile as a hummingbird in a forest fire. Things were going to shit. The SAR bird had been hit only moments after the lead Blackhawk went down. That "Big Sky, little bullet" theory wasn't remotely as comforting as it had been that morning. My youth left me.

Colonel Matthews called me on the net.

"Six-Four, I need you to go in and take Six-One's place over the target."

I was expecting that call to come. We had practiced this exact contingency just a few days before with a mock shoot-down of Six-One, and I was rolling out of holding even as I answered, "Roger, Six-Four going in." Even with everything I knew now, my mind's eye flashing me unholy images, my hands and feet didn't hesitate. We broke formation. No one in the helicopter said a word. Ray, Tommy, Bill, and I all knew what had just happened to our friends. One bird was down in the city, another was hit, and the ground force was decisively engaged. We were playing for keeps on this one. I broke the silence on the intercom.

"It may get a little sticky in there. Let's all keep our heads in the game."

There was no response.

I headed back for the target site at full power, running right along the rooftops. We were going to provide fire support for the ground elements, but I realized that everyone had been told now to consolidate at the crash site. Platoons, squads, and sections would be racing door to door toward that new position. It would be very hard to distinguish friend from foe in such a melee. We couldn't just cowboy in there, spewing four thousand rounds a minute. Tommy and Bill's electrically controlled miniguns could be armed only by me throwing a switch in the cockpit. I spoke to them very carefully.

"Okay," I said. "I'm arming your guns, but we're *not* doing any shooting until we figure out where everybody is. Roger that?"

They grunted a "Rahj."

Within seconds we were back over the target area, flying a wide circular pattern, trying to locate Cliff's crash site and *clearly* spot the enemy before we opened up. We were in a hard left bank with me up high in the right seat, so I was peering past Ray and down into total confusion. It was just smoke and dust and indistinguishable, sprinting forms. I tried to raise Super Six-Two, Cliff's and Donovan's wingman, but the air-to-air net was jammed up and the AMC kept telling us to vary our pattern and minimize exposure time. I jinked up and down, getting high, getting low, trying to make us hard to hit, all too aware that the Somalis were now shooting at us from every rooftop and street corner.

Something slammed into my helicopter.

We didn't know what it was or where it had impacted, but the helo bucked hard, like a small sports car going over a large speed bump. We'd been passing by the Olympic Hotel for the third time, doing fifty knots at about seventy-five feet, when an RPG round rocketed into the tail section. But that was thirty-five feet behind me, the aircraft was eighteen thousand pounds of metal muscle, and it certainly wasn't coming apart. At least not yet.

I looked quickly around the cockpit, while Ray did the same, both of us testing the controls and checking the gauges. Everything was "in the green": no flight control problems, engine malfunctions, or weird noises. No one in my bird said a word, and then . . .

"Super Six-Four, you're hit bad." It was Matthews up in the C2 bird. "You better put it on the ground." From his position high over the battle he had seen the rocket impact just below my tail, raking pieces away in pinwheels as it detonated.

No shit, I thought as I rolled out of the turn. Just ahead, maybe a mile off, was what appeared to be a clear area, certainly large enough to land a Blackhawk. But the aircraft still seemed to be flying normally, and I was facing the decision to crash it in the middle of a firefight or fly just two more miles to the safety of the airfield. I didn't hesitate or discuss it with anyone. It was my decision to make. We'd go for the field.

Still, I kept my eye on that midway point. It looked sort of like a city park, which was what it had been, long ago when the place was prosperous. Now, as we closed on it, I could see that it was covered with tin shacks and huts. But none of that mattered, because within a few seconds the world went completely to hell.

The RPG had smashed into the rear gearbox, a fixture the size of a big watermelon and full of oil and gears, where the drive shaft came in to have its speed and direction ratios altered for the tail rotor. The bottom of that box had been blown off, the drive shaft bent and twisted. I heard a rapidly accelerating whine, an unearthly, building scream, and then the tail rotor assembly completely disintegrated into vapor with an earsplitting BANG.

The nose of the helicopter immediately started to spin to the right. The tail rotor on a Blackhawk counters the torque created by the main rotor system, and the pedals control the pitch of the tail rotor. As we passed through the first ninety degrees of rotation, I instinctively countered with left pedal, and I knew we'd lost it. I'll never forget looking down to make sure I was pushing the pedal, and seeing my boot jammed all the way to the floor. My body was reacting properly, but my helo was not. I keyed the mike.

"Six-Four has lost the tail rotor. We're going in hard."

I looked over at Ray and said, "I guess we better pull 'em off." I was referring to the engines, because the only way to counter that spin was to shut them down and eliminate the torque. But just as the Blackhawk manual describes such an emergency, if you don't kill the engines right away the centrifugal force will make it physically impossible to reach up for the power control levers. I'd always thought that sounded a little extreme. It wasn't.

Super Six-Four started to spin so fast that the sky and ground became nothing but two blurred stripes of blue and brown in front of my eyes. It was like riding a merry-go-round and looking straight out to the side from your horse, while the teenage operator goes nuts and hauls it up to fifty revs per minute. I was hurled against my harness, my hands desperately yanking and twisting the controls, and I looked over at Ray to see him fighting the force with every muscle, his gloved hands quaking as he tried to reach up for the power levers.

I knew I was going to die, and I must have clenched the mike key as I screamed his name, shooting a paralyzing chill through everyone on the net.

"Raaaayyyy!"

And then the rubber and the steel met the road. . . .

Chapter 1

DOWN AND DIRTY

Somalia

I WOKE UP IN THE SILENCE OF MY OWN GRAVE.

At least that's what I believed in that first moment, because in my last flash of consciousness I had clearly seen the clawing hand of the Grim Reaper. I did not know where I was. I did not know *who* I was. It was like emerging from an altitude chamber with a case of hypoxia as my mind began to stagger, slowly, through the darkened hallways of my concussed brain. And when my eyelids finally fluttered open, I was stunned to take in the light.

The chopper's windshield was almost completely gone, pierced and disintegrated by a slab of corrugated metal that had stopped only inches from my face. Yet my first sense of emotion wasn't relief, but fury at the disfiguring of my helicopter by that rusty blade. I reached up to shove the thing from my cockpit, and then the pain swept over me like a wave of molten lava.

My back was broken.

Super Six-Four had come down like Dorothy's house in *The Wizard of Oz*, spinning fast, falling even faster, and finally slamming its nine tons of steel into the hard-packed ground. Two of my vertebrae had smacked together on impact, displacing the disk between them and pulverizing each other. Every muscle in my back must have tried to prevent that catastrophe and been ripped apart in the effort, and it felt like some evil giant had me on his worktable, squeezing my spine in an iron vise. I stopped moving and just tried to breathe without passing out.

I sure as hell was fully conscious now, although my thoughts and reflexes seemed to trudge through a sort of syrupy fog. Slowly I moved my aching head and glanced around the cockpit, and found I was sitting level with the floor. The pilot seats in a Blackhawk are designed to stroke downward in a major crash, and mine had done that and more. Its supports had snapped like the legs of a child's chair under the girth of a fat man. My right leg felt strangely numb, and as soon as I tried to move it I knew that the femur had broken clean in half over the edge of my Kevlar seat. My M-9 pistol was still strapped to my right thigh, and as its weight shifted I could feel the splintered ends of my bones grinding against one another. But it didn't hurt all that much. My crushed vertebrae were monopolizing my pain centers.

I was dead sure that I couldn't get myself out of the cockpit. A Blackhawk's hard enough to get out of when you're healthy. You have to contort yourself and maneuver your limbs around the seat and the controls. Now I could barely move. I unhooked my harness and took off my helmet, feeling rivulets of cold sweat running down my temples. Some guys come back from every mission soaked through, while I rarely break a sweat. Today was different. I peeled off my Nomex gloves and then, for some strange reason, I slipped my watch from my wrist, with my wedding ring still encircling the band, and laid them on the console. To this day, I'm not sure why I did that.

Maybe I knew that "time" was about to become a non-issue here. Or maybe it was the ring, and I didn't want to be distracted by thoughts of home. It was like something a man might do before surgery, or certain death.

I saw my MP-5 submachine gun lying on the floor near my left foot, right where I'd left it. If I had abided by written safety procedures, that "Skinny Popper"—our callous nickname for the compact German weapon—would have been behind me, strapped down somewhere in the back and inaccessible. So I was grateful for having a touch of the renegade in me as I reached for it, made sure it was locked and cocked and laid it across my lap. I could hear some thin, muffled shouts in the distance. The Somalis would surely try to overrun us, and it looked like I'd just have to fight it out right there where I sat. And then I remembered that I wasn't alone.

I looked over at Ray. His helmet was gone and he was slowly edging himself off his seat, which had collapsed to the floor just like mine. The acrid smell of spilled jet fuel mixed with dry dust was in the air, and I heard someone moaning unintelligibly from the back of the chopper. It was Bill Cleveland's voice, but nothing he muttered made any sense. There wasn't a sound from Tommy Field. Ray looked at me.

"I tried to pull them off." He meant the engines.

"I know it."

"Couldn't do it."

I glanced up at the power-control levers. "You got 'em halfway."

He didn't say anything for a moment, and then: "Left tibia's broken, I think."

"Right femur here. And my back, too."

"Yeah," he said, and then he slowly maneuvered himself until he was sitting in the door sill with his back to me.

"I'm movin', Mike," he said.

"I'll be right here."

Ray nodded, and then he gripped the sill with his hands and carefully lowered himself to the ground. I couldn't see him anymore, and I would never see him again.

I knew we were about to battle for our lives. We were down in the middle of Mogadishu, and there was no doubt in my mind that the Somalis were coming for us. I was dimly aware of the echoes of gunfire in the distance, the chatter of small arms, and the ominous double booms of RPGs. There was a badass fight going on out there, a real slugfest. But I didn't think, *Oh my God, this is it, it's over.* I was focused only on the things I had to do, setting my gun in position and getting ready to shoot it out. I felt no sense of despair or hopelessness, just a grim determination to hold them off as long as I could. I was ready.

And just then, Randy Shughart and Gary Gordon appeared on the right side of our chopper. They were Delta operators, and though I didn't know them personally or by name, I certainly knew who they were. More than once I had briefed them and other members of their teams prior to assaults into the city. Since they were wearing no helmets, I recognized them instantly. Randy was carrying a high-tech sniper rifle and Gary had a CAR-15, the short-barreled version of the M-16 assault rifle, and their load-bearing harnesses were slung with ammunition and grenades. They were the kind of professionals who could pick off a rabbit from a roller coaster with a BB gun. To me, they were Batman and Robin, only much better, and they just walked up to my aircraft like they were out for a stroll in the park.

Rescue Force! was the first thing that leapt to my mind. *Already!* I figured that only a few minutes had elapsed since Super Six-Four had been hit by the RPG, yet here were the Best of the Best, on the ground and setting up to get us all the hell out of there. Now there was cause for some real optimism, and a sense of elation swept through me. I was thinking that we'd all be all right, that it was over, and I assumed that Cliff Wolcott and Donovan Briley were alive and soon we'd all be swapping tales about what we'd been through.

Maybe it would be bedside by bedside in an army hospital, but what the hell. *We took a couple of punches,* I thought. *But we're still rollin'.*

What I didn't know then was that Shughart and Gordon were the Task Force's last hope to defend our crash site. They had been circling overhead in Super Six-Two, watching the Somalis streaming into the area's perimeter, taking shots at the African gunslingers and bringing them down, while more and more of them just kept coming on. They knew we wouldn't last long before being overrun, and they had put in three urgent requests to the Air Mission and Ground Force Commanders to be inserted on our crash site. At last, Colonels Matthews and Harrel had acquiesced to what they must have thought would be a suicide mission.

Piloting Super Six-Two through a hailstorm of AK-47 fire and Rocket-Propelled Grenade rounds, Mike Goffena and Jim Yacone had put Randy and Gary down nearby, and almost immediately their chopper was hit hard by an RPG. One of the helo's crew chiefs had already been struck in the hand by small-arms fire, and now a remaining Delta operator on board had his leg blown off, but Goffena—with Yacone unconscious and slumped in the seat beside him—somehow nursed that chopper back to a seaside port facility and furrowed it into the ground, more or less in one piece. Some incredible flying was done that day.

Randy and Gary didn't say very much. They knew the situation was critical and they were there to work, not chat. They asked me about my injuries.

"Well, my right leg's broken," I said. "And I think my back."

"Uh-huh." They nodded and set themselves in position to lift me out of the cockpit, but I didn't fear those hands reaching in for me. I wasn't in much pain at that point, because I guess shock had set in and my body's physiology must have been intercepting those screaming messages to my brain. They acted as if they were in no particular rush, and they raised me up gently, as if they were handling an ostrich egg. They carried me to an open spot of ground to the right of the cockpit and set me down carefully in the dust. One of them recovered a large survival kit from the bird and they tucked it up behind me to support my back.

It was my first chance to get a lay of the land. No, we hadn't made the airfield, but somehow we had made it to that open area I had seen that looked like a small park. Yet now I could see that the whole space was covered with tin shanties, homemade shacks with walls and roofs of corrugated metal. By some miracle, we had come down in the only uninhabited flat spot between a cluster of huts.

To my right was a long, high wall of that same gray and rust-red tin. To my left, Super Six-Four sat in the pale dirt, its belly smeared into the ground, its big rotors dead still and drooping like wilted palm fronds. We had crashed flat and level, which was about as good as it could get, but the landing-gear struts had absorbed as much impact as they were designed to and then the whole strut assembly had snapped off. The chopper lay there like a big truck with its tires ripped away, and you could barely see a sliver of light under it. The tail rotor and vertical fin had disintegrated in flight, and what remained of the tail boom was tucked up against the wall behind me.

I couldn't see anyone in the cargo bay. Tommy Field's minigun had swung around hard and struck him full in the chest upon impact. It was a very heavy weapon and it had crushed his entire rib cage. Someone in the C2 bird flying overhead saw him briefly sit up, then fall flat back into the bay. Something else inside the chopper had torn up Bill Cleveland really bad.

Just in front and to my right was a long shack and a large tree, its high leaves rustling in the hot wind and throwing some shade onto me. The only open area was between that shack and my helo's cockpit, a clear field of fire. Randy and Gary knew what they were doing. They handed me my MP-5 and the single spare magazine, a total of sixty rounds of 9mm ammo, but they didn't say a word as they walked off around the nose of the helicopter.

I heard Bill's voice again and I twisted my head around. Shughart and Gordon had placed him on the ground behind me, and he was still incoherent and in great pain. Some of his flight gear had been removed and his trousers were soaked in blood.

I looked at my lifeless leg, knowing that it was already swelling and stiffening in the sun. *Well, at least I'll be getting out of here and going home.* Just that morning I had wanted to go out on every mission, but now with a broken femur I knew I wouldn't be flying for quite some time. I tried to buck myself up, but that minute of respite gave me too much time to think. I suddenly missed my family very much, and especially my young son, Joey.

I did not want to die here, and even as I fought it, the fear began to well up. I was badly injured and scared, and there was no doubt about it, I did *not* want to fall into the hands of the Somalis. Just a few weeks before, they had overrun some Nigerian troops, and rumors about what they'd done to them were too gruesome to believe. And the Somalis had done that to *fellow Africans*, so I couldn't even imagine what they might do to *us*. The images of mutilation that flashed into my mind terrified me.

Randy and Gary came back around the nose of the helo. I wasn't sure what they were doing, but I assumed they were looking for an area large enough to land an aircraft and get us out of there. They were calm and deliberate, talking to each other like a couple of surveyors planning a new parking lot, but I knew they were frustrated. They had four badly injured men on their hands and it was impossible to move us, even a short distance.

From the other side of the tin wall to my right I heard Somali voices. It sounded like they were trying to get at us, but I didn't think it over for more than a second. My MP-5 was set on single-shot mode and I put it to use, firing four quick rounds right through the wall. I didn't hear the voices anymore. When I stopped shooting, Randy and Gary looked at me, as if surprised that a badly injured chopper pilot might actually be useful in a firefight. They didn't speak, but they moved around the front of the helo again until they were out of sight.

At some point, Karl and Keith, the two Little Bird pilots, came back into the picture. They had already pulled off an incredible rescue at Cliff and Donovan's crash site, but they came right back in to see what they could do for us. I never saw or heard them, but they landed about a hundred meters to the right of our downed helicopter, which was as close as they could get due to the dense concentration of shacks and trees. They stayed on the ground for about a minute, but began taking so much fire that they had to get the hell out of there or lose their bird. There was nothing else they could do.

From beyond the far left side of Super Six-Four, I began to hear more frequent fire of AK-47s, that deep, hollow bang that comes from the throats of those Russian weapons. It hammered in ones and twos, yet more often, and was answered by precision sniper shots and "double-taps" from Randy's and Gary's guns. But I had my own problems. The Somalis were definitely trying to get at me now from the other side of the tin wall; I could hear their chatter and the quick flip-flops of their sandals and sneakers. I fired through the wall again, the tin rattling as my rounds punctured it and lances of light pierced back through the bullet holes. A little farther down, a pair of mahogany hands gripped the top of the wall and a dark head appeared above it. I fired again and the intruder disappeared, but my weapon jammed. I worked the bolt and a perfectly good round fell into the dust. *Damn.* Wasting ammunition was a luxury I could not afford.

K-k-k-kung. A burst of AK fire echoed from the far side of the chopper. *B-dap, b-dap.* It stopped. I looked over at my helo, at my seat collapsed there in the cockpit. It had worked exactly as advertised, stroking down with the crash and taking enough of the hit so that I'd been injured but not killed. It was cocked slightly to the right, probably because of the lateral spinning impact. I decided that I would like to meet the genius engineer who had designed those pilot seats. For just a moment, the distraction opened a brief window of hope, a glimmer of the future.

Then something moved on my right and I spun and fired four rounds. But while my trigger finger kept on pulling, the weapon just clicked. A wisp of pungent smoke curled from the barrel like a ghost. My first magazine was empty, and I switched to the second. *Only thirty more rounds, Durant. You better choose your targets very carefully.*

I looked to the left of the big tree out in front of me and I could see another Somali, crouched down and slinking toward the aircraft. It was obvious he hadn't spotted me yet, and he carried one of those worn-out-looking AKs, just holding it down by his side. I wondered where they'd gotten all those damn weapons as I slowly gripped my MP-5 two-handed and tracked him in the ring sight. We had all come to believe that the Somalis did not fear death, and this man clearly didn't, approaching with a thin, confident smile as if stalking some kind of defenseless prey. But we were not defenseless yet. I fired two rounds at him and he disappeared in a small cloud of dust. I know I hit him. He didn't come back.

I fired at some more shadowy figures, and then again. My weapon jammed. I pulled back the cocking lever and shook it violently, then chambered another round that seemed to seat properly. The thing was stressing me out. It had fired just fine at the range, but it was clear the damn gun needed a good cleaning. I couldn't claim that I hadn't had the time for some basic maintenance, and I could hear the ghostly echoes of so many drill instructors: *Keep your goddamn weapon clean!*

Four or five unfired rounds were scattered around the ground where I'd ejected them while clearing jams, mixed with spent brass casings that glittered in the sun. An African voice called out from the other side of the wall. *Blam blam.* I let loose. Tin rattled, and I heard the heavy patter of running. *Blam blam blam.*

The weapon's bolt locked to the rear. It was empty. I stared at it, horrified, yet I don't recall ever thinking about the M-9 pistol that was still strapped to my shattered thigh. There were two full pistol magazines there and another thirty rounds, but for some reason my brain refused to take that in. In the end, that failure in cognizance probably saved my life.

Something arced through the air above me, fell through the tree branches, and bounced on the ground just to my right. *Grenade!* I panicked and began to flail the now useless MP-5 in circles around my head, contorting and twisting like a man with a tarantula on his neck as I tried to sweep the horrible thing away from me. I thought I felt the weapon clang off of something, and I turned and covered my face with my arms as it exploded with a concussive bang off to the right, covering me with dust and hammering at my eardrums. I didn't feel any shrapnel wounds, but I lay there breathing as hard as a decked tuna.

My spirit, which only minutes before had been buoyed up by the arrival of Randy and Gary, now spiraled down into the ground just like my helicopter. At first I had been happy just to survive the crash, then accepted that I'd fight to the death, then swelled with elation at the promise of rescue. Now we were taking heavy fire, we'd almost been overrun, and they were throwing goddamn hand grenades in here! I was dripping sweat, in pain, half paralyzed, and out of ammo. The stench of spilled jet fuel and gunsmoke and rotting garbage and sweat would be the only escorts to my death. Randy and Gary were out there somewhere on the other side of the chopper, desperately trying to hold off the "Injuns." The bursts of AK fire were starting to roll together like a thunderstorm. I was alone. It was turning into the frigging Alamo.

"Damn. I'm hit."

It was Gary's voice, from the other side of the chopper. A Somali bullet had found him, yet it wasn't so much what he said but how he said it. He sounded almost irritated, like this was just going to make things harder for him. It wasn't a scream or a plea, just a statement of fact, like someone who'd nicked himself with a vegetable knife. At that point I am sure he realized how desperate our situation had become. No one was coming for us—not anytime soon, anyway. The ground convoy and the troops pinned down at Wolcott's crash site all had their own problems to deal with, and there were many more lives at stake. The unfortunate truth was that we were only a small part of a much bigger and bloodier picture.

Only minutes before, Gary and Randy had jumped from a hovering helicopter to rescue us. They had fought their way through a maze of paths and shanties, driving off seemingly countless Somali gunmen. They had already done more than any two men could be expected to do. They had put their own lives on the line to try to help their fellow American soldiers.

Gary Gordon died on the other side of that helicopter. I don't know exactly when, and I don't know exactly how, but I never saw or heard him again. He died before I even learned his name.

I will never forget him.

Randy Shughart came back around the cockpit, striding toward me and showing little more than professional concern in his expression.

"They're throwing grenades in here," I told him, but he didn't seem too worried about that. He was focused on our critical shortage of ammo, and he looked at my now useless MP-5.

"Are there any weapons in the aircraft?" he asked.

"My crew chiefs keep their M-16s between the seats."

He went off to the helicopter without a word, climbed in, and started digging around. Moments later he returned, carrying the longer M-16s and a CAR-15, the short-barreled submachine gun I had seen in Gary's hands. He handed me the smaller weapon, and for some reason it felt much better in my grip than my own MP-5. He held up a PRC-112 survival radio.

"What channel is the fire net on?"

It was odd. He didn't even have to shout. There was gunfire echoing from the far side of the aircraft, but in hesitant ones and twos.

"Channel Bravo," I replied.

He worked the radio, and suddenly I wondered if we'd been communicating with anyone at all out there. We *had* to be. I'd assumed that Randy and Gary had at least been talking on their own internal radio net. But maybe the communications were bad because of our location and the distances involved? *Surely* we'd contacted one of the other helicopters by now.

Could we be cut off? Wild thoughts began to race around in my brain. *Does anybody even know what's going on down here?* The gravity of our situation began to really dawn on me, and I simmered with anger and frustration. *We're gonna be overrun. It's gonna happen soon. How far away is that damn reaction force? There are hundreds of American troops in this damn city! What the hell are they doing?!*

Fortunately for me, I didn't know the truth about what was going on out there. If I had, my pounding heart might have simply succumbed with terror. Back at the first Blackhawk crash site, Cliff's and Donovan's corpses were jammed into the crumpled remains of their cockpit. Yet no U.S. serviceman would be left behind in enemy territory, not by this unit, dead or alive, and some of the Rangers and Special Forces had fought their way to the wreck. Other elements had been pinned down en route by relentless fire while, just like me, they waited with their injured and their dead for relief. But the vehicles in the ground convoy were being beat up so badly that they had to turn around and go back to the compound. The lightly armored Humvees and Five-Tons were riddled with bullets and RPG shrapnel, hauling dead and gravely wounded Rangers, their cargo bays slick with blood. They would have to regroup, rearm, muster more personnel, and come back out. It would be hours before any kind of help could make it to our site.

Randy made a call on the fire support net, which gave him a di-

rect line to the Little Bird guns and the fire support officer. A Little
Bird was flying high over our position.

"A reaction force is en route," came the return call from one of
the helicopters. The voice sounded familiar. I was sure it was one of
the Little Bird pilots named Chris.

Now, *that* was encouraging. All we had to do was hold out a little
bit longer. We needed help, but help was on the way. *We just gotta
keep them from overrunning us. We gotta hang in here just a little
while more. . . .*

Randy probably knew right then and there that "a little while
more" would not be soon enough. He squinted at the radio, stuffed
it into his combat harness, hefted his weapon, and moved off around
the nose of the helicopter. He left without saying another word. I
would never see him again.

Once more, I was alone. As far as I could tell, there was only one
man among us still on his feet, and he had walked off to make his
last stand. Directly to my right front, another Somali was trying to
climb over the wall. I couldn't understand why they so desperately
wanted to get at us, hurling themselves into the open like that. They
seemed to be coming from everywhere now, a veritable plague of
killers.

I aimed the CAR-15 and pulled the trigger, and the burst of automatic fire took me by surprise. Randy had put the weapon on burst
mode and I hadn't checked it, but it surely was effective. One moment the Somali's head was there, and the next moment he was
gone. I can't say for certain, but I think I killed that man.

I looked at the weapon in my hand and thought, *This is what we
need, not that MP-5 piece of crap.* The heavier "bangs" of 5.56mm
ammo seemed much more effective than the 9mm "pops" from my
MP-5. The small German weapon might be fine for urban antiter-
ror work, but this American piece was a robust field tool. It felt better and it didn't jam, not once. My confidence came back. I fired a
few more rounds at a flashing figure to my front. I fired a burst at one

to my left. And then the CAR-15 ran dry. It had been Gary Gordon's weapon, and he'd used up half the magazine before he was hit.

Desperately, I looked all around, shocked to be out of ammo. *Again.* Just meters away from me there were *six thousand rounds* of 7.62mm minigun ammunition in the chopper. But I had no way to fire any of it. Those miniguns would have been so damn effective, but they required aircraft power to operate. Tommy Field had nicknamed our helo "Venom," but Venom would never fly again and her battery wasn't enough to run those guns. We had to have AC electrical power. We might as well have had six thousand rocks. *Ammo, ammo everywhere, and not a round to fire. . . .*

Suddenly, it grew very, very quiet. Up until this point there had been quite a bit of gunfire, ebbing and flowing in volume, some from us and some from them. But for some reason it all stopped for a few moments. *Maybe they've given up,* I told myself. I could hear my own lungs, rasping at the air like sandpaper on plywood. *Maybe the reaction force is coming on and driving them away.* I had no idea if this might be true, but the fantasy was encouraging. My mind worked hard to suppress the rising panic, but my thoughts weren't remotely clear or focused. I couldn't move. I couldn't hide. I couldn't make myself invisible. There were a few good 9mm rounds lying around me, but I never thought to reload the empty MP-5 mags, and my pistol never entered my mind. I no longer had any control of the situation. All I could do now was wait for that reaction force. *It's only a couple of miles from there to here. They should be able to make it in time. They'll be here any second now . . .*

My body jerked and I clenched my fists as a huge volume of gunfire suddenly shattered the silence. It came from the far side of the chopper and it rolled in like a hurricane of the worst sounds that Satan could conjure. Volleys of AK-47 fire hammered at our helpless bird, echoing off the clustered shanties, the heavy rounds piercing the chopper's steel skin and ricocheting everywhere. The only thing armored on that Blackhawk were the seats, and I watched, helpless and horrified, as it was punctured over and over again and it bucked like a downed elephant under a hail of poacher fire. Flying bullets plucked shorn metal and glass into the air and kicked up clots of dirt all around me, and it was like being on the wrong end of the firing range at Fort Bragg while an entire company of infantry let loose at you.

The Somalis had plainly changed their tactics. They seemed to have realized that they weren't going to take us one at a time, but it had become clear we were few in numbers and lightly armed. The regular soldiers of the Somali National Alliance had arrived and taken over, organizing a coordinated assault.

It went on and on for maybe an entire minute, a short span of time that stretched into an agonizing eternity. I couldn't see anything through the hulk of the smashed chopper, so I can't say for sure, but Randy Shughart was probably the only American left fighting over there, alone against a countless number of enemies. He couldn't fight them all. It was only a matter of time before he went down. And when Randy finally fell, the shooting stopped. The last volleys of gunfire echoed off into the sparse trees. When the dust cleared, the Somalis would count twenty-five of their own killed at our crash site. In those last moments of his life, Randy had done some pretty damn fine shooting.

Then the most terrifying minutes of my entire life began. I doubt there is a more horrific thing one could experience. I still lie in bed at night and feel that flood of suffocating anxiety. Time seemed to stand absolutely still. My skin crawled and every vein in my body throbbed with terror. *What did they really do to those Nigerians?* I couldn't move. I could barely breathe. *How much pain can a man endure before his mind shuts down and retreats into the sanctuary of unconsciousness?* I knew they were going to kill me. I just didn't know how.

Death was on its way. I could *hear* it. They were a mob of hate-filled men and women, and I couldn't see them yet but their voices grew louder and louder, yelling and screaming, and the sound that really made my blood run cold was the clatter of debris being thrown out of the way as they advanced. It was like some multilimbed Hydra, stomping toward me, thundering the ground and furiously tossing away shards of metal and wood as it drew near. It was the sound of approaching death, just overwhelmingly terrifying, and I knew that as soon as they came around the nose of that helicopter and saw me, they were going to chop me to pieces. That's what they had done to the Nigerians. That's what they did to *everybody*. We had heard eyewitness accounts of them playing soccer with the skulls of their enemies.

The howling racket of the mob's rage grew louder and louder, and I knew there was absolutely nothing I could do to save myself. There was a large survival knife in the chest pocket of my vest, and I could have plunged it into my heart and ended it right there, but somehow I never even considered that. My life was surely lost, but I would not be the one to take it. A fully loaded M-9 pistol was strapped to my broken thigh and within easy reach, but for some reason my brain still refused to recognize its existence. Maybe one small part of my psyche reasoned that if I was holding a threatening gun in my hand, any thin hope of being taken alive would be lost. That enraged mob would riddle me with a thousand bullets.

I was no longer a soldier fighting with my comrades against a common enemy. I was merely a man alone, facing a horrifying death. I did not know for certain that everyone else was dead, but I could do nothing to help them now. Within less than a week, American M1 tanks and armored personnel carriers—equipment that we'd requested and been denied—would finally arrive from the States. But for Ray and Tommy and Bill, and those two incredibly courageous Delta men whose names I did not yet even know, it would be one week too late.

I could think of no other course of action. I put the empty weapon across my chest, placed my open hands on top of it, and stared up at the hazy blue sky. In seconds, the Somalis would come for me. Not an organized military enemy, but a mob of enraged civilians and militia with only one thing on their minds: vengeance. A few clouds drifted by overhead. There were no helicopters in sight. I heard the rising victorious cries as the Somalis swarmed around Super Six-Four, the poundings of hundreds of fists against her battered hide, a rattle like a swarm of feeding locusts. I did not sob. I did not pray. No tears coursed down my cheeks. For me, in that one frozen moment in time, all that I could do was wait for their arrival.

My Joey will never know his father. . . .

The first Somali came around the nose of the aircraft. My eye caught the movement, and I raised my head up and looked at him. I tried to stay perfectly still, but I had startled him. He and his co-horts must have thought that they had killed us all. The man took a step or two backward, then realized that I was not a threat, and the crowd surged forward, descending on me like vultures on a cadaver.

There may have been a hundred of them, or even a thousand. I could not tell. I couldn't see what was happening around me. The sky above became a blur of screaming heads and flying fists and feet, punching and kicking at me. I didn't cry out or try to resist, I just went limp and tried to absorb the blows. *How do I make it through the next five minutes?* There was nothing I could do for the other men now; I had to focus on my own survival. *If I can survive for five, then I'll worry about the next five.* I decided to act as passively as I could. The situation was volatile as nitroglycerine. Only minutes before, I had been trying to kill them and they had been doing the same, and now I would just have to endure their unbridled fury.

They seemed to divide quickly into two groups, one bent on tearing me apart and the other intent on stripping me of anything of value. I saw flashes of incongruous clothing, men wearing T-shirts with Nike and Adidas logos, women wrapped in dresses with prints nearly as loud as their screams. Someone kicked me hard, while two more started to claw at my flight gear and clothing. My flight vest would not come off; it was closed by the kind of plastic clasps you find on a water skier's vest, and the Somalis had never seen such things. They tore at it so violently that I knew if I didn't help them they would rip me limb from limb simply to get it off. I opened the clasps for them, as well as the carabiners that held my extraction harness together, and then I was lying there in only my brown T-shirt and desert flight trousers and boots as they waved my vest high overhead and shouted victoriously while others swarmed in to try to capture the prize. I was carrying no personal effects, no wallet or good-luck charms. And it was a good thing that I'd removed my wedding ring, because they would have severed my finger to get it off.

I cannot remember how many times they struck me or clubbed me. But it was many, many times.

A snarling face bent in and a man ripped the green badge loose from my neck cord. That badge gave me access to the Task Force Ranger compound, and taped to the back of it was my military identification card. My metal "dog tags" went with it, and as soon as he saw the green badge in his hand he stuck it in my face and shouted.

"Ranger! Ranger! You die Somalia!"

His scream curdled my blood, but it shocked me even more that this man could know so much about our security and procedures. There was nothing on that green badge but a *number*. I wondered how many of these were now hanging around the necks of our enemies. But I didn't wonder for long, because two men began to work on my boots. They barely tore the laces open before bracing their feet in the dirt and twisting and pulling. I watched them tear my left boot off. I closed my eyes when they went for the right. The pain of my broken femur shot up through my shattered spine like a high-voltage electrocution.

I looked up as a man raised something high above his head. For a second the sun haloed around the object, and then he swung it down on me like a club. It smashed into my face, breaking my right eye socket and cheekbone. For many years I have held my peace—

for the sake of the survivors of the men who were killed—not refuting the claim that I was struck with the butt of a rifle. But the truth is long overdue.

That object was not a weapon. It was soft and very heavy.

It was the severed arm of one of my comrades.

I did not cry out or try to defend myself. My assailant was poised for another blow and obviously preparing to beat me to death, but I stared into his eyes with such hatred and defiance and disgust that he froze, backed away, dropped his "club," and disappeared.

Someone fired a shot in the air. It didn't exactly bring things under control, but it must have stilled the blood lust that was surging through that savage crowd. I was lying there barefoot now, with only my T-shirt and flight trousers remaining. In those climatic conditions of heat and humidity, our medics had recommended not wearing underwear, and when the Somalis opened my trousers to drag them off and saw that I was naked, they inexplicably stopped. It was an absolutely surrealistic moment as someone slowly zipped my fly back up, and the last vestiges of my filthy uniform were left in place. Their choice to honor modesty, while mutilating and desecrating the dead and the defenseless, utterly dumbfounded me.

Someone threw a handful of dirt into my eyes and my mouth. The grit blinded me, and I choked and sputtered it from my throat. Someone else wrapped a filthy rag around my head. I felt many hands clutching at my legs and my shoulders, and then they hoisted me high up into the air. My crushed vertebrae ground hard against each other, and as they stretched me out like a prisoner on the rack, my broken femur cleaved into the back of my leg, the sharp bone puncturing right out through my skin.

I left my body.

I do not remember fainting, but the flood of agony triggered a response that would only be explained to me much later by a survival psychologist. The human mind has some defensive talents that only the dying or near dead can relay, and mine took me to a place high above my tortured form. I looked down on myself and the surging horde, watching it all in perfect detail, that sea of howling, triumphant inhumanity and those thousands of hands passing me aloft like a bloody sacrifice to their unholy gods.

For those brief moments, the pain was swept away.

And then, so was I. . . .

Chapter 2

A PRISONER OF HATE

October 3, 1993

I RETURNED TO MY HOME IN NEW HAMPSHIRE.

The delusion lasted for only seconds, but it was refuge, a brief retreat to a peaceful corner of my soul. My small, serene town of Berlin nestled there in the cleavage of rolling green mountains, where the bittersweet smoke from the paper mills drifted through the towering pines. Almost every "Berliner" was of French Canadian descent and Catholic, and the differences we had were small compared to the bonds that made us one huge family. In the autumn we hunted deer and birds and rabbits, not for trophies, but for the dinner table. In the winter we skied and rode snowmobiles and played hockey until our faces were apple red and our lips bright blue. In the spring we fished in crystal-clear streams and rivers, swollen with ice-cold runoffs from the northern peaks.

For a moment I was a junior in high school again, with no plans for college, just a carefree kid who dreamed of flying army helicopters someday soon. My only nightmares were of fumbling the deciding pass in a high school football game, or of having my hero, hockey legend Bobby Orr, chastise me for missing an easy goal. It was the heart of summer in 1977, when all of us were free at last from math and English and chemistry, and the Vietnam War was no longer on the nightly news. The days were long and lazy, and there were beer parties at someone's house nearly every night. My homely Datsun B210 was scraped and battered from careless encounters with guardrails, but I was happy to have wheels of any kind, and in spite of my abuse its souped-up cassette player still blasted out "Stairway to Heaven."

I lay on my back on a large flat rock, overlooking a river bend called Emerald Pool. The water below was glassy and cold, and the happy howls of kids echoed through the trees as they leaped from a cliff into deep eddies below. Birds chirped and the waters splashed and bubbled, and as always in the summertime I loved to just close my eyes and feel the sun's rays baking my face, inhaling the scent of the forest. I heard a soft voice, my eyelids fluttered open, and there was Laurie, my high school girlfriend. She was striding toward me up the hill in her frayed blue jeans, tight tank top, chestnut hair, and glossy tanned skin. Her smile was wide and snow white, and I felt my chest flutter with the promise of romantic adventure as I raised my hand and she reached out for me. . . .

Then suddenly her smile turned into a vicious snarl, her fingers grabbed for my crotch, and she screamed and squeezed with all her might.

I was violently snapped back to reality, being carried aloft on the thundering wave of a mosh pit from hell. That suffocating rag was wrapped around my head and I couldn't see a thing, but the surging crowd engulfing me sounded like an urban riot. The fingers snatching at my genitals belonged to an enraged Somali woman, and her shrieks made my blood run cold as she leaped into the air and dove right onto me, trying to tear my testicles from my body. But I was half crippled and helpless, utterly unable to defend myself. Someone wrenched her off me, though not before she tried to castrate me again, and I heard her wails as she was left behind in the dust, without her trophy. I was grateful that I still had my flight trousers on, but I was also pessimistic as a fat, caged turkey on the last Wednesday of November.

They're going to tear me apart. . . .

All around me people were chanting and screaming, their sandals and sneakers pounding the dust and the slings of their rifles rattling. I was being carted around by a group of crazed gunmen and we were parading through the streets, while bony hands and gnarly switches slapped at my body as if I were a piñata. I clung to the sharp bones of someone's shoulders, my biceps convulsing, trying to relieve the unholy torment coming from my back. It was a bizarre, unearthly sensation. I was me, but I wasn't. I was living this, but I couldn't *possibly* be alive. I was nothing more than a bloody trophy, being displayed with far less dignity than the slaughtered deer I had hunted as a boy.

I did not utter a word, and I tried very hard not to groan or cry out with the incredible pain. I did not want to remind these people that I was still their living, breathing nemesis, a creature of loathing who could be made to suffer further for their losses. If I behaved like a corpse, maybe it would quell their urge to turn me into one.

The entourage rushed onward, and it seemed to me that even *more* babbling voices and stampeding feet joined the procession. The stench of smoldering rubber and burning wood seeped into my nostrils and an image leaped into my mind of a huge iron pot of boiling stew, with my own severed head floating amid steaming hunks of camel meat. The terror surged in my gut, and if I could have somehow wrenched myself from my captors' grasps and run like a cheetah, I would have. But with my broken leg and crippled spine, I knew I wouldn't make it five feet before they diced me up into desktop ornaments. The fear gripped my chest like an iron claw, but I shoved those ghastly images away. The worst trait a combat chopper pilot can have is a vivid imagination.

For Christ's sake, Durant, I snapped at myself inside my head. *Just go with the flow.*

As if I had a choice in the matter.

I had no clue as to how far or in which direction we were moving, but I knew that each breath could be my last. And I savored every one of them, while gunfire hammered in the distance and the simple act of sucking air made the sweat run in rivulets from my armpits. The grim reality that every pilot has to deny in order to focus and fly into combat had happened to me—I was shot down and badly wounded, an American in the clutches of an infuriated enemy, a hated symbol of Caucasian Western power, fallen from the sky into a swarm of African tribal rage. I was a man in a land of no futures, without a hint of what might happen next, and I could not prepare myself for any coming event.

Then all at once I was sailing through the air. My body smacked down onto a hot iron slab, my head bounced hard, and I bit my lip and writhed as the pain thundered through my spine. My palms recoiled from sun-broiled metal, but the slab wasn't a torture rack or the top of an iron stove—it seemed to be the floor of a flatbed truck of some sort. A coarse canvas tarp was tossed over me, smothering the dim light that filtered through my blindfold, then the engine gunned and the truck rumbled off through the wild streets of the Mog.

It was a ride not unlike many I had taken before in gypsy cabs and other modes of transportation, throughout the world in cities where there are no rules—where the horn and cussing are as important as the steering wheel, where the vehicle never moves more than a few feet without having to negotiate some kind of obstacle, where the driver starts and stops constantly and the trip is a vibrating stagger from one pothole to the next. But now my vertebrae were crushed, my leg broken, and my face smashed. It was a rough and painful ride, but I was so glad to be away from the mob that I would have stayed on the

back of that truck all day rather than go through that insane gaunt-
let again.

Unfortunately, my mode-of-transportation preferences were not on
anyone's list. Within minutes the vehicle skidded to a stop, the pack
descended on me again, and I swallowed my groans and made myself go limp as they dragged me from the flatbed onto their bouncing shoulders. The immediate reappearance of the crowd was surreal.
Had they been running alongside the damn truck the whole time?
Or had the entire city become an endless wave of clutching hands,
just waiting to pass me from one victorious riot to the next as news
of my capture was shouted from rooftop to rooftop?

They were sprinting with me now, every pounding step of theirs
a thunderbolt through my torn nerve endings. But suddenly those
hundreds of voices dropped to just a dozen. Because I was blinded
by that rag, my other senses seemed to become acute, my hearing
sopping up every hint of change in tone or environment. We were
entering a closed space, a room of some sort. *Oh shit, here it comes
again.* I braced myself and gritted my teeth as they swung me into
the air, like overzealous parents tossing a child into a pile of autumn leaves, and I smacked down onto an unforgiving, hardpan
floor.

Lightning exploded behind my eyes, and the neural current
surged through my body from my feet to my forehead. I was breathless, twisting on the floor, trying like hell not to wail. I wondered if
a man could die from the shock of pain alone, and I begged my
brain to take me up and away from my battered shell again.

Take me back to New Hampshire.

Take me anywhere but here!

No such luck.

A dozen hands searched every pocket of my trousers, checking
every wrinkle of my sweat-soaked T-shirt, groping for some over-
looked item of value. Hot breath hissed in my face, threatening me
with death in that phrase that had become their litany: "Ranger!

Ranger! You die Somalia!" But I did my best to stay completely passive and nonconfrontational—the single, basic, and most crucial lesson from my survival training that was right there at the forefront of my brain.

"Those first few minutes of capture are critical. . . . Don't piss off your captors!"

I heeded that voice in my head, but I didn't think my captors could get much more pissed off.

The Somalis were known to chew the narcotic leaves of a tree called *khat*, which gave them a feeling of euphoria and made them utterly fearless in combat. But even without the drug-induced state they were in, I was sure they'd kill me in an instant if I would only give them a reason. The harsh voices around me seemed to be arguing in their warbling, African babble, and I gathered they really had no idea what to do with me. Then more pairs of feet stomped into the room and new voices entered the picture, their tones even louder, more overbearing and strident. The situation was clearly still as volatile as the spilled fuel from Super Six-Four.

Some years later, American intelligence officers would tell me that at that moment a rival and more powerful clan took possession of me. But at the time, I just lay there like a blind man at a Mafia standoff, hoping they wouldn't settle the dispute with gunfire.

You guys just sort this out. . . . I'll hang around for a while.

For a brief moment, I wondered about my men—Tommy, Bill, Ray, and those two courageous Delta operators. Had any of them survived the onslaught at the crash site? *It's possible,* I told myself. *It could be. There was so much confusion and gunfire, maybe some of the guys got away.* I remembered that Bill had been lying on the ground behind me, but I hadn't actually seen Tommy or Ray again, or witnessed the fates of Gary and Randy with my own eyes. Could any of them have possibly escaped this mass fury that seemed to engulf the entire city? *If any of you boys are still out there,* I coached silently, *you'd better lay low till nightfall, 'cause in this slum you'll stick out like cockroaches in a fruit salad.* But those thoughts left me as the rag was tightened more firmly around my head, the Somalis yanked me up into the air, squeezed me through the door, and we were on the run again.

Slam. I landed on the floor of the flatbed. Maybe it was a different truck, but it didn't much matter—it sure as hell wasn't a shiny new Ford with a pillow, a blanket, and a six-pack of Bud in the back. We rumbled off on another bronco-bucking ride through the labyrinth of streets. I tried to keep track of the turns and distances, but it was impossible. The driver braked and veered sharply, as if he were trying to lose someone. *How goddamn long is this going to go on?* I wondered in frustration, unable to track the passage of time. *Maybe it's only been ten minutes? Or maybe it's already been two hours?* There was just no way to know. Yet after a while, even through the thickness of my blindfold, I began to discern that the light was finally fading. The Sabbath sun was making its descent at last, and this godforsaken day was coming to an end.

If I ever make it out of this alive, Sundays will never be the same.

I thought about the ironies of fate, and how a man's life could take some wild, unforgiving turns in the space of just a few hours. I was stunned by my own transition—from a healthy, self-assured, eager young warrior of that morning, to a battered, wounded, shit-scared cripple by the late afternoon. Some of us were certainly dead. Some of us were surely lost. But I was still alive, and very soon now, it would be night. My comrades in the skies above had electronic eyes, while our enemies would be left to grope in darkness.

Outstanding! I thought to myself. *Now we have the advantage. The odds have been tilted in our favor. We own the night!*

But it would be years before I would realize just how desperate the situation had become for all of Task Force Ranger, and that the plight which I was in that day was inconsequential compared to that of the remainder of the force, pinned down and surrounded in that very same city.

———————

THE TRUCK STOPPED AGAIN. There was gunfire in the distance, but it was like the muffled soundtrack of a war movie coming from an outdoor drive-in. We were certainly still inside the city, but that was all I could be sure of. Night had fallen as it does in Africa, a blackness so thick you can almost feel it. The wind had died down, yet I could still smell the sea. Dogs howled from somewhere, but I knew they were wild and on the move—there were no house pets in Mogadishu. My second wild ride of the day was over. It was time to face the next unknown challenge. The engine idled while I waited for the pack to descend on me, yet the crowd of wild rioters failed to appear. Instead, a smaller group of murmuring men roughly lifted me up, the pain sloshed through me, and I balled my fists and gnashed my teeth as I was carted from the flatbed.

My captors were squeezing me through another doorway. I held my breath for the inevitable impact as they grunted under my weight, crossed some kind of a room, and threw me against a wall. *Sweet Jeessus.* I slowly exhaled into the pain, willing it to recede as I let my body slide down flat and settled onto a floor as hard as marble. The door slammed, someone tore the rag from my head, and I blinked and squinted into darkness.

All around me were shiny, shadowed faces and glinting gun barrels. The Somalis were gesticulating wildly and snapping at each other. Even with all of their efforts to hide me from their rivals, or from the overflying eyes of our aircraft, they hadn't calmed down much. I sensed an urge to end it all right there and dispense with this half-dead American and the problems my presence was sure to bring.

I flicked my eyes from one furious face to another, wondering how much I might be worth to them. A truckload of grain? A whole hangar full? Should I suggest to them that I'd be worth much more alive than dead? *Hey, maybe you guys would consider exchanging me for a Mercedes with a CD player and a Mohamed Aidid hood orna-*

ment? As a kid I had always been something of a jokester, but now I knew that I was just half delirious and my snide side was rearing its ugly head. Wisely, I decided not to say a word, because they might just all spin on me and let loose with those AKs.

Keep your mouth shut, Durant. . . . It only gets you in trouble.

Still arguing, the Somalis walked out of the room and left me alone for a few moments. The sudden solitude was a blessing, even though I knew it wouldn't last. I tried to straighten my broken leg, feeling the dampness of blood and syrupy fluids stiffening on my flight trousers. It was obvious that the bone had broken through the skin. Running was definitely not an option, and even a combat crawl was a fantasy. I cleared some of the dirt from my eyes and spat it from my mouth. My face felt like a mask of crusted blood and sweat-caked dust. I was filthy, all busted up, and in very bad shape.

I swept my eyes through the darkness. *What can I do to get out of here?* The gunfire in the distance was growing steadily in volume, and I tried to imagine what might be going on out there. If the mission had been successful, all of Task Force Ranger would have been long gone by now. But I knew that some of my friends had been shot down before me, and maybe some more after my own crash. No one would be left behind, and I concluded that was why the battle raged on.

Get them out, boys, I urged silently. *Get us all the hell out of here.*

Of course, I had no idea at the time what that effort really entailed. Donovan's body had been pulled from the smashed cockpit of Super Six-One, but Cliff's was still wedged so firmly inside that men were working on his metal coffin with bolt cutters and fire axes, and all of that in the middle of a fierce firefight. The exfil convoy was all shot up, regrouping now and gathering additional support to go back out into that melee and recover the wounded and stranded Rangers and Delta operators. Reinforcements, consisting of more Rangers, 10th Mountain Division soldiers, Navy SEALs, and Malaysian and Pakistani tanks and armored personnel carriers, were fighting their way toward Cliff's and Donovan's crash site. And throughout, pilots and crews of the 160th were flying mission after mission, providing fire support to the ground elements and trying to keep the Somali hordes from overrunning them all and making Custer's Last Stand look like nothing more than a rained-out corporate picnic.

The best friends I had were still out there, all of them flying the toughest combat missions of their army careers. Just south of Cliff's crash site, ninety-nine Rangers and D-boys were pinned down in the buildings bracketing Marehan Road. They had a number of critically wounded and they were nearly out of water, IV bags, and ammo. My good friend Stan Wood and his crew had their helicopter, Super Six-Six, loaded up with supplies and took off from the airfield for the battle zone. Stan knew he would probably be shot down, but he figured that if he crashed in the right place, at least the customers would be able to recover the goods.

The Rangers tossed infrared chem lights into the road. Stan swooped in, his blades nearly shaving the low rooftops, his chopper's belly roaring past the shot-out windows. While a couple of D-boys in the back pushed the resupply packs out the doors, the Somalis opened up on Stan from everywhere. Bullets chunked through the rotor blades, pierced the gearbox, and spewed fluids from the engine. One of the men in the back took a round in the neck. But the drop was so precise that the Rangers merely had to reach out from their cover and drag the kits back inside.

When Stan got back to the airfield, there were so many jagged holes in his aircraft that he lost count after forty. He cursed in frustration at the shot-up mess of Super Six-Six, because the unit was down another Blackhawk. He looked around for Dan Jollota, who just that afternoon had barely nursed his smoking SAR bird back to the seaport, but Dan was nowhere to be found. Jollota had "borrowed" a spare Blackhawk, reassembled a SAR team, and was flying nonstop missions searching for survivors from our crash site. From all reports, he was a man possessed and he flew continuously for nearly forty-eight hours, stopping only to refuel and re-arm.

Stan considered calling Dan's wife, Jane, to give her a situation report. But as it turned out, he didn't have to. He ran into her at the compound.

Unlike most of the wives of the men in the 160th, Jane already knew exactly what was going on. Captain Jane Jollota was a company commander in the 101st Airborne and stationed right there at the other end of the airfield. She and Dan had both been deployed to Somalia and had to leave their fifteen-month-old son in the care of Jane's parents. She was a chopper pilot herself, she knew what Dan was doing, and she didn't need an update. The fight was still young.

There would be no dearth of courage in Mogadishu that night.

I blew out a sigh of frustration and lay there flat on the floor, looking once more around the darkened room. It was empty, but I couldn't tell much more about it. There had been no electricity in this part of the city for quite some time, and the only revealing light had come from the dim oil lanterns that the Somalis carried in and out with them. As my eyes adjusted, I could see that the space was shaped like an octagon, the concrete walls solid to a height of about five feet. Above that were several rows of blocks with diamond-shaped ventilation holes that allowed the air and the sounds from the outside world to pass through. There was nothing else in there — just a hard floor, those walls, and a flimsy door.

No serious breaching required on this one, boys, I thought hopefully as I imagined a Delta team exploding through the door. *You can just burst in like linebackers.*

But no one was coming to my rescue, at least not yet.

What I didn't know was that the events at our crash site had actually been recorded by the long-range cameras of the P3 Orion. There was already a grainy videotape of my body being carried away in the melee. Yet even as I was seen being swallowed up by the surging crowd and billowing dust, the other barbaric acts taking place at that site were also observed by horrified Americans back in the JOC. It would be some time before I would learn about the dismembering of my comrades, or how the next morning their corpses were shackled with chains and dragged through the streets of Mogadishu. But my commanders and fellow Task Force officers would witness it all. Enraged and frustrated, they had no idea where I might be, but they held out slim hope that I still breathed.

The door to my "cell" opened and the Somalis surged back inside, carrying their primitive oil lamps and inspecting me like some strange insect pinned to a microscope slide. There was obviously still a vociferous disagreement about what to do with me. Two of them were very hostile, jabbing their AK-47 barrels in my face and growling over and over again in broken English: "Ranger, Ranger, kill many Somalis! You die Somalia!" I don't know how many times I heard that threat, but I certainly had no reason to doubt them. One of them spat on the floor and they hustled out of the room again, leaving me blinking and breathless.

So this is it, Durant. I closed my eyes and slowly shook my head, feeling a powerful sense of disgust and disappointment. *So this is heaven's door.* I was too young to have ever seriously envisioned the end of my life, but I definitely hadn't pictured it in a hellhole like this. *Looks like you're going to die here. It's just a question of when and how.*

A younger Somali came in alone, carrying another small lamp and a three-foot chain. He apparently had been ordered to restrain me, which certainly seemed superfluous, given my condition. He bent down and placed my hands together over my stomach. I don't know why I thought to do it, but I kept my elbows clamped at my sides, creating a gap between my wrists. So, even though he wound the chain tightly, the gap remained as he slipped a padlock through the links and snapped it shut. I kept up that counterpressure while he tugged

at the lock to check its effectiveness. Satisfied, he left the room, closing the door behind him.

All right, Durant. Let's see how smart you are.

I curled my right hand and squeezed it hard against my left palm.
I twisted it back and forth and pulled at the same time. It took a lot
of effort and my skin chafed and tore at my wrist, but I slipped my
hand out of the chain! *Outstanding,* I thought. It might not seem
like such a big deal, but at the time it was an incredible morale
boost. It was only a small victory for me, but significant. They had
captured me, I was defenseless and at their mercy, but I had out-
smarted one of them already. If I could do that, what else would I
be able to do?

And still, I harbored no illusions about my desperate situation. I
didn't know where I was and I didn't think my comrades could possibly know either. The fate of my crew and those two Delta men
seemed worse than grim. Only a few hours before, I'd been thinking
about such meaningless things as my suntan and if I'd make it home
in time to run the marathon. It was all too clear now that I'd probably never make it home. And if by some miracle I did make it back,
with these injuries I wouldn't be running another marathon for a very
long time, if ever. Yet I didn't feel remorse or self-pity. I felt somewhat
stupid and naive, like a man who'd blissfully gone through life ig-
noring the facts of death.

Outside the room there must have been some kind of crushed
rock or gravel. The folks at survival school had taught us to focus on
such details, and the warning sound of crunching footsteps gave me
just enough time to wrap the slack chain around my freed wrist. This
time, a different Somali came in and *again* I was searched from head
to toe. It was as if none of them trusted the thoroughness of any
other, and I resigned myself to the fact that I'd be frisked by each new
visitor. But his dismissive glance at my chain told me that my plan
was working. I wasn't home yet, but I had done something that the

enemy didn't know about, and it gave me a small psychological boost. He squatted there and jabbed a threatening finger at me.

"Ranger! You die Somalia!"

By this juncture, I had heard it all before and it was making less of an impression.

"What about the others?" I asked him. My voice sounded thick and gravelly to me.

He frowned and stood up, as if surprised that I had the audacity to speak. "*Udders?*"

"My friends. My comrades. The *other* men at the crash site."

He shrugged and left the room. A few moments later, he came back with yet another Somali.

"The others," I asked again. "What happened to the other men?"

The second man shook his head, and they both left. I didn't know if he, too, had failed to comprehend the question, or if he was telling me that they were all dead.

I slipped out of the chain again and tried to make myself a little more comfortable. My leg had begun to swell, it was bloated and stiff, and I adjusted it to relieve the pain and examined the rest of my injuries. I could feel the broken bones under my right eye. My vision seemed all right, but the bones suddenly dropped away where my eye socket met the bridge of my nose. For a second the vision of that swinging "club" flashed in my memory, but my rational brain wanted to reject what I'd seen. No human I had ever encountered could commit such a wanton act. Maybe it had been a wooden truncheon after all? Or the limb of a tree, or a rifle butt? No. I knew exactly what had happened. But no matter what, I decided that the wives and loved ones of my men would never hear that horror from my lips.

It would be many years and many nights of tears before I would accept, and relay, the most horrific events of that day.

I was lost in thought as another Somali entered the room, taking me by surprise. I quickly mashed my hands together, hoping he wouldn't discover my freed wrist. Yet this man did not seem quite as aggressive or as angry as the rest. He was older, and he was the first one I saw who was not hefting a weapon. In the midst of this highly charged atmosphere, he appeared calm and self-satisfied, as if he was a knight who had slain an infamous dragon. He squatted at my side and pointed at his own lips.

"You want wah-terr?"

I hadn't even thought about water, but I knew I needed some. If there is a military person out there who doesn't know the importance of water, he or she has not been paying attention. It's the most critical element of survival, and we all know it. I nodded, and while he was out, I squeezed back into the chain.

He returned momentarily with a large bowl and handed it to me. I lifted it with my chained hands and gulped down most of it. My fingers were trembling, from the fear and pain and the repetitive surges of adrenaline that had coursed through my body. But I will never forget that bowl of water. It had more sludge floating in it than a sewage treatment plant and I knew I would probably be sick from it, but risking bad water is better than drinking no water at all. I thanked him for his kindness. His face was one I needed to remember—I might have to depend on this man to stay alive. He took the oil lamp with him and left me in darkness.

I could still hear the sounds of a firefight in the distance, but now it seemed to be getting closer. What had before been simmering in the background was coming to a boil. *K-k-k-kung, k-k-k-kung* . . . *bdap, bdap, bdap, bdap.* There was a myriad of weaponry going off. It was familiar, but also different in a way that at first I could not figure out. And then it occurred to me that I had not been downrange since basic training more than a decade before. Sure, I had fired thousands of rounds from helicopters and hundreds at the small-arms range and back home in New Hampshire, but until today I'd never heard the sound from the target's perspective. In all of my combat experiences, I'd always been at the controls of a helo, and enemy fire was something you could hardly see and certainly not hear above the noise of the aircraft, unless it was very, very close. Now I could hear not only the guns themselves but the impacts of their rounds, chunking off shards of cement, ricocheting from rocks, and rattling tin as they rang off into the night.

I was clearly on the wrong end of this typhoon of gunfire. By the sound of it, the battle was unfolding less than a mile away. And even more significantly, it was getting louder by the minute.

Then there was a new sound that hadn't been there before, the unmistakable *whoosh* and *boom* of a 17-pound high-explosive rocket. The distinctive buzz saws of chopper-mounted 7.62 miniguns were followed by the awesome roars of those 17-pounders. My mind began to race. What if an "eye in the sky" had seen me being carried away? Could someone in one of the helos have spotted them putting me on that truck? Maybe they had tracked my movement by air while it was still light enough? Did they know exactly where I was and had they already developed a plan to swoop down here and assault this meager prison? Could a rescue be imminent?

That's it! That's why the sounds are getting louder! My heart began to hammer as I raised my head, my ears pricking up like a bloodhound's. *They're coming to get me. It's all gonna be over soon!*

I had to make some quick decisions. What would I do in the next critical minutes? I was convinced the Somalis would try to kill me before my friends broke through their outer perimeter, and my eyes darted around the room, searching for options. Should I crawl to a dark corner near the door, so that when my captors burst in to finish me off, I could buy a few seconds in the confusion? My comrades were on the way, I was sure of it! There was certainly high risk in this venture, but nevertheless I silently cheered their arrival as the heavy gunfire continued to march nearer and nearer. Those thousands of rounds of 7.62mm never sounded so good, and explosions were erupting at regular intervals every few seconds. I could actually hear the unearthly screams of large projectiles in flight.

I struggled up onto my elbows, crabbing backward, pushing my

shoulders against the wall, and edging up a bit. And it was then, as
my forearm rested on my thigh, that I felt something strange. There
was an *object* inside my flight trousers? *What the hell is this?* I
wrenched my hand from the chain again and slid my fingers into my
pocket. The pocket must have folded over on itself at the crash site,
because, unbelievably, there inside was my army issue pocketknife!
I couldn't believe it. The Somalis had searched me *fifty* times but
had missed this? I looked up at the dark ceiling and mouthed a
"thank you" to whoever was watching over me. I tucked the knife beneath my leg and knew that I now had one final option.

If anybody comes in here to put a bullet in my head, I pledged, *that
mother's gonna get a big surprise. . . .*

Suddenly my captors outside were engaged in the battle. I could
hear rounds being fired from the other side of the wall, and the
yelling and chaos grew to a fevered pitch. The bright flashes from
their spitting gun barrels pierced through the ventilation holes above
my head and lit up my cell like a lightning storm. I could feel the
might of the U.S. Army approaching my door. It would all be over
in a few minutes, and for the very first time that day, I prayed. I
prayed for God to spare me and spare the lives of my comrades. I
prayed for just a bit more of the mercy that had kept me alive until
that moment. I had been a "casual Catholic" before, but I would become a faithful servant forever if I could just have three more minutes of protection until I was on board a Night Stalker helo and we
were all flying off to freedom.

Yea, tho I walk through the valley of the shadow of death . . .

And then, when the firing reached its peak, and I knew that within
seconds an American would come charging through that door and
it would all be over, the sounds began to change.

I squinted and listened hard, but I could no longer hear those
rockets in flight. The men in the compound outside had stopped firing. The familiar clatter of American weapons began to fade ever so
slightly, and then I realized what was happening.

The men of Task Force Ranger had no idea where I was. My location was clearly *not* their objective, and they continued their deliberate march right past me and into the distance.

They were gone. It was over. No one knew my whereabouts, or even that I was still alive. There was no rescue force en route to my prison. The sense of utter desolation was overwhelming. I was alone, in the hands of the most ruthless and vicious enemy I had ever faced, and for a moment I felt my heart and my hope sinking into a bottomless void.

But it was way too early in the game to surrender to despair. I got a grip on myself and prayed another silent prayer for my own survival, for my family, and for all the soldiers who would fight this night. I slipped my wrist back into the chain, took a deep breath, and tried to figure out what to do next.

The door suddenly swung open and a pair of Somalis rushed into the room. They were typical *mooryan*, young Somalis who lived for *khat* and combat. Their dark faces and throats gleamed with sweat, and there was an arrogant swagger in their steps. One of them was very young, probably only fifteen or so. He was thin and wiry, his cheekbones protruding from his face, his eyes wide and wild. They both gripped AK-47s, and I could smell the freshly burned carbon in their gun barrels.

The older one babbled at me as he gestured at the younger one. It was hard to understand his African mixed with bursts of incongruous American slang, but he was trying to show me that some of the Somalis doing the fighting out there were no more than young boys.

"This kid fight much years, much years," he nearly yelled as he gestured like a ranting dictator. "He brothers dead. All brothers dead!"

I did not say a word. I did not want to aggravate this already very angry man. Had I been in the mood to argue, I would have pointed out to him that a fifteen-year-old with an AK-47 can kill a man just as effectively as a gunman twice his age. *We didn't create the turmoil that decimated this kid's home and country,* I thought. *YOU Somalis did that without our involvement, and we only came here to help resolve the situation.* Yet I hardly moved, just watching them both until the acrimonious tirade was over and they left. I doubted that that young boy would live to see his eighteenth birthday.

At that point I was so exhausted, in pain, and pissed off that I wished they'd all just leave me alone. I felt as if I had lived ten years in the last ten hours, and I was fed up with visitors.

Somebody get me a Do Not Disturb sign from the Olympic Hotel and hang it on the frigging door.

Yet when the man who had given me the water returned, I was actually relieved to see him. He was definitely different from the rest, more mature and neatly dressed, in a plain clean shirt and unsoiled chinos. By the light of his lantern, I could see some gray in his thick, curly hair. He was still unarmed, and he didn't charge into my room as if there was a giant scorpion inside. He looked at me as if genuinely concerned for my well-being, although I was far from trusting any of them.

"My name is Mohammed Gait," he said.

I nodded politely, thinking, *I'll tell you my name when I have to.*

He squatted beside me and offered me a cigarette.

Although I've smoked only a handful of cigarettes in my entire life, this seemed like an appropriate time. He held a match to the end of it and I inhaled the smoke. I'm no connoisseur of tobacco, but this thing tasted terrible, and I thoroughly enjoyed it. There was just something about doing it that made me feel a little better. He lit one up for himself and we smoked in silence for a while.

I decided to speak to him without revealing any details that might compromise the other men at my crash site. If the Somalis didn't know exactly how many men had been there, then at least one of

them might have survived and still be out there somewhere—
wounded, hiding, or on the run. But at least I could try to find out
what the Somalis *did* know.

"My friends," I said. "Can you tell me about my friends?"

Mohammed Gait frowned and cocked his head. He touched his
ear, as if he hadn't heard me or didn't quite understand. I had finished my cigarette, and he took it and smudged it out with his sandal, lighting another one up for me. For a would-be marathoner, I
was doing a lot of smoking.

"The other men," I attempted again. My lips were cracked and
dry, my throat still coated with grit. "The other men who were
with me."

His brow furrowed, as if the answer to my question was obvious.
Most probably he already knew exactly what had happened to my
comrades. But I truly didn't, or else my mind still refused to accept
the horrible truth. I knew that they were either injured or shot, but
when the crowd had overrun the crash site, I could not really tell
what was happening to them.

All at once he nodded, as if at last grasping my intent, and then
he shrugged and shook his head.

"I do not know," he said. He left me one more cigarette, and then
he rose and left the room.

I slowly slipped down to the floor and lay there, looking up at the
ceiling. I lit up my last smoke. The specific pains of my back and my
leg and my face had become one full body throb, a fierce companion I would have to live with for now. I tried not to lose hope, searching in my singed memory for an image from the crash site that might
tell me someone else had survived. But what came to me again was
the shadow of that heavy object swinging into my face, and my mind
pushed the images away.

With the distant chatter of machine-gun fire still echoing from the
streets, I thought about home. I conjured up the most pleasant things
in my life. I thought about my son, Joey, kissing my cheek. Those

kisses were like gold. If there was anything that I wanted to feel again, it was that—his precious little lips on my skin. And my wife's hair, the smell of Lorrie's hair. Of all the things about her, why I thought of that I can't explain. And finally, I tried to recall the sweet scent of freshly mown grass. Maybe it was because the smells of Mogadishu— the fetid garbage, the dried sweat, the explosive residue, and the coppery stench of blood—were so awful. I'm not sure why those particular things entered my mind, but I hadn't smelled pretty hair, been kissed, or seen grass in a long, long time.

The last thing I remember thinking about on that first night was Christmas in New Hampshire. It had always been my favorite time of year, when all of my uncles and aunts and cousins would gather and celebrate and play practical jokes on each other and exchange piles of gifts. And we kids would raise a ruckus outside in the snow like a pack of happy pups, and everything was right with the world. I could almost see the winter moon, shining on a frozen pond. If I could just feel those few things, if I could do those simple things just one more time, nothing else would matter.

I could still hear the gunfire raging in the distance. So close, and yet so far. My eyelids were shuttering as I listened for the slightest hint that the column might turn my way again. I felt the ashes of my cigarette singeing my fingers.

Haven't you ever heard, Durant, I chided myself as my trembling hand crushed the butt out on the filthy floor, *that it's dangerous to smoke in bed?*

I had to surrender hope, at least for the night, and at last I drifted off to sleep from the sheer exhaustion of it all.

It was the end of my first day as a prisoner of hate. But I had no idea if it would be one night of captivity or a thousand.

Chapter 3

KOREA

November 1985

THE WOUNDED SOLDIER IN THE BACK of my chopper was going to die.

There was no doubt about it. If we didn't get this kid to a hospital pad soon, we'd be delivering a corpse. It was late at night, already the dead of winter in South Korea, and this young American infantryman had been drinking and partying with his buddies in a small northern town called Tong Du Chon. As they were wandering around the "ville," someone had thrown a concrete block from the window of a building and it had landed on this soldier's bare skull. His buddies had carried his twitching body to a taxi and hauled ass to the clinic at Camp Casey, just a stone's throw from our outfit, the 377th Medical Evacuation Unit.

I had just shut down my Blackhawk, and I was glad to be on the ground. The skies were black and stone-cold brittle, hurling huge flakes of snow from a ceiling of swollen clouds, and we had barely made it back to the pad after another mission that turned out to be far from urgent. There was a system for evaluating the decision to use a chopper for medevac in Korea. If an injury was termed as "routine," ground transportation would probably suffice. If it was slated as "priority," at least one soldier was hurt pretty bad and a quick flight to the clinic was in order. If the situation was "urgent," someone was going to lose a limb or expire if we didn't get that chopper to his location and medevac him to a sophisticated medical facility. Still, it was always up to the pilot in command to evaluate prevailing weather conditions and decide if putting up a chopper was worth the risk.

I was twenty-three years old, a Warrant Officer One, and had been flying medevac missions in Korea for eighteen months. I was young, but at this point I'd flown one hundred and forty-nine missions, making life-or-death decisions every day. I was thawing out in the ready room, my gloves still on, when a doctor on staff at the clinic called and asked for the pilot in command on duty at the 377th. That was me. I took the call.

"Mr. Durant here. What's up, Doc?"

He didn't laugh. He wasn't in the mood for cartoon humor. "I've got an extremely urgent situation here, Chief."

I rolled my eyes. My heart rate was still up from our near-fatal attempt to land in the blizzard.

"Sir, we nearly just punched into the snow. The wind's at twenty-two knots and it's pissing ice marbles out there. We can't go."

"All right." He sighed heavily. "Then this young man's going to die."

I didn't say anything for a moment. Then I asked, "How bad is it?"

"Head injury. This soldier has to get to the hospital at Yong San, and I mean *now*. He will not survive the drive. It's your call."

"I'll be right up."

I hung up and looked at my copilot. He was a CW4 and had been flying army helicopters for fifteen years, but he was new to medevac, which technically made me his superior in the cockpit. My grim expression told him everything.

"You've got to be kidding me," he said.

"I'll be right back. You'd better get the crew back out to the bird and fire it up."

I stalked outside, blew out a steamy breath into the freezing air, and hustled on up to the clinic in the ankle-deep snow. When I got up there, some of the nurses I knew looked at me, but without their usual smiles, and they turned away. Inside the doctor's office, the captain clipped the X ray up onto the viewer. I blinked at it.

The young soldier's head was cracked in half right over the top, from one ear to the other. The two separated halves of his skull, front and back, were displaced in height by about half an inch. I mean, this kid's head was busted, and after seeing the X ray, I realized that this really was an urgent medevac. His brain was hemorrhaging and they'd need to drill holes in his skull to relieve the pressure, surgical procedures that just couldn't be done at a field clinic like Camp Casey's.

I didn't think about it for long. I hadn't become an army helicopter pilot to avoid a high-risk occupation. On the other hand, I had my doubts that we'd actually make it through that blinding fury out there.

"All right," I said. "We'll try it."

Fifteen minutes later, we were airborne and headed down toward Seoul. The injured soldier was bundled up in the back, his litter affixed to the "carousel," a heavy upright slab of steel that rotates for easy access to the wounded. Our crew chief and a medic were back there keeping an eye on him, but they couldn't do much more than shiver and stare at their watches. The doors were shut tight, but the Blackhawk's heating system was having little effect.

My copilot and I were flying with night-vision goggles, which made it much easier to spot ground lights and vehicles on the roadways below, but the NVGs also let us see exactly what kind of frozen hell we were charging into. Even on a clear summer day, South Korea was a pilot's bad dream. Camp Casey was in the northern part of the country, just a few klicks from the 38th Parallel and the De-militarized Zone. Why they called it "demilitarized" was anyone's guess, because both sides of it bristled with antiaircraft batteries, surface-to-air missiles, and fixed armor emplacements. If you screwed up your navigation and strayed over the DMZ, the North Koreans would shoot you down. If they missed and you managed to cross back, the *South* Koreans would shoot you down. There were moun-tain ranges and high peaks that seemed to just pop up like icebergs in a foggy sea, and the entire country was crisscrossed with high-tension wires. On a night like this one, with high winds, icing con-ditions, and a raging blizzard, flying was a full-blown nightmare.

Then there was Papa 73. The Papa stood for "P," and the "P" stood for Prohibited. It was an invisible ring of restricted airspace around Seoul, designed to protect the South Korean president and his residence from attack by North Korean aircraft. If we flew into it, there would be no contact made and no warning of any kind— we'd get a missile up our ass. In order to reach the hospital on the south side of the city, we would have to fly a predetermined, cir-cuitous route from our northern approach.

Outside the cockpit, the snow had become a solid mass of hori-zontally hurtling globules. It was just like driving a car on a slick road in New England in the middle of a blizzard, except without the se-curity of feeling the ground. And very much like that situation, if you use your headlights you'll find yourself in the midst of a solid white dome, and blinded. In a helicopter, you don't fly on instruments un-less you absolutely have to. It's not like a commercial aircraft, where the objective is to take off, fly above the weather, and then land at a well-designated airport. The whole purpose of army chopper flying is to remain low and fast and stay close to the ground, without hit-ting it. We had no radar to tell us when a mountain or a tower might suddenly appear, and in poor visibility that warning would come too late.

As we approached the forbidden Papa 73 at an altitude of about two hundred feet, I could still see some dim lights on the ground. Just north of the kill zone, I made my first left turn to begin slipping around the perimeter of antiaircraft batteries. I knew the pattern well, and it would take us between two unforgiving mountain ranges, but as long as we could still see the ground, we'd go for it. There were some American army bases I had memorized as waypoints. There below were the tents and Quonset huts of Camp Redcloud, and not far beyond that, the dim flickers of Camp Stanley. A slim road followed the general path between two ridgelines, and I kept my eye on that road and a vehicle slowly making its way south through the storm.

Then the vehicle lights disappeared. In a second, the road was gone as well. Then, the mountains themselves were swallowed up into billowing clouds of opaque white, and the only thing I could see was the cockpit glass.

It was my hundred and fiftieth mission as a medevac pilot in Korea, and at this point I thought it might be my last. . . .

As FAR BACK as I can remember, I always wanted to be a helicopter pilot. Sure, other dreams flash by when you're a young kid in a small New England town—firefighter, policeman, sports hero, brain surgeon—but the idea of flying for a living had always enthralled me the most. My father was a full-time First Sergeant in the Army National Guard, and many of my uncles and cousins served there as well, but I didn't have fantasies about flying off into battle and coming home a hero with a chest full of medals. I grew up during the Vietnam era, when none of the kids around me wanted anything to do with wearing a uniform. So it wasn't about patriotism or flag waving or anything like that. My feelings about duty, honor, and country would evolve over time, but back then the army was just a way for me to get the best flight training without having to pay for it.

Through his service in the Guard, my father had become acquainted with an army helicopter pilot named Joe Brigham. Joe had retired as a CW4 and had opened his own air transport business down in southern New Hampshire. My family would spend every summer in a camper-trailer at a campground down there, and us kids would enjoy the entire vacation on the river and in the woods. Joe's family had a trailer down there too. I remember everyone out there by the campfire, swigging beers and telling jokes in their lawn chairs, to the tune of the soft chatter of crickets and the rush of the river.

Joe owned several aircraft, including helicopters and airplanes, which he leased, rented, or flew to provide services. He did everything with those helicopters, from recovering crashed airplanes, to setting pylons for ski lifts, to slinging cranberries out of cranberry bogs by air. Later on, he even shuttled people to the NASCAR track in southern New Hampshire and flew helo scenes in movies. You name it, he did it with those helicopters and airplanes.

One summer, when I was about fourteen, Joe asked me if I'd like to work part-time for his company. I jumped at the chance, even though the job wouldn't involve any flying for me or the other boy he'd recruited. A light plane had crashed in the mountains of a state forest, killing its occupants. Our job was to hike up to the crash site, carrying tools, and take the plane apart so Joe could come in with a helicopter and sling the wreck out of there in manageable parts. It was a cool job for a small-town kid, and I thoroughly enjoyed it. The fresh blood inside the crumpled cockpit obviously didn't make much of an impression on me.

Near the end of that summer, Joe had to ferry a helicopter from one end of the state to the other, and he offered to take me and my father along for the ride. We flew over lush forests and rushing rivers, climbed over the towering, rocky, and windswept peak of Mount Washington, and as I watched the sun and clouds reflected in the big blue lakes below, I remember thinking that this would be one out-standing way to make a living. Not long after that, Joe flew me down to a National Guard base to take a look at the army's new helicopter. The Blackhawks were just coming into military service, and when I saw my first one I thought it was the sleekest-looking thing I'd ever laid eyes on. I put my hands on its steely hide, and I knew what I wanted to do with my life.

I was barely seventeen when I sneaked off to a briefing at the local army recruiting office. The army's "sales pitch" was slick—I'd be at-tending all of these advanced and top-secret training schools and have all sorts of incredible adventures—and I swallowed it hook, line, and sinker. I wanted to get into flight school right away, but the recruiter told me that was not possible. I would have to join up and then apply for flight school while in service. Still, my test scores were pretty high, and I was confident that eventually I would make it. College was not an option for me—I wanted only to fly, and I signed that commitment paper on October 25, 1978.

A year later, shortly after my high school graduation, I found my-self in basic training. But I quickly discovered that the army had its own way of doing things, and that the road to flight school would be an uphill struggle. After Basic, I was sent to the Defense Language Institute in Monterey for Advanced Individual Training and an in-tensive course in Spanish. It was only during a long stint as a Span-ish voice intercept operator with the 470th Military Intelligence Group in Panama that I was allowed to apply for flight school. I'm convinced that the flight school assessment begins right then and there to test a potential pilot's perseverance and motivation, because my own application packet and those of my comrades seemed to get "lost" at least twice in the process. But I applied again, and then once more, before finally being accepted as a pilot candidate in 1983.

At Fort Rucker, Alabama, all of us hotshot pilots-to-be were treated like green recruits at boot camp. It was the army's final test to make sure you really wanted to fly and that you deserved the honor. We were up before dawn for PT, endless formations, dress-right-dress, and the whole nine yards. For two months, the only aircraft we saw were the ones drifting by outside our classroom windows, as we endured tedious courses in officer conduct, military law, and obsessive-compulsive paperwork procedures. Finally, when we were just about ready to die from boredom, they took us out to fly.

My first helicopter was a TH-55, a bubble canopy two-seat trainer. It was painted bright orange like a hunting vest, as if the manufacturer were warning: "Look out! There's an idiot behind the controls!" That first flight was called your "nickel ride," probably because it was just a taste and lasted about as long as one of those mechanical rides for toddlers you see out front of the grocery store. But I took to it right away, feeling at home in the cockpit and at the controls the way kids nowadays slip right into Nintendo. We learned to take off, hover, and land, and within seven hours of flight training the Instructor Pilot got out of his seat and said, "All right, Warrant Officer Candidate. Solo." If you managed to take the chopper up, fly around the pattern, and land without killing yourself, you graduated to the next stage of flight school. We all survived.

Next came training in Bell UH-1s, the ubiquitous Hueys that had been flown by the thousands in the Vietnam War. The Huey was still the warhorse of the army, and although the Blackhawks had entered into service, the UH-1 was still regarded by us trainees as an advanced aircraft. If you could handle a Huey, you were a bona fide army pilot. I was very proud when I received my wings, and even more so when I was selected, along with one other pilot, to advance to a four-week Blackhawk course. That was the helicopter I wanted to fly.

In the spring of 1984 we all received our orders. Pilots were sent out to Germany, Hawaii, Panama, to the 101st and the 82nd Airborne Divisions. I was ordered to Korea as a medevac pilot, and that was just fine with me. I was single, ready for faraway places and adventures, and flying medevac meant real-world missions—a fine way to *really* learn how to fly.

On April Fools' Day I reported to the First Platoon of the 377th Medical Evacuation Unit at Yong San near Seoul. The unit was still flying Hueys, and I was one of the first Blackhawk pilots to arrive. Over time, the 377th would staff up with more Blackhawk pilots until we had enough personnel to accept the new birds. But for now, I would be back in a UH-1. Almost immediately I was put on standby status and sent up to Camp Casey for a seven-day, round-the-clock rotation. I was twenty-two years old and most definitely the unit's "FNG"—fucking new guy.

The winter was waning in Korea, but it was still pretty cold and there was ice on the roads. Camp Casey sits comfortably in a small valley, but there are some high hills of one and two thousand feet nearby, and considerable mountain ranges just to the north. On that very first night, I was standing by as a copilot when the phone rang in the ready room. There had been a serious vehicle accident involving a troop transport on one of the winding roads in a nearby valley. Some serious injuries were involved, and it looked like one soldier might lose an arm. We took off just after 2:00 A.M.

At that time, we did not yet have the night-vision equipment that would soon become standard. Flying at night in helicopters without night-vision goggles is interesting stuff when you're going to unprepared landing areas. You're flying into black holes, landing on the side of the road somewhere, and you have no idea what's down there. It's risky business, but I hadn't been flying long enough to really appreciate the dangers. The pilot in command was an experienced CW3 in his midthirties, and I was a "slick wing" Warrant Officer One. Unlike with fixed-wing aircraft, where the left seat is reserved for the chief pilot, in an army helicopter the choice of seating is up to the pilot in command. But it doesn't matter where you sit—he'll be sure to tell you who's running the show.

The mission was precarious, but this wasn't a combat situation where we'd have to zip in and get out under fire, so we took our time evaluating the landing zone. The thing about vehicle or training accidents was that the folks on the ground were not usually prepared to bring in a helicopter. We couldn't rely on them to understand how large the landing area would have to be, or that it should be relatively flat, with no large obstacles, wires, or fences in the area. They didn't have signal beacons or know how to set up an approach pattern. If we could make contact with them we'd coach them with simple instructions, but more often than not they had no radio gear compatible with ours. At any rate, you couldn't trust any coordinates they'd relay, because they often had no clue as to where they really were. At the time, global positioning systems weren't yet in service and ground troops were still navigating by map, eyeball, and stars. On this night, the infantrymen at the accident site had set up three vehicles in a wide triangle pattern with their headlights on. That was pretty good, but not having full faith in their judgment, we swept in with our big landing light on and checked out the zone before committing.

The one unknown—and the biggest hazard with helicopters—is how dusty the ground might be. When you come into an unprepared landing area and there's loose dirt, you never know what's going to kick up. Every place in the world is different. In some areas the covering is very fine and becomes airborne in a rotorwash cloud, but you're able to see through it. In other places the dirt is more dense and creates a "brownout" effect, and when you get down into it you can't see a damned thing and you lose all outside reference. And yes, we are all instrument rated, which means we can fly using our altitude, heading, power, and attitude indicators, but it's very high risk to try to physically land a helicopter on instruments.

You've got to be able to see outside. But if you get to the point where you've committed yourself, where you're down below the trees and you suddenly lose sight of the ground, you've just got to feel your way down. You stay on the approach that you've set up and you hold your course and take it all the way in. You've got a controlled rate of descent, so even if you do lose outside reference, you just hold what you've got until you feel the skids or the wheels touch down. It might be a little abrupt, but if you keep your cool and don't overcontrol, you'll be okay.

Unfortunately, what happens to some pilots is that they get to that point—they're fully committed—and then that brownout kicks up and they change their minds. Oftentimes, that's why helos crash, because the crew overreacts and they try to pull out. The danger is that in a helicopter, when you make one control input, you have to make other opposite or coordinated control inputs to keep the bird upright. You have to coordinate the movement of the cyclic with your right hand—the control stick between your knees that provides a mix of directional and speed control; the collective with your left hand—which adjusts altitude and power; and finally the tail rotor pedals—which at low speeds and at a hover point the nose of the aircraft in the desired direction. If you make one control input all by itself, the impact on the other control surfaces causes the aircraft to do things like pitch, roll, and yaw. And if you're not compensating for that, now the aircraft is suddenly going to be flying sideways, and you don't know it because you can't see. You hit a tree and the party's over. So, once you're committed, you make that damned landing.

I wasn't overly nervous or edgy on that very first mission, I was just eager to do it. It was just a natural fit for me. I still consider myself to be blessed with the career I ended up in—I liked it, I always felt comfortable with it, I was good at it. It was just the right thing for me. That first mission was kind of when it all came together, and it went well.

The injuries of the three accident victims were serious and their status clearly urgent. Their two-ton truck had skidded, smacked into a tree, and rolled down an embankment. Their lives were hanging in the balance and one soldier was in danger of losing a limb. The pilot and I stayed in our seats, keeping the aircraft at idle, letting the blades turn just enough to keep the systems warmed up and running. We lowered the noise and cut down on the blade wind, because most of these injured people are scared enough to begin with. Some of them have never flown in a helicopter before, and now they're hurt and scared and you want to minimize any further environmental shock. You try to make it a little less traumatic for them. But you very rarely shut a helicopter down on a medevac, because starting it up again takes time and always has inherent dangers, system failures and the like. Their buddies loaded them onto litters in the back of our chopper and we flew them down to Yong San and the hospital at Seoul.

The impact of my job satisfaction really hit me that first night. After we shut it down, debriefed, wrote up our reports, and turned in, I kept thinking about those injured soldiers who'd ridden in the back of our chopper and I couldn't sleep, wondering about how they were. The next morning, I called the hospital and found out they were all going to make it just fine. I felt fantastic, like some super-hero. It was an incredible payoff for a job well done, and making those follow-up calls became a habit for me for some time.

I would not realize until much later that medevac personnel have limited emotional reserves to spend.

OVER THE NEXT eighteen months, I flew one hundred and forty-eight missions, starting off in Hueys and winding up in the bird I was born to fly, the UH-60 Blackhawk—coincidentally, the new birds were delivered on my birthday in July of 1984. The 1st Platoon 377th was responsible for the northern sector of South Korea, the entire zone along the DMZ. We flew at dawn and at midnight, in super-heated summer air that soaked our coveralls through with sweat, or in whipping winter winds that froze our auxiliary power units and made our teeth chatter. There were gunshot wounds out there, soldiers lost on snow-covered peaks, overturned jeeps, and meningitis victims with raging fevers. We didn't ask a lot of questions, we just flew in and got them out.

Of course, with a lot of medevac missions, you'd get there to find out that the victim wasn't that badly injured. There were personnel on the ground making unqualified medical assessments, and you would suddenly discover that you had put yourself and your crew at risk for no good reason. Every medevac mission has inherent dangers—you're going into unprepared landing areas, there's no briefing, you're trying to do it fast, and the ground personnel you're dealing with are untrained. Still, we never held a grudge. Maybe the best thing about being a medevac pilot is that folks are always happy to see you.

In the backs of our choppers were our silent heroes, the medic and crew chief. They never complained, never questioned a mission, never balked before leaping into the cargo bay and taking off on a rainy, windy night. The medic was cross-trained as a crew chief. He understood the aircraft, and if needed, he could take oil samples or pull chip lights, the indicators that would warn us of a malfunction in the system. Conversely, the crew chief was cross-trained as a medic and could assist with the wounded in the back.

These men had the faith of monks, trusting us pilots to get them there and back without killing them. On one particular mission, a small town had been flooded by winter rains and mountain runoffs. Some of the South Korean civilians had been swept away and drowned, while others had made it to their rooftops and were clinging to the shingles. Our crew loaded up a "jungle penetrator" onto our Blackhawk's hoist and we flew off toward the village. The device looked like a ship's anchor, with three steel arms that swung down from its center weight. While we hovered over the rooftops, our medic rode that penetrator down into a blinding rainstorm, until he and the chief had brought up every civilian into our bird.

Flying medevac in Korea was a character-building experience, probably the best first assignment for a junior pilot. I had to evolve quickly, shouldering responsibility, making critical decisions in an isolated environment. Had I been sent to another assignment, such as the 101st or the 82nd Airborne Divisions, I would have been flying multiple ship missions. In that situation you're pretty much a "duck" in a row, following the lead aircraft. There are some more challenging technical aspects to that kind of task, such as close formation flying under night-vision goggles, but all of the decision part of it is taken out. But within three months of arriving at the 377th, I was promoted to pilot in command. As a twenty-two-year-old "kid," I was taking phone calls telling me that someone's life depended on my assessment of the flying conditions and probability of mission success. It was a tough environment out there—mountainous terrain, brutal winters, broiling summers, high altitude, lots of wires, and a real-world threat. If you made a mistake and turned right for five minutes longer than you should, you were going to get shot down. I was in the "decision seat," and I liked it.

It wasn't long before I became a unit trainer, teaching other pilots how to negotiate the DMZ. There was a complex "corridor" system that had to be memorized without the use of a map. The DMZ slopes up between South and North Korea from west to east, with another unmarked strip below it called the "No Fly Line." Between the No Fly Line and the DMZ is a strip, varying in width, into which unmarked air corridors are cut. If we had to, we could fly up into those corridors, just teasing the DMZ, and execute evacuations.

There were many of these corridors laid out all across the peninsula. Every medevac pilot had to memorize the corridor layout, be able to cruise the No Fly Zone, fly up into each corridor, and return unscathed. There were no red flags or warning signs marking the DMZ below. If you crossed the point of no return, the South Koreans were supposed to fire warning shots across your nose. But if you were off your game, the North Koreans would happily let you come across, shoot you down, and take you, your crew, and your chopper captive—providing you survived the crash. I flew hundreds upon hundreds of hours learning that corridor system, and then hundreds more teaching other pilots to do the same. It was an intense, dangerous, and mentally demanding challenge.

I don't remember ever training a pilot who wasn't up to the task. They were very young men and women, but the best of America's youth. I didn't think about it back then, but I realize now that they were all brave souls.

But it wasn't all hard work. The standby rotations lasted seven days, and then we'd be back down in Seoul for a week until the next rotation, clearing our minds and entertaining our bodies. I hooked up with a crowd of about fifteen civilian and service personnel who all lived in the same billet area. There were other officers, a fixed-wing pilot, and the kinds of army nurses people envision from *M*A*S*H*. We blew off steam, laughed a lot, drank some, and danced. We went on small excursions together, taking winter ski trips and summer island hops. For a time, I had a fine relationship with a nurse, and together we all experienced some of the most fun we would ever have in the service.

After a year in Korea, I was still young but a veteran medevac pilot. I had learned a lot about flying, but I hadn't yet absorbed all the lessons that make it possible to do that job over a long period of time. I was no longer calling the hospitals or clinics after every mission to find out the status of my "patients," but that was primarily because I had learned to assess their injuries pretty well myself. Yet if a situation appeared to be highly critical, and we had gone through hell and high water to execute the mission, I'd still make that call to hear that ultimately gratifying phrase from a doctor: "He's going to be okay." Then, one rainy day in the spring of 1985, all that changed. . . .

The Blackhawks in our unit had been grounded. There was a problem with the tail rotor drive shaft in the new helicopters, so none of them would fly again until that had been worked out. Huey pilots and their choppers were hustled on up to the 377th, but they had never flown "The Zone," so us Blackhawk pilots sat in the back as mission managers, coaching the Huey pilots through their medevacs.

It was a mild spring day when the call came into the ready room. Up near the DMZ an M-113 armored personnel carrier had been attempting a crossing of the Imjin River, but the sixteen-ton vehicle had swamped and sunk below the waves. Everyone had made it out but one soldier, who was still trapped inside the steel hull. It was a possible drowning incident, slated "Urgent," and we had to be on the scene.

The skies were clear and the approach was easy as we landed on the south side of the wide, muddy river. There were lots of army vehicles and personnel milling around, but I could see no sign of a patient awaiting medevac. I jumped out of the back of the Huey and an infantry captain approached me.

"It's gonna be a little while," he said. "They're hooking up a cable."

I looked down the long embankment to the water's edge, where a wet-suited diver was wading in, holding a grappling hook in one hand. The hook was attached to a thick steel cable that ran back up to a tank retriever, a heavy treaded vehicle with a winch on the back end. The water was fast and swirling with clouds of brown. There was no sign of the sunken APC. It certainly *was* going to be a while. I turned to the Huey cockpit and swept my fingertips across my throat, telling them to kill the engine. The pilots shut the chopper down.

"Who's down there?" I asked.

"One of my men." The infantry captain was pale, staring at the river, his jaw set hard.

"How long's it been?"

"About forty-five minutes." He walked away.

I couldn't imagine how that diver was even going to find the APC in that muddy water, but he went on in, maybe following the angle of the tracks from the far embankment. Forty-five minutes was an awful long time for a man to be under water, but it was possible he was still alive. He might be breathing off of an air pocket trapped inside the vehicle. The water would be icy cold, and sometimes low water temperature can hold a body in a sort of suspended animation. I stood there watching, reaching pretty far for hope.

M-113s have heavy towing eyelets mounted below their sloping engine covers. The diver hooked up the cable, surfaced, and signaled with a twirling finger, and the tank retriever's winch started to whine. The cable went taut and the APC started to emerge. First, its antenna broke the water like a periscope. Then the front corner poked out. And finally, the top of the vehicle was above the waterline. Its hatch was open and umber water sloshed from its steel mouth.

Wang. The steel cable suddenly snapped, whipping back from the river and sending soldiers diving for the mud. It twisted crazily and coiled itself up, then lay there like a black, dead serpent. The APC slowly rolled back into the river, its open hatch, front corners, and antenna disappearing once more beneath the waves.

"Shit," someone hissed, and then the whole process began again. Men cursed and smoked and stamped the ground while a new cable was spooled and the diver went back in to hook it up. By now it had been realized that the weight of the water in the APC was too much for the winch. This time, they would just drag it out until it surfaced, dive inside, and retrieve the victim. But before that happened, another precious forty-five minutes went by.

As per regulations when executing a river crossing, the young soldier inside the APC had been wearing an inflatable flotation device, a life vest. But when the vehicle swamped, he hadn't waited long enough before yanking the inflation tab. The vest ballooned up in a split second, making his exit through the narrow hatch impossible. Inside the hull, he was jammed up against the steel ceiling, and the divers and some of his buddies had to go in with survival knives and cut the vest off of him to get him out.

Six men hauled him up on the embankment. They laid him practically at my feet, and for that first split second, I just stared at him.

He was a young black kid, but his color all over was a deep, bruised blue. Frigid river water ran from his soaked fatigues and sloshed from his combat boots. His body was stiff like tire rubber, his sightless eyes half open, and the first thing that came to my mind was the memory of the big trout I had fished from New Hampshire lakes, and how they looked long after they'd ceased breathing. This young soldier was clearly dead, and it was the first time I'd ever seen a dead man up close.

But army regs stated that without a doctor on the scene, no victim could be pronounced dead, and all efforts to revive him would continue until a qualified physician made that pronouncement. We jumped right into it. I sliced his fatigue shirt away with a knife while our medic pushed in with the defibrillator. He pressed the paddles onto the kid's chest and yelled "Clear!" while the rest of us backed off and the juice shot through the cables. The soldier's body arched hard, white foam spewing from his mouth and nose. We held our breath and stood stock-still while the medic checked his pulse. He shook his head, and we went at it again, paddling the kid five times before I finally said, "All right. Let's go."

The flight to the hospital pad took about half an hour, and throughout that flight until the second we landed, our medic, crew chief, and I tried everything we could think of. The medic performed mouth-to-mouth, and the crew chief and I took turns pumping the soldier's chest with our crossed palms. We cranked his limp arms, expelled water from his lungs, talked to him and prayed out loud, and tried by sheer force of will to get one breath out of him.

Nothing worked. We had barely touched down when a crew of stretcher bearers sprinted with him to the hospital. He was barely through the hospital doors before an army physician pronounced him dead on arrival.

Something changed for me that day. That mission was different from all the others that had come before, when every effort had resulted in a sense of satisfaction. I had become accustomed to calling the hospital and hearing those words of affirmation, that we had made the difference between life and death. On this day, while we hadn't done anything to cause this soldier's death, we hadn't been able to save him either. It was my first mission failure. The patient had died.

I began to understand what medical professionals go through every day. As a doctor or a nurse, you have intimate contact with the most critical patients. You have to be compassionate *enough*, but you have only so much emotion in you. Even as a medevac pilot, just turning my head from the cockpit to check on my patients, I had begun to get too emotionally involved. I would continue to care, but caring too much might cloud my judgment and place the lives of my crew at risk.

I decided that I was not going to make any follow-up calls, ever again.

BUT ON THAT November night of my hundred and fiftieth mission, I was about as emotionally involved as I could be.

We had a kid in the back of the chopper with a massive head injury, we were approaching Seoul's forbidden zone Papa 73, and we had just "punched into" the snow, losing all visual contact with the ground. If we didn't take immediate action, all of us would "buy the farm." I had no choice but to execute an Inadvertent IMC recovery.

The Inadvertent Instrument Meteorological Conditions recovery is standard operating procedure when you can't see a damned thing anymore. You instantly switch to flying on instruments, climb straight up, contact air traffic control, and have them put you on an instrument flight plan. Then you fly a strictly instrument approach into a designated and properly equipped airfield. If you don't do that, and instead try to regain visual contact with the ground, you're going to hit a mountain. Lots of pilots die that way.

I keyed my mike switch. "We're Inadvertent IMC," I said to my copilot. "Start to climb." But he was already adding power to the rotors. Our forward motion slowed while our rate of climb increased and the blizzard just enveloped our Blackhawk like a mountain landslide burying a skier.

Making that instantaneous transition from visual flight rules to instruments isn't always easy for a pilot, but we slipped into it quickly, maintaining a steady rate of climb and eyeballing the altimeter. The mountain range to our immediate right was high, a couple of thousand feet, and we'd have to get over it without slamming into its hide. Everything was going okay, and we were about halfway to altitude, when I suddenly realized a terrible consequence of our maneuver.

"Shit," I hissed into my mike. "What's the worst thing you can do for a head injury?"

My copilot looked at me.

"Altitude," the medic chimed in from the back.

We both turned our heads for a second, to see our crew chief and medic hovering over that young kid's immobile form, while they stared back at us through steely squints. With the pressure of brain hemorrhaging already killing him, a reduction of outside pressure would only hasten his demise. But there was nothing more to be done except to haul ass and get it all over with quick.

We did what we could to expedite and made contact with Seoul air traffic control. They had already spotted us as a blip on their radar, but they weren't expecting to have to vector us in. Fortunately, on a night like this we were the only crazy sons of bitches flying. But communication with the Koreans was always a crapshoot. Their professional expertise was fine, but their language skills were questionable, their English so heavily accented that instructions from them were hard to discern. The risk was that they wouldn't understand what we said, or vice versa, and our lives were in their hands.

"Cumm lite on won-too-ninah" crackled in my headset.

"Say again, approach? Come right on one-two-niner?"

"Uh-fummahtivv! Cumm lite on won-too-ninah!"

On any other night it might have been funny, but my copilot and I weren't laughing. With each new instruction from air traffic control, we confirmed with each other what we thought we'd heard, held our breaths, and made the turns. Worse still, we could no longer be vectored into the medical pad at the hospital, and had to reroute to K-16, Seoul's military air base, located even farther south of the city.

It seemed like forever until we broke out of the blizzard and settled onto the runway at K-16 in a mushroom cloud of billowing flakes. Our blades were iced over, the cockpit glass nearly opaque white, and the whole chopper looked like something left in the freezer beyond its expiration date. There was snow everywhere, probably eight inches on the ground after three hours of nonstop spewing from the clouds.

Miraculously, the kid in the back of the chopper was still breathing. There was another torturous wait while an army ambulance drove down from Seoul to K-16 and picked him up. After that, I decided that we'd find someplace to sleep in the airfield barracks and fly back to Camp Casey the next day.

In the morning, I broke my new ironclad rule. I called the hospital. The young soldier had made it into surgery alive. And as far as I know, he's alive today. I walked out of the barracks into an incredibly beautiful day. The sky was blue, the sun was sharp, and the wind was mild. There was two feet of fresh snow on the ground. My copilot showed up, sipping from a steaming cup of coffee and breathing in the pure morning air.

"Let's crank it up," I said.

"Roger that."

It would be a perfect day to fly.

I loved flying in the early sunlight above fresh, clean snow.

Chapter 4

ANOTHER DAY, ANOTHER BULLET

October 4, 1993

THERE WAS NO SNOW IN MOGADISHU.

There was only pain, thirst, cold sweat, and hunger, the first sensations I felt after being kicked in the ass by a pissed-off Somali wielding an assault rifle.

My eyelids snapped open and there he was, standing just beyond my bare toes. It was that teenager, the most dangerous junior high school kid I'd ever seen—only this kid had probably never been to school. He was holding his AK-47 in the cocky, casual manner of a bird hunter, with one long finger twitching over the trigger. It was like waking from the worst nightmare you could possibly have, only to discover that you haven't been dreaming at all. He grunted something unintelligible, then his eyes ranged over me as if assessing my ability to do any further damage to his world. I followed his gaze to my side, where my wrist chain and lock lay in a heap on the floor. Someone else had apparently decided during the night that my crippled body required no shackles. The kid looked at me again, as if he only wished he had permission to put a bullet in my head. He bared his very white teeth, turned and spat on the floor, and went out.

Good morning, Somalia.

The flat, dull gray of dawn began to seep into the room. I could still hear the rattle of gunfire in the distance, but not nearly at the feverish pitch of the night before. Within minutes I could see everything around me quite clearly, but as I looked myself over, I thought that maybe the darkness was preferable. My right leg had swelled to twice its normal size, completely filling out my normally loose-fitting flight trousers. It looked like the leg of an inflatable doll, not a single crease in it, and the tan twill was blood-soaked and caked stiff. I could almost feel the infection starting to crawl through my wound. After that would come gangrene.

At the very least, I'm going to lose this damned leg.

I tried to reposition myself to ease the pain. With the chain removed I could use both hands and move my body a bit to reduce the agony. But the relief was only temporary as shock waves coursed through me from my back and right thigh.

Jeeeez. I clamped my eyes shut and ground my teeth. *You are in very bad shape, Durant.*

It was already clear that my right femur was broken in two, yet in spite of that extreme injury, my back seemed to hurt even worse. I couldn't tell what was wrong with it exactly, but it was like my spinal cord was pulsing out screams to every muscle from my buttocks to my shoulder blades. A night of fitful sleep on a rock-hard floor had apparently made matters worse. If I didn't get some medical attention soon, I wouldn't survive this, and the amputation of my leg would be purely cosmetic.

I needed water. It had been five years since I'd gone through survival school, but most of what I had learned there was already ingrained in a kid who had grown up in the woods hunting and fishing with his dad. Many elements of survival were second nature to me, and the first thing I knew I needed was hydration. A man could go for long periods with nothing else, but lack of water would spell the end—and with these kinds of injuries, much sooner than under normal circumstances. I found myself thinking with nostalgia about the bowl of sewer water that Mohammed Gait had brought me the night before.

And then an amazing transition took place outside my "cell." The sun's early rays began to slant into the room through the ventilation blocks above my head. The fighting that had gone on throughout the previous night ceased altogether and was replaced by the chirping and singing of birds. All around me the city began to waken and the unfettered laughter of playing children echoed off the grimy walls. It was such a sharp contrast after that night of bloody warfare, and these children seemed utterly unaffected by it. I was unaware of the full death toll—that seventeen Americans and three hundred and twelve Somalis had died fighting in those very streets while I slept in a semicoma of exhaustion—but I was certain that these kids had been exposed to that savagery. Yet there they were, giggling and shouting and chasing one another.

I listened to those incongruous sounds for maybe an hour. It was so strange to think that in the midst of all this chaos, life went on in some bizarre form of normalcy for these people. The high, musical voices of those children reminded me of my young son, Joey. He was one year old now, safe at home and unaware of the terrible predicament his father was facing on the other side of the world. I wondered if he would grow up with me there to love and shepherd him, or if he would have only a few faded photographs and the recollections of my friends and family. And just as the emotion began to choke me, the door opened.

Mohammed Gait entered the room, looking very calm and well rested for a man who lived in a combat zone. But I was focused primarily on the large wooden bowl he carried. It brimmed with a hazy white liquid that I assumed was goat's milk, and I managed to prop myself up on one elbow as I drank it down. It was very sweet and warm, and although it hardly rinsed away the foul combination of cigarettes and dirt that stained my mouth and throat, it was nourishing liquid and I was grateful for it. I wiped the corners of my mouth and nodded as he retrieved the empty bowl and squatted beside me.

"How are you, Ranger?" he asked.

I was not a Ranger, but I didn't bother to correct him. I formed the recognizable symbol for "okay" with my fingers.

He raised an eyebrow at me, then looked at my swollen leg and reached out to inspect it. My whole body tensed, and he withdrew his hand and draped his elbows over his knees.

"Your friends," he began, and then he paused like a surgeon emerging from the operating room with bad news. "You are the only one."

I waited for the rest of it, hoping that he meant I was the only one captured. Gait came up with his pack of cigarettes and offered me one. I heard the voice of one of my instructors from SERE School — Survival Evasion Resistance and Escape — in my head.

"You don't have to be subservient to your captors, but you do have to be cordial. Politeness is a tactic, not a surrender."

"No, thank you," I said. They were my first words of the day.

Gait began to tell me about the others. He didn't speak English very well, but I understood what he was trying to say.

"I am sorry, but it is only you. Your friends not living. We thought maybe one alive, under your helicopter, and run away by night. But that is not true."

I watched his mouth and his eyes and listened very carefully. My breathing was shallow, as if I did not want to inhale the truth.

"You know," he continued, "many Somalis very angry with the U.N. and the Americans. Many, many Somalis die in this fighting. Our women, they are the most angry. They are also the most cruel. A Somali woman must make her revenge upon a person who kills her son or husband. She must take something from that guilty person. There is no trial, no jury. This is justice in our world."

He smoked for a moment, as if formulating his next words carefully.

"Your friends had no pain. They were not living. But some, their bodies were beaten, dragged in these streets of Mogadishu. Some, they were cut, into parts, and pulled along. I saw this."

The birds had stopped their singing and chirping outside, but the laughter of the children seemed deafening. I did not know if what Gait was telling me was just a horror story to weaken my defenses, but it certainly churned my stomach and filled me with rage and loathing. He wagged his head and clucked his tongue once, as if he disapproved of such savagery.

"You must understand, but the people have not control. They were very, very angry. No one could stop them."

At that very moment, the truth of Mohammed Gait's words was being shipped by air courier from photojournalists in Mogadishu to their offices around the world. Within hours, the images of my comrades' corpses being dragged through the streets by celebrating Somalis would be seen by millions. The Africans did not realize it at the time, but their hideous revenge would completely alter the world's perception about who had committed atrocities in Somalia. They were literally biting the hands that were trying to feed them. No one would forget those images. No one should.

Gait finished his cigarette, stood up, and squashed it with his sandal. He picked up the empty wooden bowl, looked down at me, and shrugged.

"The people look for you. They know you are prisoner somewhere and want to kill you. You have much luck, to be a prisoner of the militia."

He left the room. If he had been trying to convince me that I was fortunate to have been captured by his faction, it had worked. I'd had a taste of the unbridled fury of the civilians, and it was likely that I would have been dead by now had I remained in their hands. But there were still hundreds of them out there, perhaps thousands on the hunt for me, and my prison could still become my tomb if just one of those children outside happened to chase a wayward ball in here and discover me. Things did not look good.

The broken bones in my face began to make their presence known, creating a hangover throb between my eyes. But the soreness was minimal compared to the constant waves emanating from my back and leg. I touched the open, encrusted slit below my eye and wondered what my face looked like.

Forget it, Durant. A chopper pilot doesn't have to be pretty.

My ears still rang with Mohammed Gait's words: *Your friends not living.* Part of me believed him. After all, I had taken part in that savage firefight at the crash site and I had heard the final fusillade of gunfire and witnessed the ensuing insanity of the riot. But another part of me denied it, trying to logic it out. After all, I was the only one who knew exactly how many Americans had been there. If one of the men had successfully escaped, the Somalis would have no way to take that tally. I decided that Mohammed Gait was the first major player in the mental chess game of captor-captive. It would be his job to provide me nourishment, to soften me up. He would undoubtedly offer me the bleakest news, in order to draw me toward him. I decided that he was lying.

A Somali came into the room, holding something that looked like a thick, brown pancake. He handed it to me and left before I could nod my thanks. It seemed to be a hunk of bread of some sort, covered with a coating of powdered sugar. I took a bite of it. Aunt Jemima would not have been impressed. It tasted like an old sneaker sole and the sugar did little to disguise the scent of mold, but I managed to choke down another couple of bites. I set the half-eaten hunk on the floor beside me and almost immediately a line of large, rustling ants marched out from a crack in the floor and swarmed my leftovers. I watched as hundreds of them clustered on the bread and flicked the sugar grains into the air, reminding me of the riot swarming over Super Six-Four. But at least these ants weren't enormous or crimson colored. They weren't fire ants.

The same Somali returned, this time with a large banana. He tossed it onto my stomach and left. *Now we're talking,* I thought as I peeled it and devoured the sweet fruit. I scraped every inch of the pulp from the peel with my teeth, then left the skin for the ants. If they were occupied with the foul bread and the banana peel, maybe the scent of my festering wounds wouldn't attract them for a while.

With the accumulating nourishment of the goat's milk, the bread, and the banana, I began to feel a bit better. The throb in my head receded a little and I felt somewhat stronger, able to think more clearly.

All right, what are your options? I asked myself. *Severely limited,* I answered. *You can't even roll over. Maybe you can crab backward a little, but it would take half an hour to make it across the room. Just let them feed you all day,* I decided. *Gather your strength, but display no obvious improvement, and see what the night brings. Maybe they'll start to drop their guard.*

Since they were feeding me, it was obvious that they wanted to keep me alive—at least for now. I knew that a dead prisoner of war would be a worthless prize. If they had wanted to execute me, they would have done it by now. I began to feel optimistic. My next objective would be to get them to summon some medical attention. Maybe I was going to live through this after all.

The door opened again.

Outstanding! More food! I thought as I raised myself up on my elbows. *How about some steak and eggs?*

But the only thing that appeared was the barrel of an AK-47, stabbing into the room between the flimsy door and its sill.

Blam! A huge flash exploded from the barrel, the thunder of the weapon shaking the concrete walls. Shards of cement splintered from the floor and something slammed into my left shoulder.

I was utterly shocked, my eyes wide and frozen in horror, my breath paralyzed in my lungs. My ears were half deafened from the explosion and my head rang while I waited helplessly for the coup de grâce. But nothing more happened. The door slammed shut and the footsteps of the angry coward who had taken a potshot at me pattered quickly away.

I lay there, just trying to breathe, my thoughts racing. *Is that bastard coming back again?* Some very anxious moments passed. *Am I in for another round, or has that coward made his little statement?* And then, there again, was the laughter of playing children.

As the dust literally settled on me, I carefully assessed my fresh wounds. The puncture in my left shoulder felt like a fresh wasp sting, and a piece of something had struck my right thigh. The bullet had obviously ricocheted off the floor, sprayed me with cement shrapnel, and lodged in my arm. I twisted toward my left shoulder and pushed up the sleeve of my T-shirt. There it was, the back end of the heavy bullet sticking out of my skin. I grabbed it with my fingers.

Shit! It was hot as hell, and I let it go. Blood started to run down my arm.

I waited a minute for the spent round to cool, my eyes riveted on that flimsy door. Nothing around me seemed to have changed. The sound of gunfire was so common in the city that no one had even reacted to it. I grabbed the bullet again and pulled it out of my arm in one quick yank. I looked at it. It had mushroomed somewhat, probably from hitting the floor, but it was basically intact. My arm was bleeding, but it wasn't a gush. I couldn't move enough to see the shrapnel wound on the back of my leg. I put the round on the floor next to me and lay down again.

Just moments before, I had experienced a delusional surge of optimism. Now that was gone in a flash.

When the hell is this all going to end?

The door opened again and I flinched hard, but it was just one of the younger Somalis. His weapon was slung from his shoulder, and

I calmed down a bit as he looked around, as if someone had alerted him to a disturbance inside. I remembered that the night before, when the Somalis were outwardly angry and threatening, they had made gestures at me representing gunshots. Like children playing cowboys and Indians, they had extended the index fingers from their fists, cocked their thumbs like hammers, and said, "Pssst."

I waved the Somali over to me, pointed at the door and then at my fresh shoulder wound, and said, "Pssst!" I gestured at the spent round on the floor, hunched my shoulders and raised my palms, silently demanding, "What the hell is going on here?"

He looked at my arm, at the spent bullet, creased his brow, and shrugged at me. His expression was one of annoyance, as if to say, "If people are shooting at you, it's your own damned fault." He went out, presumably to report the incident to a superior.

It wasn't long before Mohammed Gait showed up again. By this time I had concluded that Gait was, at least temporarily, responsible for my welfare. I let my outrage flow as I showed him my fresh bullet wound.

"Do you people know what's going on in here?" I demanded. "You warn me about your angry civilians, but it looks like your militia wants to kill me too!"

He frowned as he peered at my wound.

"I do not know about this," he said. He seemed somewhat remorseful, so I suppressed my urge to dress him down like some plebe at West Point. Maybe on some other occasion a bullet wound in the shoulder would have seemed pretty serious to me, but compared to my other injuries it was a shaving cut. I was more outraged by it than injured.

We didn't have long to discuss the incident, because at this point a new character entered the drama. He was preceded by four bodyguards, and as he swept into the room the other Somalis, Gait included, retreated a bit and nearly bowed with respect. He was middle-aged, wore a pencil-thin mustache, and the wide fringe of hair surrounding his bald head looked freshly cut. His colorful, short-sleeved shirt sported pastel palm fronds, and his beige trousers were crisp and clean. He reminded me of a Miami Beach tourist. He seemed well educated, and his mannered English was delivered in soft tones.

"My name is Mr. Abdi," he offered. "And yours?"

It was clear that this man held some kind of higher position, well above the tactical level. It was time for me to give up one of the "Big Four"—Name, Rank, Service Number, and Date of Birth.

"Durant. Michael J. Durant."

"Is there anything you need, Mr. Durant?"

"I need a doctor."

"Yes, I can see that," Abdi said. The Somalis surrounding him seemed to be listening very carefully, trying to understand his nearly whispered English. "And is there anything else?"

"I need to be set free."

"Of course." He nodded, as if expecting me to say that very thing. "We will provide you with medical attention, and I will make sure that you are treated as well as possible."

You can start by telling these assholes to stop shooting at me, I thought.

"Thank you," I said.

"You are welcome." He smiled slightly. "Tell me, Mr. Durant. Do you remember the prisoners of war in Iraq during your Operation Desert Storm? Do you remember that they appeared on television?"

Uh-oh. I knew what was coming next, but I wasn't prepared. Of course I remembered those videos of the allied pilots who'd appeared on Iraqi television, looking all beat up and scared shitless as they tried to figure out what to say in order to stave off execution. I had been to SERE School prior to the Gulf War, but I did not recall being trained on how to handle video exploitation by the enemy. I tried to quickly analyze if it would be a good thing to be seen alive and in

captivity on television, or if I would simply be serving as their propaganda tool.

"Yes, I remember that," I said cautiously.

"Good." Mr. Abdi seemed to brighten a bit. "Then you would be
willing to make such a video appearance."

"No. I would not," I said as politely as I could.

A long silence ensued. Abdi's expression hardly changed, as if he
knew that it would only be a matter of time.

"I see," he said. And then he left, along with his entourage.

So, this is how it begins, I thought as I was left alone again in the
room. *They want a videotape, some sort of statement from me.*

The process of interrogation and psychological intimidation had
just begun, with a simple "request" from this guy Abdi.

*They want me to say something on camera that they can use for their
own political ends. Well . . . they're not going to get it.*

But I knew that there were many ways of breaking a prisoner
down, attacking his will, getting him to comply. You could make
him wait for days or even weeks, leaving him in a dark hole, starving
him into delirium, and thoroughly unnerving him before you asked
a single question. Or sometimes physical torture would be applied
immediately, again unaccompanied by any interrogation, until the
prisoner was a quivering mass of bloody bruises and just begging to
spill his guts. These Somalis weren't very subtle. They had already
showed their hand, plainly telling me what they were after. Of course,
I was already enduring plenty of physical torment as a result of my
injuries, so on that score they were halfway home. As for breaking me
psychologically—good luck.

My fresh arm wound throbbed, as if the flesh there had been
snagged in a rat trap, and some blood still dripped off my elbow.
Still, I was suddenly much more worried about betraying my comrades, my unit, and my country than about my own pain, torture, or
death. The Somalis weren't going to give up on their videotape just

because I'd refused, and I had no way of knowing when they'd come back and start working on me in earnest. I needed tools, and I needed them quick. It was time to recall every lesson I'd learned in SERE School and put them to use. I closed my eyes and tried to concentrate, returning to nineteen bleak days and nights in the winter of 1988.

I HAD NEVER been so cold in my entire life.

If hell could feel like being naked and abandoned on an arctic iceberg, then I was in it. In the rolling mountains of North Carolina in December, the dawn cuts through you like a knife blade, especially if you're wearing only camo fatigues, one pair of socks, and standard-issue combat boots. I opened my eyes, hearing the low whispers and mumbled curses of other men, and reluctantly stuck my head out of my sleeping bag. The ground was covered in six inches of gray frigid fog, and up above through the towering pines hawks wheeled in lazy circles, like vultures waiting for a fresh corpse. I crawled out of my cocoon, and the morning air charged through my flimsy fatigue shirt and into every pore, sucking any warmth away. Almost immediately, I began to shiver like a brittle autumn leaf. Within seconds, the exposed skin of my face and hands became mottled pink and contracted, taking on the texture of a chicken wing in an icebox.

I reached into my sleeping bag for my canteen. I had kept it in the bottom of the bag, certain that my body warmth would at least assure me of a lukewarm morning swig of water. I unscrewed the plastic top. The water was blocked by a plug of solid ice.

There were six of us on my Evasion team, all hailing from various special operations units and considered high-risk personnel by the Department of Defense. We had already been through the first section of Survival Evasion Resistance and Escape, learning how to land-navigate through unknown territory, locate potable water, hunt and trap small animals, and differentiate between edible plant life and the attractive-looking goodies that could put you in the hospital. From my boyhood in New Hampshire, I already knew most of that stuff and was confident that I was "good in the woods."

But now we were into the Evasion phase, six of us on the run with nothing more than our survival knives and single canteens of water. We had been given the option to take one further item, either a sleeping bag or a field jacket. I had chosen the bag, reasoning that I could wrap it around me during our daylight humps through the mountains, then get a reasonably warm night's sleep. Our task was to make it to an objective, many miles away, and in theory make contact there with friendly forces. We had started out light-footed and optimistic, charging through the mountains from dawn till dusk, and then carrying on well into the night, until finally collapsing for four hours of fitful slumber. We knew we were being hunted and had tried to move over hard-packed trails, leaving few signs, burying our feces, zigzagging and crossing half-frozen streams over slippery rocks. But a man needs fuel to keep up that kind of pace, and those winter woods were bleak and utterly barren. By the third day, our jogs had turned to staggers, our tactical whispers to murmured oaths. By the fourth day, I had eaten no more than a single acorn.

There were other teams out there, also trying to make their objectives. But it wasn't a competition, and it quickly became clear that this wasn't a game any of us could win. The SERE cadre were professional man hunters, and they were properly dressed and warm and relentless. Even if we managed to make our objective, we were going to be taken prisoner. As we six unshaven, filthy, hungry, and demoralized men gathered up our meager belongings for one more attempt to evade, I thought of that book about the rock-and-roll group The Doors: *No One Here Gets Out Alive.*

"Place your hands on your heads and drop to your knees!"

A powerful voice barked from the tree line of our small clearing and all of us stopped moving, frozen in a stunned tableau. Through the thick morning fog I could dimly see a cordon of figures around the perimeter, wearing leopard camouflage, Eastern bloc web gear, and gripping AK-47s.

"Do it *now*," the voice snapped again.

I laced my fingers together on top of my head and slowly lowered my knees to the icy earth. One of our team apparently thought he might gain some points by attempting an escape, but he made it only five feet before a stiff arm sent him sprawling onto his back. Someone grabbed my arms and wrenched them behind me, tying my wrists together with a coarse rope. A heavy cloth hood was yanked down over my face.

"Well, maybe at least our POW cell will be warm," the fresh prisoner to my left grunted hopefully.

"Fat chance," I replied. An open palm smacked me hard on the back of my skull. . . .

SERE School was the brainchild of Colonel James "Nick" Rowe. In the autumn of 1963, while serving as a young lieutenant with American Special Forces in Vietnam, he had been captured by the Vietcong after a vicious firefight in the U Minh Forest. During five harrowing years of captivity, Rowe had suffered physical torture, intimidation, endless interrogations, threats of execution, and crippling beri beri and dysentery. He had watched some of his comrade prisoners slowly die and had been moved from one primitive jungle POW camp to another before finally making his escape. Returning to America and to the service of his country, Rowe had written a book about his experiences called *Five Years to Freedom*. It was to become the new bible for American service personnel who might be captured in future conflicts.

At the time of Rowe's capture, the only guide for American troops was the Uniform Code of Military Conduct. If taken prisoner, a man was to reveal nothing more than the "Big Four": Name, Rank, Service Number, and Date of Birth. This ironclad code was referred to as the "John Wayne Standard," but Rowe quickly discovered that it was totally unrealistic. You couldn't expect a prisoner suffering physical torture and psychological torment to say only four things during the entire length of his captivity. And if a soldier did try to maintain that code, he was probably going to antagonize the enemy until they killed him.

That was exactly what had happened to Nick Rowe's comrade, Rocky Versace, another American officer captured during the same fateful firefight. Rocky's performance as a prisoner had been strictly hard-assed, and while incredibly courageous, it had also doomed him. He had spit in the faces of his Vietcong captors, both literally and figuratively, until ultimately they had killed him.

"Rocky didn't need to die," Nick Rowe would say in the opening lectures of his new SERE School. "Rocky should have come home. But he didn't, because we failed to train him on what he could and could not do or say to keep himself alive."

Based upon his experiences and observations, Nick Rowe began to develop new and realistic methods for soldiers to survive captivity, while still maintaining their own codes of honor and doing their very best to avoid betraying their country. He reasoned that the U.S. government and the American people wanted their soldiers to survive and return to their loved ones. They didn't want stoic heroes coming home in body bags.

"We don't need to have people dying for things that have no tactical value." That was Rowe's whole thrust. If a soldier had been in captivity for any length of time, in most cases the tactical information he possessed would quickly become worthless. Especially in today's world of instant Internet communication and cable TV technology, the enemy could simply access the Net or turn on CNN to learn most of what he needed to know. It was all there: Unit names, strengths, locations, and even how the U.S. military planned to do business were being discussed openly on morning TV shows by retired general officers. So to have a soldier in the field get shot and killed because he didn't want to say anything more than the "Big Four" did not make sense. The Code stated that a prisoner was *re-*

quired to give those four items of information, and beyond that, "to do his best to resist." How a prisoner could still resist the enemy without sacrificing his life was what Nick Rowe wanted to teach.

Rowe convinced the leadership that the army needed more advanced training for high-risk personnel, so he recruited a number of key people with experience like his own and set up the SERE School at Fort Bragg, North Carolina. It would focus on four major issues: how to Survive with minimal resources; how to Evade capture; how to Resist if you are captured; and how to plan and execute Escapes if you are in the hands of the enemy. Most of the course is actually focused on the academic elements of survival, evasion, and escape. The last phase is the RTL—Resistance Training Lab—but that's the part that everyone remembers. It's the most physically and psychologically demanding, and about as close as you can get to the experience in the real world.

SERE School was one of the first courses I attended after being posted to the 160th SOAR(A). Many of its elements were then—and remain today—highly classified. At the time, graduates of the course wouldn't even talk about it to the uninitiated. If you failed the course—didn't make it through due to a physical problem or didn't complete the required number of RTL hours—you did it again, and again, until you made it.

At the beginning of the course, I was cocksure that I was going to make it through. By the end of the fifteenth day, a number of tough guys had already been thoroughly humbled and I wasn't quite so cocky. It was clear that a few folks wouldn't last. Some of the survivors, after days of sleep deprivation, hunger, and torment, had actually begun to believe that they were prisoners of some unknown enemy entity.

After all, none of our captors appeared to be Americans. They wore foreign uniforms, carried foreign weapons, and spoke fluently to each other in a Slavic tongue none of us understood. When they addressed us in English, it was heavily accented.

"You there! What do you think you are doing?!"

I realized that a man was yelling, possibly at me. All of the Evasion teams had been rounded up and hauled off in a long, freezing forced march to the Prisoner of War camp, a collection of bleak concrete structures surrounded by guard towers and rows of razor concertina. For the past four hours, all of us prisoners had been kneeling on the camp's parade ground, a wide pitch of frozen earth that had turned to thick, freezing mud with the rising of the winter sun. Our arms were trussed behind us at the elbows and the wrists, and we sat upon the heels of our combat boots, which had the laces removed. We had been ordered to sit silently, backs erect and heads up, while our captors harangued us for hours on end. The pain in my legs had receded to complete numbness, but my knees still felt like they were going to pop, and the muscles at the base of my neck ached so much that I had momentarily dropped my head to relieve the pressure. I looked up.

"Yes, you!"

One of the captors was glaring down at me from his perch on a mound of raised earth. He was a huge man, over six and a half feet tall, with a bushy dark beard and eyes like dead, black coals. He wore a black beret and a woolen uniform that appeared to be East German, and he was stabbing a riding crop directly at me. His heavily accented voice was like rolling thunder.

"Answer me! What were you doing?!"

Throughout my younger years back home, I'd always been something of a jokester, playing pranks on my high school teachers and generally letting my mouth get me in trouble. I never committed any serious infractions, but I can't remember how many times I received detentions for wisecracking. In the army, I had quickly learned to save my clever remarks for my peers in the barracks, and in the presence of my commanders, to shut up and snicker inwardly. But today, with the giddiness of hunger and fatigue upon me, I just couldn't help myself.

"Praying, Sir?" I answered.

The man whom we would soon refer to as "The Bearded One" stomped down from his dirt mound, grabbed the scruff of my shirt, and hauled me onto my feet. My legs were like jelly and wouldn't support me, but he had incredible strength and dragged me back to his position, spun me around, and hooked his thumb and fingers around the base of my neck.

"You prisoners!" he boomed. "This will be your first lesson today!"

He twisted me to the right. There was a large flagpole cut from a raw birch at the edge of the parade ground. From the top, the POW camp standard whipped in the wind. It was black with a skull and crossbones over Cyrillic letters, like a pirate's flag. The Bearded One gripped my neck, trying to force me to bow to the flag. I went stiff as bone.

"You will show respect," he growled in my face.

No way. I wasn't bowing to him or his flag or anything else. He lifted me right off the ground, until the toes of my boots were dangling. I couldn't move or speak. I just hung there like a limp rag doll, as he took his free arm, swung it out wide, and rapped the backs of his knuckles into my solar plexus. I squeezed my eyes shut as my body jerked and pain flooded up through my chest.

"You will show respect!" his voice thundered.

I tried to breathe again as his knuckles whipped out for another blow. My feet jerked with the impact, as if I were hanging from a gallows. But I still wouldn't bow. I thought they might be videotaping the entire episode and would use it against me later on. He turned on my comrades.

"You prisoners! Assume the position!"

The entire group of ragged prisoners struggled into a push-up position. I watched them splay their raw hands into the freezing mud. *Damn!* I thought. *He's gonna torture them all until I give up.* And sure enough, he started to count, very slowly. But my Evasion team had prepared for something like this. While we were still out in the woods, we'd agreed upon a silent signal that we could use in captivity. If any one of us touched the side of his nose, it would mean *We're okay, keep on truckin'*!

". . . Thirty-one!" The Bearded One roared. "Thirty-two!"

It was torture just to watch them. Their arms were trembling and their breaths steamed from their flaring nostrils. One of my comrades looked up, grinned at me, and stroked the side of his nose on the upswing. I smiled inside, and I still wouldn't bow.

There were unspoken rules for the SERE School cadre. They could do just about anything to break a prisoner, short of causing him or her permanent physical injury. But finally my comrades collapsed. They were starved and exhausted, and they just couldn't do it anymore. For all I knew, in the next moment he'd make them all strip down and go for a swim.

"All right," I grunted.

The Bearded One let me set my boots down until I dipped my head at his goddamn flag. He dropped me in a quivering heap at his feet.

"You *will* show respect!" he thundered out over my crumpled form, and I had certainly learned the lesson in a manner I would not likely ever forget. . . .

For the next endless days and nights, all of us were kept in a single, large concrete cell. The walls were so freezing cold that we kept away from them, huddling together in the center like frightened poultry. The steam of our breaths filled the dank air; we were exhausted, sleep deprived, and hadn't eaten in a week. The only toilet was a hole punched in the cement floor, and all of us, men and women alike, were forced to relieve ourselves in front of the entire group. It was designed to demoralize, debase, and degrade us, and it was very effective.

Systematically, our captors dragged us from the cell for interrogations. It was then that we tried to apply what we had learned in the SERE classrooms—appearing to fully resist at first, then giving up meager bits of information, and finally offering carefully constructed cover stories that would throw our interrogators off the scent. But since our cadre had developed the course, it wasn't a game we could win.

They came for me in the middle of the night. Because of the severe temperature we had been allowed to wear our unlaced boots, but my uniform had been replaced by hospital-type pajamas that were several sizes too large. To keep the bottoms from falling off, I had tied the waist together with a couple of half hitches. That kept them from falling down, but it also left a gaping hole in the front where the fly snaps had long before been ripped out. As I was blindfolded and bound and taken through the meat locker cold to a room somewhere in the labyrinth of buildings, I knew that my genitals were completely exposed. But under the circumstances, my modesty wasn't high on my list of priorities.

We entered a room, someone threw me into a chair, and the blindfold was removed. In the dim light I could see two people a few feet in front of me, facing the other direction. The first interrogator spun around and with an angry and determined look came at me rapidly. This was not going to be good.

It was then I realized that my interrogator was a woman, and a very attractive one at that. She stopped short when she saw that the "family jewels" were completely exposed to the elements. I couldn't ignore the humor of the moment, and a huge grin spread across my face. It was the only time in SERE School that I saw one of the cadre break character.

"And what do you think you are going to do with *that?*" she demanded as she worked very hard to suppress her laughter.

But by this time I had learned to show respect, and I suppressed the urge to offer some snide remark. At any rate, she instantly returned to her role and the interrogation began in earnest. Three hours later, after having endured endless screams of beratement, having lied repeatedly and been caught contradicting myself, and after finally being rewarded with buckets of ice-cold water, I was thrown back into my cell like a puny trout.

On the last day of SERE School, those of us who had passed received our damp graduation certificates in a driving, freezing rain. I came away with tools that I never believed I would ever really need, but even in those first seconds of capture at the crash site in Mogadishu, those lessons would come rushing back to me. Throughout my captivity, I would summon them nearly every hour.

I never did get to personally meet Colonel James Nick Rowe. Not long after my SERE School graduation, he was assassinated by terrorists in the Philippines while on an assignment for the U.S. government. But I thanked him silently every day in Mogadishu, and I asked that God bless him, as I tried to plan my next move. . . .

ALL THROUGHOUT THAT long October day in Mogadishu, the certain knowledge that I would be forced to make a video statement hung above my head like the Sword of Damocles. I knew that eventually I would be thrust in front of a camera, but how to respond was the nagging question. The one good thing about a videotaped statement, I reasoned, was that you needed the prisoner to be alert and alive in order for the film to be effective. The one bad thing was that you could torture the hell out of him first, give him a short break, and *then* turn on the camera. Looking around my cell, I was grateful that the power grid had long before failed in this part of the city. There were no functioning outlets to plug into, so at least they couldn't use electroshock on me.

That-a-boy, Durant. Keep looking on the bright side.

As the noonday sun began to bake my cell, various Somalis came and went. Some of them were young toughs, brandishing their weapons and telling me in no uncertain terms that this room was going to be my grave. Some of them were older and unarmed, at times simply standing there and observing me silently, at other times conversing across my prone body as if I wasn't there.

I was offered no more food, but that was fine, as I had no appetite. At one point a pair of Somalis appeared and repaired the primitive lock on my door. It still looked as though a good push could knock the whole thing off its hinges, but they obviously thought it was sufficient to discourage any would-be assassin. I took it as a positive sign and it made me feel a little better, knowing that not just anyone could open that door unhindered. I believed Mohammed Gait's claim that I would have been a dead man in the hands of the civilians. If the people holding me were part of Mohamed Aidid's Somali National Alliance, then they had every political reason for wanting me alive. Back at the Task Force, we had previously been briefed about the SNA's desire to capture an American. If I hadn't been shot down, it was probably only a matter of time before one of us was somehow abducted.

There was no point in ruminating further about that damned video, so I decided to get as much rest as I could. I closed my eyes and lay very still, trying to will my body to conserve its energy, while I silently scripted my cover story over and over again in my head.

Soon after that, the first interrogators arrived.

There were two of them, men I hadn't seen before, both about thirty years old. They were dressed alike, in T-shirts, baggy blue jeans, and sneakers. One of them had a Nike logo on his shirt, and the other, Adidas, but aside from that they could have been brothers. One had a pen and a sketch pad, while the other was wearing a holstered handgun, so I knew they weren't students from the local art school.

Frick and Frack, I thought. *Okay, here we go, Durant. Don't give up the whole store, just the sale items.*

They settled on their haunches to my right and left flanks.

"What is your name, Mr. Durant?" asked Frick.

I thought the redundancy was funny, but I didn't say so.

"Durant, Michael J."

"And what is your rank, Durant Michael J.?" Frack joined in.

"CW3."

"See Double You . . . ?"

They paused for a moment, exchanging some patter in Somali and searching for English vocabulary.

I wonder if they're going to ask, "What is your favorite color?" Monty Python would love this. . . .

Without their even asking, I gave them my service number. "My date of birth is 23 July 1961."

Frick jotted down some notes while Frack came at me again.

"You are pilot of helicopters?"

"I'm sorry, Sir. But in accordance with the Geneva Convention, I am not required to give that information."

The "brothers" exchanged confused frowns.

"What is the name of your military group?"

"I'm sorry, Sir," I said again. "But in accordance with the Geneva Convention, I am not required to give that information."

"But this is not Geneva," said Frick. "This is Somalia, and *we* require it."

I made them work for it. I made them work very hard. It went on throughout the day, and they would occasionally leave the room and then return for more questioning. At times they brought in other men, who allegedly had better English skills, but I'd just ratchet up my vocabulary. Yet I was consistently polite.

You will show respect.

"I apologize, gentlemen, but the disposition of our personnel and the particular nomenclature associated with our tasks is of such a sensitive nature that my duties as an army officer preclude me from delineating such details."

This sort of thing elicited fierce exchanges between my interrogators, but I was careful to provide them with enough information to let them feel that they were getting somewhere. By the end of that first, long session, they were pleased to have "discovered" that I was a Lieutenant Colonel in the 101st Airborne Division (*they* settled on that rank because the term CW3 meant nothing to them), that I had been ferrying a number of soldiers into downtown Mogadishu, but I was ignorant of the identities of these men or their intended mission. That, of course, was a fabrication. My claim that we had not fired a single shot from our helicopter was the truth, but I didn't tell them that we had simply been trying to avoid killing our own troops.

The information that they got was useless, very basic, and, for the most part, inaccurate, but they must have been quite satisfied.

They brought me a large bowl of spaghetti.

By this time I was ready for some nourishment, and I dug into my "reward" with a plastic spoon. Spaghetti is actually my favorite food, and while this wasn't exactly my mom's cooking, it was decent and full of carbohydrates. I didn't know how long this hospitality was going to last, so I felt that I should eat as much as possible. But I hardly put a dent in the huge bowl.

The evening swept in quickly, draining the sunlight from my cell and replacing it with dark, gloomy shadows. The children outside had abandoned the streets, but the eerie silence was unpunctured by gunfire and, to my disappointment, there were no sounds of Night Stalker rotors in the air. The rapid drop in temperature brought a chill to my skin, but if I lay very still, the throb from my back and leg was bearable.

With darkness my interrogators returned, looking like Halloween goblins as they carried their swinging oil lamps. Once again the same set of questions was posed, and my answers were consistent with the afternoon session. I knew that these men were not highly trained intelligence officers, and their lack of English skills gave me some advantage. When they attempted to get me to elaborate further, I was cordially tight-lipped. It was important to make them feel that there was much, much more to be learned. Their plans for me were still unclear, and an empty vessel is easily "discarded."

But I kept on thinking about that video. *They're going to do it*, I told myself. *You know they're going to do it.* I suddenly remembered a film I had seen from the Vietnam era. It was of an American naval aviator who had been forced before the cameras while being held for seven years in Hanoi. While reading a prepared statement, he had blinked his eyes repeatedly, sending out a Morse code message: "TORTURE." But I had a problem. I didn't know Morse code, or any other code that I could use. I tried to think of a way to signal, but I just couldn't come up with anything. I decided I would just focus on their questions and not slip up.

Midway through that evening, a pair of armed guards unlocked the door and escorted a man into the room. He was middle-aged, perspiring very heavily, and his eyes were rimmed with fatigue. He looked like he was burdened with the weight of the world on his shoulders, and he carried what appeared to be a blue tackle box.

"I am Dr. Abdullahi Hashi Kediye," he said.

I propped myself up on my elbows, silently blessing his arrival. Dr. Kediye asked me about my injuries, and I described them as best I could. He was clearly a compassionate person as he gingerly inspected my leg wound.

"This leg looks very bad," he said as he opened his tackle box. It contained nothing more than some aspirin-type pain reliever, a roll of gauze, one bottle of antibiotics, and some Betadine solution. "Don't eat any more bananas," he warned. "They make the swelling worse."

"Your English is very good, Doctor," I commented.

"I attended medical school in California," he said as he placed a bottle of distilled water next to me. Back at the Task Force compound, designer water had arrived by the truckloads. Here, downtown, it was an incredible luxury. "I have been treating the wounded at the Digfer Hospital. But unfortunately, this is not California. We have few supplies and virtually no surgical equipment."

So that was why this man looked so exhausted. There were probably hundreds of Somali wounded to care for, yet here he had taken the time to tend to the enemy. On the other hand, he might have been "invited" here at gunpoint.

He opened the aspirin bottle and poured four tablets into my palm, then did the same with the antibiotics.

"Use them sparingly for now," he instructed, and then he left.

Dr. Kediye hadn't done anything significant to treat me, but his visit was still encouraging. My captors were apparently concerned for my health, or at least they wanted me to think so. I drank as much of the water as I could and took two of the aspirins and two of the antibiotics. *Aspirin*, I scoffed to myself. *What I need is a double dose of morphine and bottle of Jack.*

Someone brought me a can of warm Pepsi. *Spaghetti? A doctor? A can of soda?* I put it all together. They were clearly trying to soften me up, persuade me to cooperate with them. *This is the "carrot,"* I thought, but I drank half the can of Pepsi and set it down beside me, watching the ants immediately swarm over it.

Within five minutes, the "stick" showed up.

At least six Somalis, most of whom I hadn't seen before, poured into the room. One of the afternoon's interrogators was there, not Frick or Frack, but an older guy with a nasty disposition. He immediately began to repeat the questions I had declined to answer previously, but as soon as we started to go round and round, he waved me off with a hand and snapped out orders to the other men.

Two of them came behind me and tried to lift me up into a sitting position. I grunted hard as the pain from my crushed vertebrae thundered through my spine, and as soon as they released me I collapsed back onto the floor. There was just no way I could sit up, so they hooked their arms under my shoulders and dragged me back against the wall. My leg sang arias of torment to me, and beads of sweat burst from my face. I couldn't lean against that wall, and my spine wouldn't support my weight, so I slammed my palms to the floor and tried to support myself that way and relieve the intense pressure. I was instantly infuriated, and I knew I was about to face some of the most difficult challenges of my life.

Someone threw a coarse blanket over my legs and then more Somalis crowded in. There was a man with a video camera on his shoulder, and two more with tripods, batteries, and floodlights. I was breathing hard, my mind bouncing off options like a steel marble in a pinball machine. It was one thing for me to weave fictions during interrogation sessions, but I'd be damned if I'd give them even *that* much on camera.

You can all kiss my American ass! I raged inside my head.

You will show respect! echoed The Bearded One's voice.

The lights blazed, and I went temporarily blind. My arm muscles were quaking and my mouth was bone dry, and I squinted into the white-hot lights, seeing the gleam of the camera's glass eye staring straight at me. The interrogator was standing just off to my right. The rest of them were a semicircle of silhouettes behind the harsh halo of spotlights.

"What is your name?" he asked officiously.

"Michael J. Durant," I managed to state.

"What is your military rank?"

"CW3. U.S. Army."

"Why you come to Somalia?"

I just looked at the camera, my expression set in stone.

"You kill the people innocent?" he demanded more harshly.

I was mute as a G.I. Joe doll.

"You will answer these questions!" He was getting a little edgy.

Like hell I will, I thought, but I just looked at him as stupidly as I could manage.

He waved at the video crew, and I imagined he was cursing me out. The cameraman stopped rolling and let the camera tilt back on his shoulder. My interrogator put his hands on his hips as he regained his composure. He bent down to reason with me.

"We have brought doctor for you," he said. "This doctor say your wounds are very serious. You would like us to invite him again, no? We take care of you, and then you see your family again. You only must answer questions. It is so very simple."

He stayed right there, staring at me, waiting for my response. The searing pain from my back was jolting me every time I breathed, and I didn't know how much longer I could stand it. My arms felt like jelly, and the sweat was rolling down my neck. I knew I had only seconds to think.

It was clear that I had only three options. One, I could use the John Wayne standard and give up only the Big Four. That worked great in the movies, but here my goal was survival, not fruitless heroism. Option two was to offer some political statement that would make their day. I'd betray my country, but avoid a possible beating or execution. Option three was the only logical choice: answer the questions with a meaningless, neutral response that revealed nothing.

And I suddenly realized one more very important thing. This video would be my "proof of life," something like a photo of a kidnap victim holding up a current copy of a newspaper. If I didn't give them enough to make it valuable, no one would see it. No one would even know that I had survived and was in captivity.

They turned the camera back on. Take two. I was dizzy with pain, frustrated, and infuriated. I felt like a cornered rat. Behind the sunbright lights more anonymous figures wavered, more people appeared to enter the room. I didn't know if I was delirious or not, but I thought I saw Mohamed Aidid himself standing there behind the cameraman.

You're one lucky sonuvabitch, I thought as I glared at that silhouette, *because if I only had a goddamn gun I'd end this all right now.*

The questions began again. In those next few moments, I would utter responses that would change the rest of my life.

"Why you come to Somalia?"

"I am a soldier," I said in a flat, expressionless tone. "I do as I'm told."

"Why you kill the people innocent?"

I glanced at my interrogator, then back at the camera, so that at least someone out there would see I was responding against my will.

"Innocent people being killed is not good," I said.

Someone snapped his fingers. They turned the camera off and shut down the lights. It was over. They had what they wanted. Within minutes, the room had been cleared of everyone, and I slumped down onto my back. I lay there, reviewing every second of it in my mind, and decided that I'd done all right. The only thing that video accomplished was to tell the world that the Somalis had an American in captivity. I didn't second-guess my decision to answer, and I believed then, as I do now, that it was the right thing to do. I know that Colonel Rowe would have agreed.

At the very least, now they would leave me alone. I could rest, drink some more water, and take some more aspirin, even though it obviously hadn't done a damned thing for me. But I was looking forward to a night of relative peace.

Then four new Somalis entered my cell.

Now what? Can't you people give a guy a break?

These men were heavily armed and obviously in a big hurry. One of them was clearly the team leader, and he spoke to me rapidly in a growl.

"I am Firimbi," he said. "You are not in safe place."

"There has been too much happen this area," one of his men joined in. "The people are suspecting. They will find you and kill you here. You must be moved."

I had no time to protest, and they certainly didn't give a damn about my injuries as they reached for me.

Maybe because I had barely moved during the course of the day, my body had already begun doing its best to heal itself. Maybe the splintered ends of my femur had somehow met and begun to set. But whatever the reason for the shock that followed, when they bent down and lifted me up, hauling me onto their shoulders, it felt as if everything inside me was once more tearing itself apart.

I wailed like a newborn infant.

Chapter 5

THE HOTEL NOWHERE

October 5, 1993

WE WERE GOING FOR A RIDE on the highway to hell.

A battered compact car was waiting outside in the silent, midnight streets of the city, but I didn't know that yet. All I knew was that they were shoving me through the doorway of the cell, pulling and twisting to move me quick, and it felt as if a white-hot scalpel were slicing me open from my groin to my neck. I couldn't believe how much it hurt and I hollered, trying to free that demon from inside of me. They hissed at me to shut up and I clenched my teeth and tried to think about something else, but it was just no good. The way they were handling me, I figured that now that they had their damned video they were taking me out for an execution.

At that moment, I might have welcomed a bullet.

They jogged with me across some kind of courtyard, their team leader Firimbi issuing orders in harsh whispers, their sneakers crunching pebbles as I tried to squelch my groans. It was pitch black and all I could see were the cold, passionless stars in the sky above. The rusty hinges of a car door creaked and then they were shoving me into the backseat of a vehicle about the size of an old Volkswagen Beetle. My busted leg was going everywhere, my body dripping cold sweat, and I was shaking uncontrollably. That space was too small for my stiff and grotesquely swollen limb, so they just bent it sideways and I howled like a wounded dog. Someone gripped the back of my head, shoving me up and forward, and they slammed the door.

I couldn't tell which part of me hurt the worst. It was like being squeezed into an oil drum lined with iron thorns. The far door opened, someone threw a blanket over my head, and two of them climbed in and sat right down on top of me. The other two got in the front and started the car. I took in long, slow breaths through my clenched teeth, trying to ease the pain, and I began to calm down. The two Somalis were sitting on me as if I were a seat cushion, and for a moment an errant rifle butt crushed my fingers to the floor, but all that was nothing. As long as they weren't moving me around, I could hack it.

The road seemed bumpier than I remembered, peppered with potholes and ruts and maybe chunks of cement blown from the buildings during the fierce machine-gun and rocket battles of the night before. The car coughed and crunched along, while I breathed my own foul breath inside the black cocoon of the woolen blanket. We made some turns and then stopped at what seemed to be a checkpoint. The driver spoke to someone outside the car, some sort of mutual agreement was reached, and we drove on.

The tires settled onto smooth, paved asphalt and we picked up speed. This was a decent road, maybe a highway, but although it was an easier ride I didn't like the idea at all. I believed that as long as we stayed inside Mogadishu proper, my buds would have a better chance of tracking me down. But if we drove to some militia enclave in the wilds of Somalia, no one would ever find me. Yet those concerns were quelled as we turned back into the pockmarked city alleyways, passed through another checkpoint, and stopped.

The car backed up. The engine was shut off. I heard the doors open, and the weight of the men perched on my body was suddenly gone as all four Somalis got out and walked off. I waited, alone in the vehicle, just breathing hoarsely and listening. A minute passed, then another. Where were they going? What the hell were they doing? I started to draw some nasty conclusions.

The bastards are leaving me here to die, I decided as my anger started to steam. *They've got their goddamn video, so they don't need my sorry ass anymore. They've left me out here in the middle of the city, and now they'll put the word out to the civilians. He's all yours! Come and get him!*

I slowly lifted my head, the blanket hooding me like a monk's habit. My eyes cleared the window frame and I squinted into the darkness. The car was parked in some sort of small courtyard, not a single lamp showing from any building window. My escorts were nowhere in sight. This wasn't exactly a party town, and at this hour no one would be in the streets. If I was ever going to have a shot at escape, this was *it.*

I scanned the area again, checking it out. There wasn't a single soul around. If I could make it to the airfield, or just out of the city, I'd have a chance. If I could follow the stars and just keep on moving south, toward the sea. But I couldn't walk. I couldn't even crawl.

Maybe I could drive!

I tore the blanket off my head and struggled up, trying to see over the front seat. *No way,* I told myself. *No way those keys'll be in the ignition. This isn't some clichéd movie of the week where the bad guys stupidly leave their keys in the car, just so the good guy can get away. . . .*

The keys were in the ignition.

Outstanding! My palms started to sweat, and the excitement flashed through me. But it was immediately smothered by reality. *How the hell are you going to drive, Durant? As a matter of fact, how*

you gonna get into the front seat without screaming your head off?
Even if I could get up front, my damned leg was useless, and so huge
I wouldn't be able to sit in the driver's seat.

You're going to do it, I told myself. *You will lie across that front seat,
use your hands on the pedals, and steer with your frigging teeth if you
have to. Now, move!*

I grabbed onto the back of the front seat and tensed my biceps,
preparing myself for the inevitable torture of my launch. And then
I felt the hairs on the back of my neck prickling, and I slowly turned
my head toward the window. Firimbi was standing there, placidly
gazing at me.

Checkmate.

I slowly lowered myself back down, covering my head with the
blanket again. They had stopped me before I'd even had a shot at escaping, yet I wasn't exactly shattered by having been caught. Even if
I had managed to drive that car, I probably wouldn't have made it
two blocks before being riddled with bullets. *But hey, you can't blame
a guy for trying*, I thought.

The Somalis piled in again and we rumbled off, but we didn't
drive more than a couple of blocks. The car stopped and I heard a
metal gate being opened. We rolled forward just a few feet, stopped
again, and my "oh-so-compassionate" escorts got out and opened up
the doors. *Here we go again.* I braced myself for more torment. *You
guys can forget about ever working for an ambulance company.*

They left the blanket on me as they carried me out of the car, but
I writhed with the pain and it slipped off my head. It was darker outside than a groundhog's hole, but I could see that we were going up
a small flight of stairs. We turned left along some sort of balcony. The
place looked almost like a cheap, highway hotel. A series of doors
along the balcony were evenly spaced, and there were lamps above
the frames that probably hadn't seen bulbs in years. We turned into
the last door on the right, and I hoped, at the very least, for a bed.

Who was I kidding? The room was barren, not a thing in it, just like my last accommodations. The door was the only way in or out, and on the far wall were two small windows, shuttered on the inside but without glass. A weak strip of moonlight lanced from one window onto a gritty cement floor. I held my breath for the inevitable impact, yet this time the Somalis didn't drop me. They placed me on the bare floor behind the door. I expected someone to come up with a chain and shackle me, but they just went out, whispering to one another.

It was dark and very quiet, and I lay there motionless for a few moments, just letting the pain subside. A couple of aspirins might have taken down the throb a notch, but I realized that all of Dr. Kediye's "prescriptions"—the aspirin, antibiotics, and my water—had been left behind. Worse than that, I no longer had my knife. It had been tucked beneath my body in the other cell, and by morning some Somali kid would probably be killing a chicken with it. All in all, it had *not* been a good day, and the night had been worse. In spite of this guy Firimbi's claim that I was being moved for my own good, I couldn't count on anything my captors said. As far as I was concerned, my "reward" for not spitting in their faces while they videotaped me had been to torture me and take away the only relief I had.

I forced myself to regain my composure. Anger would only fire me up, and that wasn't a useful or healing emotion. I decided to try to distract myself and think of something pleasant, but I was thoroughly drained and couldn't drum up a single comforting image.

Firimbi came back into the room carrying a straw mat. He was a pretty big man for a Somali, and I realized he was wearing thick glasses. But the mat wasn't for me. Without saying a word, he rolled it out on the floor on the far side of the room, lay down, and immediately fell asleep. In a minute, he was snoring like a lion with a nasal blockage. *This is just what I need,* I thought, rolling my eyes at the bare ceiling. *A minus-three-star hotel and a restless roommate.*

But Firimbi's lumber sawing didn't keep me from sleeping. I was exhausted.

———

I DREAMED that night of Kentucky.

I was sitting in a lawn chair, wearing a pair of loose-fitting shorts and a T-shirt, sipping ice-cold beer from a brown glass bottle. My bare feet were crossed at the ankles, settled deep in a wide pasture of that blue-green grass, and all around the perimeter were groves of sycamore trees, the summer wind waving through their caps of lush leaves. In the distance, split-rail fences crossed this way and that, while handsome horses chased one another inside a corral. Nearby, a scrap-lumber tree house sagged from the lower fork of a thick old oak, and an old tire swing hung down from one of its branches, the empty, black rubber ring twisting lazily in the breeze. The soft and constant chatter of crickets in the grass mixed with the laughter and splashes of children playing in a sprinkler. The sweet smell of roasting pork teased my hunger, while the twang of Willie Nelson singing "Whiskey River" wafted from a speaker somewhere.

But it wasn't a dream at all, not some fantasy concocted out of longing. It was a recollection, clear and perfect, with every blissful event and bit of conversation exactly as it had been.

It was back in the summer of '92, a year after we'd returned from Desert Storm. Cliff Wolcott had bought himself a small Kentucky farm, and he and his wife, Christine, had invited us all up there for a barbecue. Lorrie was pregnant with Joey. Donovan and Sharri Briley, Stan and Wendy Wood, Dan and Jane Jollota, Clay Hutmacher, our battalion commander and some of the crew chiefs had all shown up with their cars loaded with kids, food, and beer.

Cliff Wolcott was a tall, lanky guy, an outstanding helicopter pilot, and an innovative "salesman." He always had a sly grin on his face just waiting to break out, like the proverbial cat who'd eaten the canary. His hair and his dead-on impression of "The King" had resulted in his nickname, "Elvis." Cliff was an outdoorsman and loved to hunt, and for this family event we'd dug a pit in the ground, lined it with hot coals, and lowered in an enormous pig. Donovan and I had shown up early and had spent the night drinking beer with Cliff and turning the spit. It would still take all day for that pig to roast up, but there would be plenty of activities to keep everyone occupied.

We had all served together for a number of years by then. We'd fought together in Panama and the Gulf War and had been on countless secret missions in between. Our bonds had grown firm and unbreakable. We knew each other as well as any brothers and sisters do, and our platoon was just about as tight as one could ever be. Every day, we trusted one another with our lives, and we never thought twice about it.

Later that day when the families arrived, the kids rode the ponies and played games in the fields, while most of us adults ignored the volleyball net and just sat there splayed out in the lawn chairs, subsisting on beer after beer. Donovan Briley, whose Native American background had blessed him with raconteur talents, regaled us with ridiculous tales of his childhood until we were holding our stomachs and choking. And the rest of us doused the flames of his fantasies by reminding him of his antics with the unit. We laughed and sang and danced on the grass well into that night, long after the kids had fallen asleep on every couch and bed in the Wolcott spread.

We were young and very happy, indestructible and impervious to fate, and none of us imagined that for some of us it was a farewell party. A storm was gathering over in Somalia, but we were blissfully unaware of it as we drank and joked and chased our wives and kids for sloppy kisses. It was a beautiful, endless night, with nothing dark on the horizon.

It was just another July in another fine summer.

I WOKE UP that morning still bathed in the purity of my dream, almost relaxed, with a palpable sense of optimism. Donovan, Cliff, Stan, Dan, and Clay and all of our wives and kids would someday soon hold another barbecue just like that one in Kentucky. Yes, Donovan and Cliff had been shot down together in Mogadishu, but even if they'd been injured like me, I was sure they had survived. I was also fairly certain that they had not been captured, because otherwise the Somalis wouldn't have been so frantic about getting me — their only captive — to appear on camera. We would all recover from this. Eventually, I would be set free, and we would absorb the hard lessons of this battle and return to our unit and our helicopters. And yes, we would also mourn our lost friends, because we were warriors and that was the price of warfare. But we would remember them well, as we sat around another fire and drank beer and laughed, someday soon.

But dreams, as we know, are often triggered by outside stimuli, and I quickly understood why I had relived so clearly the laughter of our children. There they were again, the Somali kids laughing and playing right outside, as if they'd followed me like some crippled Pied Piper. I looked around at my new digs, now flooded with early daylight. The door was closed, affixed with a cheap lock like the one in my previous cell. One of the window shutters was open and I could see another building not three feet away. There were no birds chirping and I could hear more street traffic, so I concluded that we had moved to a more densely populated part of the city. I remembered seeing the position of the moon through the hood of my blanket the night before, and I calculated that we had moved farther west. But I still had no idea where I was, and unfortunately, neither did anyone back at the airfield.

Firimbi was still snoring across the room on his mat. I noticed that he hadn't slept with a weapon at hand, which was wise given that he'd bedded down five feet from a captive enemy soldier. He soon awoke, put his glasses on, and left the room without saying a word to me. He was clearly a hard case. If a prisoner can possibly miss a captor, I began to miss Mohammed Gait.

I lay there for a while on the hard cement floor, feeling stiff and sore and slimy in my own greasy film of dried sweat. If I didn't move at all, maybe the nerves at my wound sites would stay somewhat dormant, but for a guy who ran every morning and worked out regularly, this corpselike repose just wasn't acceptable. I had to keep my strength up as best as I could. As I lay there flat, I clenched my fists and performed weightless wrist curls. When my forearms felt taxed enough, I placed my palms together over my chest and repeatedly pumped them hard against each other. Those simple isometrics wiped me out, but I felt that I was accomplishing something.

When the door opened again, it was Dr. Kediye, and man was I happy to see him. He looked even more haggard than the day before, but his arrival assuaged my concern that the Somalis might still be considering my "disposal." After all, if you're going to push a wrecked car over a cliff, you don't bother repairing it first.

The doctor was carrying that same blue tackle box, and he set it down beside me and opened it up. It appeared to be well stocked today, which was heartening.

"How do you feel?" he asked.

"Not bad," I said, "for a guy with a broken back, a compound femur fracture, and a bullet wound."

"You have a lot of pain." He didn't smile at my false bravado, but began to carefully lay out some medical items on the floor.

"Yes. Those aspirins and antibiotics you gave me were lost."

"I will get you some more. But today, I must clean your wounds. An infection is out of the question."

I didn't respond. I knew it had to be done and I was grateful for it, but I also knew what was coming.

Kediye took the blanket off me, looked at the bloated, stiff sewer pipe that was now my leg, and tried to disguise the crease that formed between his brows. Very gently, he removed my blood-encrusted flight trousers and rolled me up onto my side, facing the wall. I could hear him breathing, concentrating, working with his instruments, and I looked back over my shoulder. He had donned a pair of surgical gloves and was being very careful to avoid contaminating anything. From a plastic bag, he removed a large pair of gleaming forceps, then tore open a sterile gauze pad. He pincered the gauze and soaked it in Betadine solution from a brown bottle. I turned back to the wall, stuck my right thumb in my left fist, and gripped it hard.

"This is going to hurt you a bit," he said.

"I know it."

He pulled the skin back from my open leg wound and slowly pushed the gauze inside with the forceps. I could feel him cleaning the shorn muscle tissue and the ends of my broken bones. But even though the pain was stunning, it was also different. It was pain with a purpose, and I just clamped my eyes shut and rolled on through it. This procedure was essential if I was going to avoid infection. When he was done, he placed a large dressing on my leg, then proceeded to scrub my shrapnel nicks and my bullet wound. He dressed everything up, helped me settle onto my back, and checked my face. There wasn't too much he could do about that. You can't set a cracked mug.

"I must go now." He seemed almost apologetic as he rose heavily, as if his joints were aching. "But I promise that you will receive more medication."

"Thank you, Doctor."

He left with his meager first-aid kit, but I immediately began to feel a little better about my situation. The Somalis were obviously worried about my condition. They had stopped the interrogations, and the guards who were now in charge hadn't once threatened me with death. It wasn't exactly Disney World, but it was an improvement.

Firimbi entered the room, leading a middle-aged Somali woman wearing a flowered yellow dress. She was short and heavyset and had kind eyes. The woman smiled at me slightly and cocked her head, as if in sympathy.

"This house," Firimbi said to me, pointing at the floor. "It is *his* house." He pointed at the woman.

I looked at him quizzically.

"*His* house," he said more loudly, as if I were deaf and not too bright.

"Ahhhh." I nodded. "*Her* house."

"Yes, yes!" he snapped. "His house!"

Terrific, I thought. *He's my new warden, he's moody, he snores, and his English sucks.* I smiled a greeting at the woman.

She looked at me and mimed eating something. I could not imagine what kind of food was available to these unfortunate people, but I was grateful for the offer and nodded enthusiastically, as if to say that anything she had would be fine. Yet it also struck me that in all the time I had been in-country, I hadn't actually seen any starving Somalis. Mogadishu wasn't like some other cities in Africa, where people who looked like sacks of bones lay begging and dying in the streets. Admittedly, my exposure to the country had been limited to the capital and nearby villages, and there was probably still famine in the country's interior, but the people in and around the city seemed to have plenty to eat.

The "house mother" went out and Firimbi bent down, leaving a plastic bowl next to my hip. It was a maroon-colored dog bowl, with pictures of Disney characters on the side. I wondered if the bowl's canine had become the victim of a barbecue like the one at Cliff's place. Was he expecting me to eat from this?

He pointed at his own crotch, made a "psssss" sound, and went out, and I understood that he was leaving me to my toilet. Until that moment, I hadn't even thought about relieving myself. Maybe the shock of my wounds and the constant courses of adrenaline had shut down my kidneys until then, but when I rolled to the bowl, which took agonizing effort, I filled it to the brim. Firimbi must have been standing just outside the door, because as soon as I finished he came in and removed the bowl, very carefully.

Yet on that first day of his presence, Abdullahi Hassan Mohamed Firimbi was not exactly a joy to behold. He was sullen and brusque, as if only following orders, carrying out an assignment he preferred not to have. His English skills were limited and I had not studied any African tongues, so we were reduced to communicating mostly with hand signals and mime. It struck me as crucial that I should have tried to learn some of the language before embarking on any such mission. Even if the assignment was a lightning assault or a quick "snatch and grab," there was usually enough time in transit to hammer some language into your brain. You never knew when you'd suddenly find yourself cut off, behind enemy lines, or fallen into captivity. In other lands, I had personally experienced the ice-breaking power of knowing just ten words of the native language. In a combat situation, it might make the difference between summary execution and the enemy hesitating before pulling the trigger.

But one thing was clear—that Firimbi had no intention of doing me further damage. I just had an instinct that there was a compassionate man beneath his bristly shell. Whether or not he was "only following orders," he was careful with me, almost gentle at times.

About an hour later, he returned with a bottle of water, a large metal bowl, and a paper bag. I drank down most of the bottle and saw that the bowl was full of water as well. From the bag, he produced a wash cloth and bar of soap, soaked the cloth in the bowl, soaped it up for me, and gestured at my filthy form. I nodded my thanks, and it felt good to get the grit off my arms, neck, and face. But my back still hurt like hell and I couldn't lift myself to sit upright. Firimbi took the cloth and began washing my legs, as though it were a perfectly natural thing to do. It made me somehow uncomfortable to have my Somali enemy washing my limbs, but I knew it was important to try to stay as clean as possible.

At one point, I winced when he applied too much pressure to my swollen leg. For some reason, it clicked in my mind that there had once been a heavy Italian influence in Somalia, and still having fluent Spanish, I blurted out, *"Dolor,"* the word for pain.

"Ahhh, *dolor!"* Firimbi nodded and clucked his tongue. He kept on vigorously washing the leg, but he brightened up a bit when he realized we might be able to communicate without him developing a migraine. He finished the job and gave me another small towel to dry myself off. I didn't feel good, but I certainly felt better.

Then he came up with a small wooden stick and held it up in front of me. One end of it looked like it had been mashed with a hammer. I took it from him, but I didn't know what he expected me to do with it, so I shrugged. He retrieved it and shook his head, commenting silently on my obtuseness as he mimed brushing his teeth with the stick.

All right, I thought. *I'll bite.* It seemed like a good idea. I could still taste the cigarettes I'd smoked two nights before. Unfortunately, the Somali toothbrush comes without toothpaste, but it worked pretty well. I soaked the stick in water, rubbed the frayed end over my teeth, and rinsed. I ended up with a few splinters in my gums, but I knew that my dentist would have approved.

And finally, before leaving me alone for a while, Firimbi handed me a disposable razor. Now, that was something I knew how to operate, and even though I hadn't dry-shaved without a mirror in a long time, the idea was uplifting. I took my time, dragging the blade across my stubble and rinsing it in the wash bowl. It certainly mitigated the unwelcome images I'd had of myself a year down the road, stumping along on a buccaneer peg leg, with sunken eyes protruding from a chest-length beard. The Somalis' treatment of me had certainly improved over the past twelve hours, and I wondered what they had in store for me.

Combat rations. That was the result of my failing to specify a menu request.

Most Americans are familiar with the old C rations that were used by the U.S. military for decades. Some of them were pretty decent, and I had eaten some as a kid and taken them along on hikes or camping trips. But now the field ration for all branches is called the MRE—Meals, Ready to Eat. Don't ask me why no military acronym is ever in a logical sequence. In this case, it must be to confuse the enemy about our eating habits. Suffice it to say that these new MREs are not highly regarded, and my favorite substitute definition for the term is "Meals, Rejected by Ethiopians." Some miserable soldier in the desert of Saudi Arabia was responsible for that bit of GI humor.

In the early afternoon, the Somali guards brought me three MREs, along with another bottle of water. The meals were ancient. Each came in a thick plastic pouch that normally has the contents printed on the outside, but these were so old that the writing had worn off and the brown pouches were scuffed and sun-bleached. However, they were unopened, theoretically impervious to temperature extremes and probably edible. I knew I needed to eat, so I rolled the dice and chose one.

Beef slices in barbecue sauce—as luck would have it, one of my least favorite MREs. Inside the main pouch were several smaller packages with their bold print intact, so the news of my gourmet repast was blazingly clear. I poked my nose into the pouch, hoping for something better, remembering the cynical title of a famous photograph from the Vietnam War of a badly wounded Marine, his head swathed in bandages, peering into a box of Cracker Jacks: "Where's my fuckin' prize?"

All right, I thought. *Captives can't be choosers.* I opened up the beef, but it looked like old horse leather and tasted even worse. The package had obviously been in the sun for a very long time, but I forced it down with great gulps of water, looking forward to the chewing gum that comes in every MRE packet. I figured it was hard to ruin gum. I was wrong. You can ruin it if you leave it out in the African desert for a year or so.

Firimbi came back in while I was finishing up my chow. He squatted nearby and watched me, looking very pleased with himself, as if he were a French chef and I'd just been blessed with his latest concoction. In order to foil any prying eyes from outside, he had kept the window shutters closed all day, and with the door locked as well it had grown hot and stuffy in the room. Both of us were shiny with perspiration, but of course he was used to the conditions in Mogadishu. The flies had already homed in on the scent of the beef and were leaking steadily into the room like a cloud of buzzing black gas.

Lots of these MREs come with a small bottle of hot sauce. I can't stand the stuff, even though many soldiers think you can make anything taste better if you doctor it up. I offered the sauce to Firimbi.

He obviously knew what it was, removed the top from the miniature bottle, and drank it down, straight, no chaser. He licked his lips, rubbed his stomach, and mumbled, "Good! Good!"

"Whatever you say, Firimbi." I smiled at him, but not too widely. I had to work this angle very carefully.

He thanked me with a thumbs-up, but it wasn't long before his grin receded to a tight-lipped expression and he left. The important thing was that I was starting to form a relationship with him, and from that point on he began warming up to me. I considered this an important tactical advantage for me. If I got in a tight situation, such as the threat of another pissed-off citizen with an itchy trigger finger, Firimbi might be more inclined to save my skin if he liked me. That is, as much as anyone could like their enemy.

I didn't know my "house mother's" name, but she sort of reminded me of Aretha Franklin, so I began to think of her that way. I was lying there alone when "Aretha" poked her head in the door, apparently just to see if I was still alive. It was midafternoon and the room was oven-hot, the air dead still and nasty. She looked at me lying there on the dusty floor, half-naked now but for my soiled T-shirt and a towel draped over my lap, trying to swat the flies from my mouth and eyes. She clearly didn't approve, and returned soon after with a rough mat for me to sleep on. It felt good to get off the floor. And then she brought in some type of pottery incense burner and placed it in the corner. It smelled pretty bad, but it did seem to drive half the flies away. They weren't gone altogether, but they were tolerable now, and she grinned when I waved at her in thanks.

I tried not to think about very much that day. I lay there in sort of a meditative state, letting my mind power down to an idle. Worrying about my status was not going to help, and planning an effective escape wasn't in the cards. Thinking about home and my family seemed to trigger depression, and I didn't need those images to give me the will to survive. I had that will without any additional incentives. The likely fates of my comrades from the crash site was a thought too heavy to bear. So I lay there and pictured a tropical beach, with waving palm fronds, cool blue water, ice-cold beer, and girls in bikinis.

I must have slept for some time, because I woke up in the darkness, in a slimy sweat and utterly surprised by a familiar sensation in my groin. I had dreamed about the punk singer and movie actress Grace Jones. She looked just as she had in that James Bond film, *A View to a Kill*, with her butch haircut, long pointy red fingernails, and gleaming black body. In the dream, we were having raunchy, wild sex on all sorts of motel furniture. I won't go into the details, but let's just say she had that wild animal snarl on her face and she was hurting me pretty bad. I wiped the sweat from my forehead and I actually chuckled. I didn't need Sigmund Freud to tell me what that was all about.

The evening wore on, bringing with it a deeper darkness. The children had gone home and the streets were very quiet. I still had two MREs left, but I thought it best to conserve them, and at any rate that shoe-leather beef had killed my appetite.

Firimbi came in and opened up the window shutters, and the entire room seemed to inhale one huge gulp of fresh air. He placed a small oil lamp in one corner, and the flickering flame threw soft

copper shadows on the wall. There was no sound of gunfire anywhere, but that didn't mean that my comrades had given up on me.
If, by some good fortune or the aid of a Somali agent, they had discovered where I was, my first hint of their appearance would be the
sudden roar of helicopter rotors above.

A pair of armed bodyguards entered the room, bracketing the
door. They somehow looked familiar to me, and then I knew why.
Mr. Abdi swept in, looking well dressed and completely in charge as
before. The guards scanned the room and withdrew, but Firimbi remained standing in one corner. Who knew what a wounded American helicopter pilot might try out of desperation? Maybe they
thought I might choke their boss with my bare hands.

You folks have been watching too many Schwarzenegger movies, I
thought.

Mr. Abdi knelt down on the floor beside me. He wore a very clean,
short-sleeved, white safari shirt, like a Spanish *camisa,* and he placed
his hands on the thighs of his pressed chinos. I was immediately concerned that he was there to make another "request." Maybe the video
had not turned out to their liking.

Forget it, pal, I thought. *My pay grade goes up if you want to film
me again.*

"Mr. Durant, I trust that you are feeling better," he said in that very
soft, nearly hypnotic English.

*Don't bother trying to use my pain as leverage. Been there, done
that. . . .*

"I'm fine," I said.

"Good. Tell me, Mr. Durant. How much do you know about my
country?"

"Not very much," I answered. We had been given some concentrated historical briefings before deployment, but it would be interesting to hear his version. And anyway, I didn't have much else to do.

"Somalia, as you may know, has a long, difficult history." Mr. Abdi
began his lecture, settling into it as if he were telling a fairy tale by

the light of a campfire. He used his hands, gesticulating dramatically, but to me it was more like a ghost story.

He told me about the period of time that his people had lived under the rule of a ruthless dictator named Siad Barre. For more than twenty-five years, he said, Barre had held Somalia in his iron grip. And while the country had fared well economically, the people were unhappy with their government.

"Anyone who spoke out against this terrible ruler was in danger." Abdi raised his finger, as if recounting a biblical tale for a child. "Siad Barre's secret police were everywhere, and the people whispered that the walls had ears. A word against the government could bring death to any man, woman, or child."

I listened quietly and respectfully, even though I knew what Abdi was trying to do. In technical terms, he was attempting to indoctrinate me, but I had been trained to resist this sort of exploitation. His expression became almost beatific as he recounted more recent events.

"Of course, all of this changed with the rise of General Mohamed Farrah Aidid. As the leader of our revolution, General Aidid overthrew the corrupt and cruel government of Siad Barre. But General Aidid would not be satisfied with the mere dethroning of a dictator. He personally chased Siad Barre to the border of Kenya, assuring that the despot would be banished. Unfortunately, when General Aidid returned to Mogadishu, a rival clan elder attempted to take control. Our civil war had begun."

And that's when you started slaughtering each other and starving your own people, I thought as I nodded politely.

I knew quite a bit more about Somalia than I was willing to admit, but I certainly wasn't going to offer my addendum to his story. After two years of bloody internecine warfare, Somalia had been plunged into a famine that was statistically the worst ever reported. Hundreds of thousands had died of starvation, and in 1992 the United Nations relief organizations had arrived on the scene to provide sustenance. But that only seemed to make matters worse, as warlords and clans fought for control over the supplies. It wasn't until December 1992, when the U.S. Marines landed on the beaches, that the situation began to stabilize. I knew that Abdi wouldn't admit that most of the people had welcomed the arrival of U.S. troops, or that there was little organized resistance. He surely wouldn't acknowledge the fact that over the ensuing six months, as nearly 28,000 American soldiers took charge of the U.N. missions, the supply lines were flowing freely and food was being delivered to all who needed it.

"The arrival of the United Nations was seen as helpful at first," said Abdi as I refocused on him and listened. "But when they tried to impose their will upon us, with the aid of your forces, the people became angry. Once again, as long ago with the Italians, they felt as if a foreign power was attempting to dominate them. One never understands why you Americans take it upon yourselves to thrust your noses into family affairs."

We were trying to deliver an oppressed people from a government of corrupt warlords, feed a starving population, and rid the area of terrorism. I struggled to keep my thoughts to myself, but this guy was starting to burn me up. *We Americans have a tendency to do those kinds of things, and we're damned proud of it. . . .*

Still, some of what Abdi was saying was difficult to refute. Even though I was a soldier whose first duty was to follow orders, as an American I was also free to doubt the wisdom of my government's decisions. Surely the way the Clinton administration was handling this issue now, with halfhearted, hesitant measures, was questionable. But I believed our motives were pure, while those of Abdi's faction were fomented by power lust. I knew that he was trying to win me over, a situation faced by most prisoners of war. His statements were exaggerated, but carefully concocted with a mixture of lies and truth. He was a professional propagandist.

"Of course," he continued, "the situation regarding the Pakistanis was an unfortunate incident." He nodded gravely and sat silent for a moment, choosing his next words.

He was referring to a horrific event that had taken place on June 5, not long before the deployment of Task Force Ranger. Aidid and his Habr Gidr clan had feared that they were losing power and fierce fighting had broken out in and around Mogadishu between the warlords. The U.N. had ordered its forces to disarm the people and a weapons-collection program was put into effect. The Pakistani contingent had drawn the assignment that day, but it was like sending a foreign police unit into a Texas city and demanding that the Texans give up their firearms. Of course, the Somali reaction was slightly over the top. The people had gone wild and rioted, slaughtering twenty-four of the Pakistani peacekeepers. There was no way to pretty that up. I had seen that behavior with my own eyes.

"Our people have so little," Abdi explained, as if angling for sympathy. "Their weapons are their prized possessions, their only amulets of power. The Pakistanis' attempt to take them away was a foolish gambit."

"So you killed them all and played soccer with their skulls."

I couldn't believe I'd said that, but it was already out of my mouth. Mr. Abdi blinked at me, and just for a moment his expression flashed with anger. But then his soft, patient smile returned, like a politician in a televised debate. He rose from the floor and lightly brushed his palms together, as if to dispel the soil of my proximity.

"In case you did not know this, Mr. Durant," he said casually, "I am General Mohamed Farrah Aidid's Minister of Internal Affairs. The Somali National Alliance has determined that you should be cared for, because you are a valuable, shall we say, 'chess piece,' in this complex political game."

You could've just said "pawn," I thought. *I'm not that sensitive.*

"Your face has already been televised around the world," he continued, almost with pride. "Everyone knows that you are our prisoner. *Insh' Allah*—God willing—you will see your family again."

His tone was completely flat and indifferent. He clearly viewed me as nothing more than a valuable American commodity to be exchanged for political concessions. I tried not to visibly react to his words, even though the idea that my face was now being broadcast all over the nightly news made my heart hammer. It was a positive thing, in that it would now make it very difficult for the Somalis to claim that I'd suddenly died of some disease or "accident" while in captivity. But it was also a negative thing, in that fifteen minutes of fame is not a career enhancer for a special ops pilot.

Minister Abdi walked toward the door. His guards must have sensed his approach, because they opened it for him and stood to attention. He turned back to me.

"Is there anything else you need, Mr. Durant?"

"I need an airplane ticket to the United States."

He smiled. "We shall leave that also in the hands of Allah. You will be freed, but only when that is useful to the Alliance." Then he thought for a moment. "Perhaps you would like to have a radio?" he asked.

"Yes." I nodded graciously. "A radio would be fantastic." I could not believe that he was offering me one.

"I will have one sent to you." And with that, he left the room.

Firimbi followed the minister out, throwing an approving glance at me as he closed the door, even though I knew he hadn't understood a word of the exchange. I lay there thinking about Abdi's visit, and on balance I was encouraged by the conversation. I realized that a dialogue had started between the Somalis and the United Nations, and maybe even directly with the U.S. It didn't matter to me. I just wanted to get out of there as fast as possible.

But thinking further, I knew that our government had a strict policy regarding such cases—No Deals. Unfortunately, that was the only logical course of action. Otherwise, if we met the demands of these thugs we'd be setting ourselves up for the next group of terrorists that decided to grab an American. I agreed with that policy one hundred percent, even under the circumstances. Even if it could cost me my life.

But I had to prepare myself for a long, long wait. I hoped that my health wouldn't deteriorate past the point of full recovery. And with any luck, if the diplomacy fell through, my buds back at the airfield would pay us a visit in the middle of the night. I was certain they were already preparing for such an opportunity.

The problem was intelligence, I was sure of it. They had no idea where I was. I knew they were trying to locate me, but it would be difficult, if not impossible. Mogadishu was a sprawling city, with thousands of buildings and huts and uncharted hideouts. And if the Somalis continued to move me around, a rescue attempt could never take place.

How the hell do I signal them? I wondered in frustration. *How can I let them know where I am?*

In the corner of the room, the single oil lamp flickered and burned out. The small space filled instantly with the darkness of the blind, and I heard Abdi's emotionless statement in my head.

You will be freed. But only when that is useful to the Alliance.

That could be next week. That could be next year. It could be long after I'd been sold off to an even higher bidder, maybe to some other country, a terrorist nation ruled by thugs pretending to be presidents. I might be a broken old cripple by that faraway Christmas of my freedom. My marriage would be long gone, my son a grown man. . . .

I was being held by the most powerful warlord in all of Africa. The chances of rescue were very slim. A hundred thoughts crawled through my overtaxed brain, carrying a deep, hollow sadness that overshadowed all hope. The sorrow for the loss of my crew and comrades welled up heavy and hard, and in the unrelenting blackness, I saw the mournful faces of my wife and small son.

As I drifted off to sleep at last, I silently cried for them all, feeling the hot tears running from the corners of my eyes and into my ears. It was the first time in a very long time that I had allowed that emotion to flow.

But I sensed it would not be the last.

Chapter 6

JUNGLES AND DESERTS

To an army helicopter pilot, the 160th Special Operations Aviation Regiment (Airborne) was the top of the food chain.

Now, there was nothing wrong with being a medevac pilot. I had been doing it for quite a while and I enjoyed it. There was great job satisfaction, and if you got hooked on being a first responder, you could serve out your twenty years in units like the 377th Med and retire after a fine career. There were plenty of other good slots for army pilots as well. If you liked multiple-ship missions, ferrying infantry or flying gunship support for massive armor formations, then the 101st Airborne was also a fine place to be. If and when America went to war, and you were a good pilot performing any of these tasks, you could be pretty sure about having your number come up to deploy.

But the Night Stalkers went into combat even if there was no war.

I first started really hearing about them while I was still in Korea.

One of our medevac pilots was a former Night Stalker who had been forced to leave the unit for medical reasons. Any information about the 160th SOAR(A) was tightly controlled and he was pretty tight-lipped, but I "debriefed" him as much as I could while spending a lot of my pay buying him beers. After just a few bleary-eyed, whispered conversations over bar tables in Seoul, I knew where I wanted to be.

The Night Stalkers were strictly a special operations outfit. They had the best helicopters, the latest equipment, and an unlimited acquisition budget. They flew mostly at night using the latest technology night-vision devices, deep behind enemy lines, racing just above sand dunes, ocean waves, or jungle canopies to deliver special ops teams. Their missions were hostage rescues, snatch-and-grabs of bad guys, and even "liberations" of enemy equipment. Their customers were the elite of the elite and strictly classified, meaning Navy SEALs, Army Rangers, or other special mission units. The existence of the Night Stalkers was officially denied, and their pilots had reputations as the James Bonds of the community. If a mission was regarded as impossible, the Night Stalkers would get it, and "impossible" had always been seductive to me.

But at the time you couldn't just "apply" for a Night Stalker slot. Someone had to recommend you. My secret source promised to do that for me, and as I neared the end of my tour in Korea I was itching to rotate back to Fort Campbell, Kentucky, and get that ball rolling.

LIKE MOST SPECIAL operations units, the 160th SOAR(A) was born out of necessity.

Generally speaking, conventional military organizations regard Special Forces of any kind with suspicion. We lack spit and polish, and we're thought of as undisciplined, arrogant loose cannons. We're often dismissed as snake-eaters with itchy trigger fingers. Some of that attitude toward us is justified, and some of it is born out of envy. But while full-scale wars are won by entire armies, the small deeds carried out by small groups of men often have a disproportionately large impact on major campaigns. The regular army might grumble at the mention of special ops, but the generals and theater CINCs cuss out loud if we're not around when they need us. Many citizens don't care much for policemen, but when the bad guys are coming through the front door, the first number dialed is always nine-one-one. When I joined the army, if our country needed a special ops air capability, there was no one to answer the phone.

In April of 1980, Operation Eagle Claw, the mission to free fifty-three American hostages being held in Tehran, had failed primarily because of helicopters. Although a combined assault team of special forces and the newly activated Delta was up to the task, no dedicated delivery system for the rescue force existed at the time and an ad hoc air squadron was assembled. The mission was extremely complex. Four C-130 Hercules transports would fly from Masirah Island near Oman into a remote Iranian desert location encoded "Desert One," carrying the assault elements as well as refueling blivets in their bellies. Simultaneously, eight Navy Sea Stallion helicopters would lift off from the aircraft carrier *Nimitz* and rendezvous with the assault element at the secret desert location. If all went well, the special operators would then transfer to the helicopters at Desert One and fly on to Desert Two, the final staging area outside of Tehran. On the next night, the raid would be executed, the hostages freed, and the entire force would exfiltrate.

But all did not go well. Most of the helicopter flying had to be done at night, and although the Marine Corps pilots had been training for Eagle Claw for months, they did not have nearly enough experience utilizing their newly acquired NVGs and their machines were not mission capable. Jockeying their Sea Stallions below Iranian radar and just above a black ocean was hard enough, but when a sudden *shaboob* kicked up, the billowing sandstorm was too much.

The grit fouled the engine filters and fuel lines of two of the choppers, forcing them to turn back to the carrier. When the six surviving helos finally arrived, late, at Desert One, another developed a hydraulic pump failure. Five helicopters were not enough to accomplish the mission, and with heavy hearts the commanders decided to go home, reevaluate, and try again later.

But there was one last insult to be added to injury. After refueling from a C-130, one of the chopper pilots became disoriented by the brownout from his own rotors. As he lifted off he began to drift, then tragically locked onto the dim beam of a flashlight on the ground, mistaking it for a directional signal. But the flashlight belonged to a wandering ground crewman, and the pilot followed him right into the wing of a fully fueled Hercules. The massive fireball killed the five C-130 crew, as well as three Marines on the chopper. All of the helicopters were abandoned to the enemy, while the remaining C-130s withdrew with the frustrated survivors of the force.

It was a wake-up call at the highest levels. America was entering an era of unconventional warfare, yet we did not have dedicated unconventional capabilities. As always, there were fine groups of highly trained commandos and special forces who could do the job on the ground, but if we couldn't insert them, support their combat missions, and extract them, they were limited in what they could do. If anyone doubted the necessity to reevaluate, they only had to look at the ghastly photos of Iranians celebrating over the charred aircraft and the corpses of our men at Desert One.

While the Iranians were laughing their asses off at us and the rest of the free world clucked their tongues, America got busy. We still had hostages in hostile territory and we still needed to get them out. Operation Honey Badger, the sequel to Eagle Claw, went into full swing, but this time the army turned to the 101st Aviation Group of the 101st Airborne Division at Fort Campbell. The 101st had the greatest number and variety of helicopters and experienced crews of any unit in the army, and was the most likely candidate to rapidly develop a rotary wing special ops capability.

Over at the 101st, the 158th Aviation Battalion was tasked to provide its new UH-60 Blackhawks and pilots for the assault element. The 229th Attack Helicopter Battalion would initially supply crews for the OH-6A scout helicopters and a light assault role. Over at Fort Rucker, Alabama, specialized personnel began developing armed OH-6s, combining equipment and crews from the 229th to form the first Little Bird organization of the task force. The 159th Assault Support Helicopter Battalion at Campbell came aboard with its CH-47C Chinooks. The large, twin-rotor helicopters would be difficult to deploy overseas, but once there they would best serve in establishing forward-area FARPs—fuel and rearm points—for long-range operations. Together, the men and birds of this new element formed Task Force 158.

The men began to train intensively, although none of them knew specifically what for. The nature of the mission was top secret, but with the Iranians on full alert now to any attempted hostage rescue, no one imagined that the U.S. would try it again anytime soon. So while the pilots, crews, and birds of Task Force 158 relocated to bases in Texas, Arizona, and California, their commanders treated them like "mushrooms"—fed them bullshit and kept them in the dark. Still, the nonstop training in desert environments offered some clues—they obviously weren't preparing for some op in the Italian Alps. Helicopter pilots might chew tobacco, listen to country music, and ride motorcycles, but we're generally good at math and speak English fairly well. There was lots of speculation and the wild rumors flew, but the men kept their mouths shut and let the chips fall where they may.

Just as the helicopter pilots in Vietnam had changed the face of modern warfare with their Hueys, the pilots and crews of Task Force 158 developed the next phase of special operations air-assault techniques. Very few of them were qualified to fly with NVGs, and no one was qualified to fly Blackhawks with those tactics. The helicopters themselves had to be modified, because their cockpit instruments and lighting were not compatible with night-vision devices. In separate locations, the Little Bird and Chinook pilots and aircraft underwent the same transitions. Ultimately, all of the elements linked up to fly coordinated training missions, at night, in all kinds of weather, navigating over routes as long as a thousand miles.

Throughout the summer and fall of 1980, Task Force 158 flew thousands of hours, honing desert environmental skills and close-formation precision navigation under NVGs. Late that autumn, the TF commanders asked the aircrews for volunteers to remain with the project. As expected, almost everyone stayed on board, and the volunteers were briefed on Operation Honey Badger. Task Force 158 would be the air component of a second attempt to rescue the hostages in Iran.

But on January 20, 1981, the hostages were released and Honey Badger was canceled.

The pilots and crews of the Task Force expected to be disbanded and return to their former units, but the army leadership wisely decided that this capability was going to be needed again—sometime, somewhere, maybe soon. A Headquarters and Service Company was formed, and combined with a Light Assault Company and Light Attack Company of Little Birds, two Blackhawk companies, and a company of Chinooks, Task Force 160 took its place on the army's table of organization.

The Night Stalkers had been born. However, as with every new birth, there was some pain involved. The 160th was trying things that had never been done before, and by the autumn of 1983 four aircraft had gone down and sixteen personnel had already been killed. The unit was nearly disbanded, until a dedicated training program was instituted, known as Green Platoon. This program would later evolve into the Special Operations Aviation Training Company and ensure that the highly skilled volunteers would be properly qualified as special ops pilots. Green Platoon trained the pilots intensively for four months, until they became Basic Mission Qualified and could serve as copilots on missions. Only after a further twelve to eighteen months of experience in an operational company would a pilot be Fully Mission Qualified and allowed to serve as a command pilot for special ops missions. Another two years minimum of exemplary performance would be required before a pilot could become Flight Lead Qualified, and plan and lead special operations aviation missions.

If you didn't have patience, perseverance, determination, and nerve, the 160th SOAR(A) was not for you. You would be constantly honing your skills, improving, improvising, developing new techniques. You had to fly right and shoot straight, 24/7. You had to be cool under fire, take harsh criticism, and offer it constructively. The unit's motto, "Night Stalkers Don't Quit," and its mission, "Time-on-Target plus or minus thirty seconds," had to seep into every aspect of your life. It was the ultimate team effort, but every member of the team had to have the skills of a quarterback, the grit of a linebacker, and the brains of a coach.

"Sure, there are other organizations that do secret missions," my contact in Korea whispered to me one night. "But no one does more 'point of the spear' ops than the 160th. If you want to go in, kick the door down, punch the enemy in the face, take stuff, and leave — you'll want to be a Night Stalker."

Yeah, that's what I wanted to be.

IN JANUARY 1986, I reported back to Fort Campbell and with another pilot from my medevac unit in Korea bought a house off base. I remember it well, because as I was unpacking my gear the television was on and I stood there openmouthed, watching the explosion of the space shuttle *Challenger*. It was a national tragedy, but considering how long the space program had been going on without a fatal mishap, I wasn't all that surprised. It was a reminder that if you spend your career in the air, you can't get complacent, and unfortunately very bad things will eventually happen.

The next day, I was ready and raring to "audition" for the 160th SOAR(A). Believing that the Night Stalkers were part of the 101st Airborne, I went over to the 101st admin building and signed in. It was a mistake. The 160th was an entity unto itself, but I didn't know that.

I called the 800 number I had for the unit. A 160th recruiting officer answered and told me to report to a nondescript building on base. I had diamonds in my eyes and wings on my feet, and when I got there the man blew me right out of the sky.

"You've already signed into the 101st?" he asked.

"Yes, Sir."

"Well, you've screwed the pooch, Durant. Take a seat and I'll lay it out for you."

As it turned out, signing into the 101st had already started a process that would be difficult to reverse. The 160th was not formally linked to that larger organization, and good pilots would not be easily surrendered by the 101st to special ops.

"Listen, you're a good pilot, but you're still pretty junior," he said. "If you were a CW4 with thousands of hours under NVGs, somebody we'd just drool over, maybe we'd fight that battle to get you. But you're a brand-new CW2, only two years out of flight school and, by our standards, still green."

He suggested that I put in a couple of years with the 101st, flying all sorts of missions, getting plenty of night hours, becoming intimate with Blackhawks and the assault mission of the 101st. If I continued my level of performance during that tour, when I came back to the 160th for assessment, he was pretty sure they would take me.

Well, I wasn't all that happy about it, but his recommendation seemed professionally sound. The 160th wasn't ready for me yet, and vice versa. I was only twenty-three years old and I planned to be in the service for many more years. I showed up back at the 101st, and I didn't mention to a soul that it was my second choice.

As it turned out, in those next eighteen months with the 101st Airborne I learned a tremendous amount about flying a Blackhawk. If you're serious about being a pilot, every time you go up you learn something new. It's the same with commercial pilots flying 747s, or farm boy crop-duster jockeys. When you think there's nothing more to learn, you should probably hang up your wings.

I flew lots of great missions in an assault battalion with the 101st. There were many challenges, including formation flying, hundreds of hours under NVGs, and delivering troops in complex tactical exercises. Some of the most difficult flying involved sling loads, where you would hover in above a given item, hook it up, and deliver it elsewhere. Every object placed different stresses on the aircraft: Humvees, 105mm artillery pieces, jeeps and trailers, rubber fuel blivets, and A22 bags of ammo and gear. Night formation sling loads under zero-illum (no moon) conditions, using NVGs in open terrain, is some of the hardest flying there is. In a large, wide-open area there are few outside references and it's hard to tell when you're drifting. You have to hover in and be precise enough to come directly over the load so that a soldier standing on it can manually hook you up. Then you have to lift it straight up without damaging the load, yourself, or any ground personnel. Eventually, I went through the four-week Instructor Pilot course during my time with the 101st, and wound up training other folks to do what I'd learned.

And, of course, as with many young pilots who've flown hundreds of hours without a mishap, I got a little too cocky. That usually happens when you near your one-thousand-hour mark. Mine happened at nine-ninety-five. I had just refueled at a FARP near Twentynine Palms in the California desert and for some reason decided to pull a slick maneuver, a backward takeoff. Instead of just doing a hovering turn into the wind, then dipping my nose and lifting off in standard bread-and-butter fashion, I was going to "shoulder it back"—spin the aircraft around as it came out backward and then roll out on course, real pretty. But I didn't know that there was a small rise just behind my Blackhawk, and my crew chief couldn't see it either. As I pulled up and started to spin, I caught the tail wheel, broke the rim, and pulled it out of the strut.

A Blackhawk has a tricycle landing gear, and if you try to set it down without a tail wheel, you're going to mess up the tail boom, and maybe even the drive shaft and tail rotor. The tail wheel was dangling straight down, and there was no way to set it down without damaging the bird. Cursing myself, I took it back to the airfield, hovered at about five feet off the tarmac, and told my crew to get out. Meanwhile, some ground personnel hustled out from their quarters with a pile of mattresses and stacked them up so I could set the tail boom down gently. One of those brave souls actually stood up and put the strut back together as I hovered in midair. I set it down on the mattresses anyway.

The damage to the tail wheel wasn't significant. The ground crew was able to repair it in a few hours. Accidents were classified by letters: Class A—a total loss or fatalities; Class B—aircraft damage or injuries; and so on down. This incident was classified as D, and there would be no formal record of it. But the lesson learned was invaluable: "Cowboying a ten-ton machine around will eventually lead to disaster."

As it turned out, a company commander from the Cav named Dick Cody had observed every aspect of my foolhardiness. He was flying above me, circling and cursing, wondering who the hell this Blackhawk pilot was. Cody is a three-star general now, and when I recently heard him tell the story of that FARP foul-up, I confessed to him that I was the perpetrator. He hasn't let me forget it.

After eighteen months with the 101st, I ran into Clay Hutmacher, who was later to become one of my very best friends. I knew Clay from my early days at Campbell, when he had been a senior medevac pilot. He was an interesting character who had begun his military career as an enlisted man in the Marine Corps, then switched to the army and went to flight school. We used to kid him that when he did that, he lowered the IQ averages of *both* services.

Clay didn't look much like a Marine anymore. As a matter of fact, he didn't look like regular Army, either. His hair was much longer than the regs allowed, he wore Hi-Tec boots instead of army issue, and had Oakley sunglasses perched on his head. His flight coverall was covered with Velcro swatches instead of the required army unit patches. He had made it into the 160th and was now a commissioned captain and company commander of their Headquarters Company.

Clay was probably the best "salesman" for the 160th the unit would ever have. But he didn't need to convince me; I was already sold. I told him what I wanted to do, and he gave me a tour of one of the aircraft and said, "Go for it, Mike."

I decided to "assess" for the 160th in June 1988. I had about eighteen hundred flight hours and more than five hundred under NVGs, which was pretty substantial for a CW2. I had "checked some good blocks," flown real-world medevac and multiple training assault missions, and was an Instructor Pilot. It was time for me to try for that next level and see if I had the stuff to fly with the best army aviators in the world, bar none.

The Night Stalker assessment phase was very much like that of all special forces units. Your evaluators watch you very carefully, but they don't tell you much. In the regular army's PT test, you had to score 180 out of a possible 300 points for three timed events: push-ups, sit-ups, and a two-mile run. For the 160th, you had to score 270 points, which meant 72 push-ups in two minutes, 72 sit-ups in two minutes, and running the two miles in around 13 minutes. But the Night Stalker recruiters wouldn't tell you what their standard was. They wanted to see how hard you would push yourself. And right after the PT test, we were given a grueling swim test. Many of the

160th missions take place over water, and the unit isn't about to give basic swim lessons. Then came a full psychological evaluation by army shrinks, designed to determine if you were basically sound and sane—relative to those traits inherent in the average military helicopter pilot. Of course, there was a very thorough check ride given by a hard-assed Night Stalker pilot. And finally, you'd get yourself up in your "dress greens" and go before a 160th board of admissions. The questions were designed to catch you off guard and see how well you'd respond under stress.

"You're on a clandestine mission in enemy territory and you've landed and camouflaged your bird. A group of nuns stumbles across your position. Do you kill them, bind them, or take them with you?"

There was no "correct" answer to such questions. The board wanted to discern if you would react quickly, do your best, and not second-guess yourself. I can't remember how I handled the nun conundrum, but by August I was in Green Platoon.

We started off with a "black day," as if all of us were fresh recruits showing up for our first hour in the army. From dawn to dusk we were harassed and harangued, suffering every indignity except having our heads buzz-cut. The message was clear: "No matter who you were before, you're a fledgling Night Stalker now, and you'll be treated like shit until you prove yourself."

My Green Platoon was the first formal class of its kind. The 160th was still so new that it was called the Special Operations Aviation *Group*, rather than a Regiment. Almost immediately the fundamental concepts of special ops made themselves clear, that the essence of Green Platoon was cross-training. What if you were shot down? You had to be able to land-navigate with a map. What if you encountered the enemy at close range while on the ground? You had to be proficient in hand-to-hand combat. What if one of your men was badly wounded and no medic was available? You had to be able to start an IV drip. What if you suddenly had to join your customers and participate in ground combat? You had to be able to shoot well with a variety of small arms. We did a lot of training in water survival, such as being strapped into the "dunker," a mockup cockpit that would simulate an "unscheduled" water landing. The dunker would submerge into a huge pool and roll over, and then you had to extract yourself and use a HEEDS bottle, a mini–scuba tank, in order to breathe and survive. We did a lot of flying and were given tasks extremely difficult to perform. When we fouled up, which was fairly frequent, it was essential that we submit to constructive criticism: "You screwed that up. You missed that checkpoint, and here's why." If you got defensive or argumentative under a withering hail of criticism, you were gone.

At no phase of Green Platoon were we ever regarded as Night Stalkers. We were constantly being tested and evaluated to see if we were going that extra mile. To the men who were already wearing the coveted maroon beret and Winged Pegasus crest, we were essentially invisible. Until you had passed through Green Platoon, which included the ultimate "reward" of SERE School, you were treated like a combat replacement at war. Until you proved that you were going to survive, none of the regulars would even speak to you.

At the end of three months in Green, there were no bugles, no drums. There was just a small ceremony where those of us who had passed received our berets, were told to show up at a regular 160th formation, and that was that.

It is a rare event when an army rumor turns out to be true, but it quickly became clear to me that serving with the Night Stalkers was definitely going to be different. The budget for the 160th appeared to be limitless. All of the aircraft were new and configured in ways unheard of in other helo units. We had the first "glass cockpits," meaning consoles with multifunctional displays. We had window-mounted 7.62mm miniguns instead of M-60 light machine guns. We had Forward-Looking Infrared Radar and Omega navigation systems instead of the old Dopplers. If we needed replacement parts, or wanted some newfangled widget that nobody else had, we got first priority and were never turned down.

The privileges of being special operators were also apparent in our personnel. We often had "relaxed" grooming standards and were issued lightweight, fancy boots and sunglasses more apropos of ski instructors than army pilots. Our immersion suits for cold-weather, over-water flights were custom-made, and even our harnesses and combat vests were black "ninja-style" instead of olive drab. Expensive, Gore-Tex cold-weather gear was standard issue, and while the folks over at the 101st were having trouble ordering up pencils, our hangars were full of more extraneous goodies than we could ever use. If you saw a pilot walking around with long sideburns, wearing a Cordura shoulder holster and a flight suit with nothing but his name on it, cutting slices from an apple with a Gerber Mark II commando blade, you knew he was a Night Stalker.

For a regular army guy like me who'd grown up in the woods of New Hampshire, it was all pretty heady, James Bond stuff. All of our missions, both training and real world, were classified. Our customers were strictly "Tier Units," the ultra-commandos who handled special tactics missions. We did not service any conventional units, but only unconventional organizations such as SEALs, Rangers, and others whose actual existence was still questioned at that time by regular army folks. I was issued an overseas driver's license and two passports, one civilian and one official, along with the appropriate "pocket litter." No one in the unit was ever issued a "GP Tiny," the general-purpose pup tent I had slept in while in the field with the 101st. When we embarked on a long-range training mission, our equipment made the trip in unmarked cargo aircraft, while we often flew commercial carriers in our civilian clothes and then cleaned out the local rental car agencies for ground transportation.

But for nearly everyone in the unit, it wasn't the toys and accoutrements that piqued our enthusiasm. It was "the mission." If America was involved in clandestine operations somewhere, the Night Stalkers were there. If a war went hot and made the nightly news, by the time those images were reaching into American homes, we would have already been engaged in special ops strikes. But even during peacetime there was a downside to being in the 160th. The guys were gone from home all the time, the divorce rate was high, and the Night Stalker memorial wall already had more names on it than any other post-Vietnam, special ops unit. I was a newlywed when I signed on in the summer of 1988, but my wife was the daughter of a sergeant major and had been born on Fort Campbell. She knew the drill, and my entering the unit was part of our "deal." Still, it wasn't easy on her or on any of the wives or significant others. I couldn't tell her very much about my work, and she was expected not to ask.

In the spring of 1989 I set off for Thailand. It was my first OCONUS (Outside the Continental U.S.) training mission and one heck of an introduction into the special ops community. Two of our assault birds were shipped off aboard C-5As to Utupao Field, an old bomber base from the Vietnam era at the southern end of the Thai peninsula. Up the coast along a fine strip of resort beach called Pataya, we pilots and crew chiefs were billeted in a five-star hotel. That's where we linked up with our customers, a team of Navy SEALs.

It was my first real exposure to the finest naval commandos in the world. What can you really say about Navy SEALs? They are a relatively small group of ultimate warriors who operate comfortably in putrid water, frigid air, or broiling sand, functioning entirely in the underbelly of the real world. What they do and see cannot really be imagined by some armchair tactician. They will accept any challenge, professional or personal. They fight like panthers on speed, and when they're done, they party as if they've been pent up all day in a cage. For these men, Thailand, with its reputation for blistering weather, wild sex, and lethal jungles, was a no-rules, happy playground. I don't remember seeing them sleep.

The SEALs were there to cross-train with Thai special forces, and from Utupao we flew them out to the darkest jungles in Southeast Asia. It was so far to the east that we could see the Laotian border, and the triple jungle canopies below concealed bands of drug runners and rebel groups I had never heard of. It was the first and only time I actually saw leper colonies designated on a Defense Mapping Agency chart.

It was fine training, with lots of over-water work, night-vision flying, live fire, and mock assaults into rugged jungle landing zones. The SEALs and Thais jumped from our helicopters at dizzying altitudes to practice HALO (high-altitude, low-opening) parachute insertions. They would execute a live fire mission and then call us in for support, so we could hone our precision skills and our crew chiefs could work out with their miniguns.

Being new to the unit, I was on board as an extra pilot, rotating into the training cycle as a copilot. Mike Goffena, who would later pilot Super Six-Two in Somalia, was my pilot in command. His was a very unassuming, quiet guy and a "good stick"—skilled helo pilot His temperament was very even, or maybe *below* even, which is a good trait for a special ops pilot.

One night the SEALs were going to practice some jungle land navigation culminating in live fire, so they asked us to stay out there on the ground with our Blackhawk. The area was full of wild tigers, poisonous snakes, and potential unfriendlies, so if anyone got hurt they might need immediate air extraction. We hunkered down in the back of our helo, our weapons close at hand, listening to the chatter of monkeys and the sounds of all sorts of creatures that roam the jungle at night.

In the morning the Thais and the SEALs were back and our indigenous hosts served breakfast: rice and fish oil in a Ziploc bag. It was some of the nastiest stuff I have ever eaten, but we weren't about to insult our hosts, so we forced it down. I remembered that that was all Nick Rowe had eaten during *five years* of captivity in Vietnam. Almost immediately, every one of us got the shits.

Then it was time for "closing ceremonies." A Thai officer in civvies showed up carrying a large pillowcase. The case was full of live cobras, and we all gathered in a large circle to watch him milk their venom. He stuck his bare hand into the case, snatched a cobra by the neck, forced its mouth open, and jammed its curled fangs over the edge of a glass. When the cobra had spewed enough milky venom into the glass, the Thai tossed him away and topped off the glass from a bottle of whiskey. He drank it down straight.

All of the Thai SF and our SEALs swigged down glasses of "Southern Serpent." I guess the venom will kill you only if you inject it straight into your veins. I wanted to try it, but we decided that flying while under the influence of lethal poison might not be a wise thing.

"I imagine this has some sort of medicinal purpose," Goffena mused.

"It's supposed to make you rock hard," offered a crew chief.

"Not necessarily a good thing," I murmured, "if you're around Navy guys."

"I heard that," one of the SEALs growled.

I was standing next to Goffena, watching this ritual, when the Thai bartender decided to demonstrate the proper method of cobra killing. He reached into the bag, snatched a snake up by the tail, and proceeded to whip it in the air like a bullwhip, ostensibly to snap its spine. But he lost his grip on the snake and it flew across the circle, smacked right into Goffena's chest, and fell to the ground at his feet. Mike just stood there, looking at the cobra slither and hiss around his boots.

"Is this part of the procedure?" he wondered aloud.

I didn't move. Being the new guy, I'd be the *last* one to run. Thankfully, the Thai recovered the snake and killed it, and we wrapped up the party and all flew back to Utupao. It was a kick-ass first mission, and I would always think of it as "a sweet taste of venom." Some time later, Tommy Field would nickname our Blackhawk "Venom," which certainly seemed appropriate.

BACK AT CAMPBELL I slipped right into an intensive training cycle, and I began to understand the "culture" of the 160th. As with all military units, there was an unspoken pecking order, even though your assignment did not necessarily denote any particular talent. If you had been flying Cobra gunships before signing on, you would most likely become a Little Bird attack pilot. If you'd been flying OH-58 Scouts, you'd wind up in a Little Bird assault company. Blackhawk pilots stayed Blackhawk pilots, and if you had flown a Chinook, there was no reason to make you into something else. These weren't ironclad rules, but they prevailed more often than not.

The Little Bird pilots thought they were hot shit. And in truth, they were. Lots of them rode Harleys, and in their leather jackets and jeans, they looked like members of a Las Vegas motorcycle gang. Maybe they had seen *Top Gun* once too often, but they earned their reputation with their performance. In a combined, after-action debrief, when all pilots were present, they were professional and thorough, offering criticisms and sometimes even accepting same with aplomb. But in their own private debriefs, they were absolutely brutal with each other. An unplanned delay or a miss on an insertion would engender a withering hail of abuse for the perpetrator. A serious breach of performance would result in such caustic dressings-down that the recipient would suffer like some pledge at a college frat house. Personally, I saw some value in that attitude, and I would later incorporate some of that in the Blackhawk companies, much to the chagrin of my comrades.

Our Blackhawk pilots were somewhat more suave and technically proficient, but all across the board there was essentially "zero tolerance" for defects. You were expected to perform at your peak, every

day, every night, all the time. And these expectations were not restricted to pilots. Our crew chiefs were some of the most dedicated,
intelligent, innovative, quiet professionals I would ever work with in
my life. They coveted no glory and were only there to do the job and
do it superbly. They worked themselves to the bone, while us pilots
got all the kudos.

Of course, there was plenty of opportunity for payback. If you
came to your desk and found a set of automobile tire valve stems ar-
rayed there in perfect order, you knew that your car was out in the
parking lot sitting on the rims. When we traveled around the United
States on training missions, rather than using military vehicles we
would rent an entire fleet of cars. More than once a pilot would
come out to his car, to find that all of the tires had been replaced with
those useless little "donut spares" you find in rental trunks. One
pilot, who shall remain nameless, had a penchant for screwing with
the crew chiefs. Being mechanically precocious, they rerouted the
window washers on his car from the exterior to the interior, carefully
setting up a new trajectory. He was driving down a highway in Texas
when he decided to use his wipers and got totally soaked with windshield fluid.

Things were a bit different back then, before "politically correct"
became a well-worn phrase. There were a few female helicopter pilots in the 101st, but there were none in the 160th, and the unit had
the atmosphere of a military "Skull and Bones." Our crew chiefs
read *Mechanics Illustrated*, but they still hung *Playboy* calendars on
the hangar walls. When we were inside our birds or on a mission, we
were all business. But when we were done, we played hard and none
of us watched our mouths. After hours, we pilots would often gather
at the Officers' Club and drink, and we'd get pretty wild some nights.
It was an opportunity to blow off steam and to say things to each other
you couldn't say during a regular army workday. Nowadays the "O"
clubs are virtually empty, because the concept of "acceptable" behavior has changed. It might not be as much fun, but apparently it

hasn't affected the army's performance. Or maybe the guys are now doing it all off base. All I can say is, it worked for us.

It was during this period that I met some of the commanders who would have great influences on my own life.

Brigadier General John "Coach" Dailey was the commander of the 160th when I joined the unit. He was a highly decorated veteran of multiple tours in Vietnam, and as an army aviator had been shot down seven times. He was intensely passionate about the 160th and didn't make any friends in competing organizations, such as Air Force Special Ops Helos. As far as he was concerned, the Night Stalkers were always the best choice for any mission. He was liked and respected by everyone in the unit. He presented me with my maroon beret at the end of Green Platoon.

Lieutenant General Bryan "Doug" Brown was the battalion commander during my early years in the unit. He was one of the original captains in Task Force 160 and had spent virtually his entire career in special ops. He was a good stick, a great communicator, and he had a "Can Do" attitude second to none. As the legend goes, during Operation Urgent Fury, the invasion of Grenada in 1983, his mission was to go into the control tower at Grenada's main airfield with a suitcase full of cash. Producing a pistol, he made an offer the Cubans couldn't refuse:

"You can take a bribe or a bullet. What's it gonna be?"

Lieutenant General Dick "Commander" Cody is without a doubt the most knowledgeable leader I've ever worked for. I had never seen any commander better prepared, and if you went in to brief him on a mission, you had to have your shit together because his technical questions were already locked and cocked. There was no way to bullshit him, because he'd immediately discover it and smoke your butt. He was the ultimate special ops pilot and had had just about every assignment possible in the community. As an Apache Battalion Commander in the 101st, he fired the first shots of the Gulf War in January 1991 against Iraqi antiaircraft sites to open the corridor for the bombers.

There were other men like these, but it was their influence and examples over the years that really formed my own leadership characteristics. They held lower ranks when I first met them, but they are all still in the "left lane" of army leadership, and for all the right reasons.

And then there were the men who would become my best friends and closest comrades.

Cliff Wolcott was already an experienced Cobra pilot when he came to the 160th to fly Blackhawks. When I met him, he was senior in rank to any of us new guys and had transferred from Charlie Company into an office called SIMO, the Systems Integration and Management Office. SIMO was the Night Stalkers' own version of "The Skunk Works," where new internal technical programs were developed for the unit. If you wanted to try a new weapon or nav system on the aircraft, the people in SIMO would write up the requirement, go after the funding, specify a contractor to do the work, oversee the project, test it, and field it to the unit. Each type of aircraft had a representative in SIMO, and if pilots and crews came up with some crazy idea, it was up to the SIMO folks to make it happen.

Cliff had the innovative idea to turn a Blackhawk into an attack helicopter. He called it the DAP, or Direct Action Penetrator, and he somehow recruited me into the project right away in 1989. We were putting rocket pods on the Blackhawk, taking the miniguns and fixing them forward so that we could fire them from the cockpit, and experimenting with a variety of different guns. Having had no formal schooling in engineering, I was fascinated by this stuff, to take various new weapons systems and incorporate them, fly them, and test-fire them. We tried an M2 .50-caliber twin machine gun and a three-barreled Gatling Gun .50, using test equipment to measure the forces and loads on the airframe. We finally settled on the Apache's M230 30mm chain gun, because the Blackhawk could carry a pair of them. In addition to all the training and real-world missions, it was a brain challenge for me, and I picked up analysis and management skills that would always come in handy.

The DAP program was Cliff's baby, and as I watched him work, it was clear that he was the kind of guy who could sell coolers to Eskimos. He could stand up, pitch something he believed in, and make other people believe it too. He was big into guns, big into hunting, a tall lanky guy who wasn't much into athletics but could finish a marathon. He always kind of had this shit-eating grin on his face, but he was no more of a wise guy than any of us. He had a long scar on his nose and a Soldier's Medal for pulling a fellow pilot out of a crashed Cobra. He was married with one young son, very family-oriented and very mission-focused. I liked him a lot, right away.

When I first met Donovan Briley I had just returned from Thailand. Donovan was still training in Green Platoon, and since he hadn't yet "passed through the portal," we didn't have much contact. But as soon as he officially came aboard, Donovan won all of us over.

Donovan was most definitely "different." Half Cherokee Indian, and very proud of that background, he had grown up in Oklahoma and had two brothers in the army, one serving with the 160th and the other a Special Forces medic. He was of average height, with a huge upper body, small legs, no neck, and a sly smirk constantly playing at the corners of his mouth. He was a funny guy and constantly entertaining us with tales about his youth: how he preferred sleeping in trees, how he would crawl up in the ceiling above the girls' locker rooms at school, just to get a peek at the wonders of nature. He was big into gadgets, and back home he had bought a scanner and liked to eavesdrop on his neighbors as they gossiped about *him* on their cell phones. He was married, with one young daughter, and he was the only one of us who lived on post.

No one was happier to be in special operations than Donovan Briley. He loved every aspect of it, from the unconventional gear to the secret missions. And although he was the company jester, he was also a "good stick" and extremely detail-oriented. There was never enough intel information to suit Briley. He could never plan enough contingencies or plug enough nav points into the system. If it was up to Donovan, every mission would be preplanned down to the last bullet. If you were a Flight Lead, Donovan was the kind of guy you wanted next to you in the cockpit.

He had begun his army career as a reservist and then gone to flight school. His forearms were covered with burn scars, because while witnessing a fiery helicopter crash at an airport in Arkansas, Donovan had reached right into the flames and pulled the crew out. He never bragged about that. It was in his file.

IN THE SUMMER of that year, I thought I was going to war.

For nearly ten years, the Iraqis and Iranians had been hammering at each other in a protracted ground war that claimed millions of battlefield casualties. Iraq had nearly destroyed the Iranian economy by launching air sorties against Iranian oil facilities, while the Iranians had resorted to targeting neutral ships in the Strait of Hormuz and the Persian Gulf. By 1985, foreign oil and gas tankers were being targeted by Iranian minelayers and Silkworm missiles, and when the Kuwaiti government asked the United States to intercede and guarantee safe passage, the phone rang at the 160th SOAR(A).

Since 1987, the 160th had been involved in an ongoing clandestine mission called Prime Chance. The objective was to stop the Iranians from mining the Gulf waters, and a combined special ops team consisting of Army and Navy aircraft, Navy SEALs, and Marines was dispatched. A pair of small oil-rig-servicing barges, the *Hercules* and the *Wimbrown VII*, were purchased to serve as Mobile Sea Bases. Each vessel had a small helicopter landing pad and just enough room to accommodate a couple of hundred men, their weapons, maintenance equipment, and special assault boats.

Little Bird gunships were the first of our helos to arrive on the scene, and during the ensuing two years they served in both scout and attack roles. The AH-6 pilots supported SEAL team raiders as they boarded Iranian mining vessels, and they also made their own rocket and gun runs against Iranian rogue freighters and "Boghammer" fast attack boats. By 1988, a pair of our Blackhawks were permanently on station aboard the *Hercules*, serving primarily in a Combat Search and Rescue mode. They had been painted gray to match the Navy colors, and were temporarily dubbed "Grayhawks."

In the summer of 1989, it was my turn and I was anxious to go. Even though Prime Chance had cooled down to life-support status, we would still be in harm's way and there was a chance to see some action. As part of a replacement crew for the Blackhawks on station, I flew out to the *Hercules* in the Gulf. To me, it looked like some contraption out of *Thunderball*. The vessel was only about four hundred feet long, and it had a huge derrick for construction and maintenance of oil rigs and an elevated landing pad. The pad was barely large enough to accommodate a single helo, but we had two Blackhawks and two Little Birds sharing space on this tiny island in the sea. The deck was only a hundred and fifty feet wide, but it was crammed with commo gear, weapons, Zodiac rubber assault boats, and scuba equipment. Navy officers and Marines were running the show, and together with SEAL team members, as well as Army air crews preparing to soon bring in OH-58D Kiowa Warriors to replace the 160th, every bunk was booked.

For the most part we remained on alert status, ready to support any over-water combat. We also took our turns patrolling the Gulf and set out floating targets so our crew chiefs could keep their gun skills up. The environment was challenging, providing me with more opportunities to learn. The waters of the Gulf can be very calm, and on a moonless night it's nearly impossible to discern where the water ends and the sky begins. Incredible sandstorms would kick up, billowing out over the sea. We described it as "flying inside a Ping-Pong ball" while trying to find this minivessel in the middle of the Gulf and land on it. But for the most part, we Blackhawk pilots served as truck drivers, hauling supplies, Marines, maintenance parts, and even mail back and forth from land bases. The Navy called it "Pony." We called it frustrating as hell.

In my three weeks of rotation on Prime Chance, I never saw or heard a shot fired in anger. I was actually embarrassed when, just for hauling ash and trash, I received the Army's combat patch. But I returned to Fort Campbell unaware that the invasion of Panama was on the horizon, and that it wouldn't be long before I earned it.

This stage of my life had been set. And as always, much of life isn't about what you do but about the people who make a difference while you're doing it. I had met Donovan Briley, Cliff Wolcott, and Mike Goffena. I would soon know Dan Jollota, Stan Wood, Ray Frank, Bill Cleveland, and Tommy Field. They were men I would come to think of as my brothers.

Within four years, all of us would be shot down, captured, or killed.

Chapter 7

THE DAY OF THE *KHAT*

October 6, 1993

I WOKE UP facing five years of captivity.

That was the reality as another dawn slowly crawled up the walls of my cell in Mogadishu. In the course of this century's history, hundreds, perhaps thousands, of American pilots and crewmen had been shot down and captured by America's enemies. They had parachuted into the waiting arms of the Nazis, crashed in Burma and been hunted down by the Japanese, endured years of torment in Hanoi, and been used as pawns by the Russians, Iraqis, and Hezbollah. Some of them had escaped, some had lost their youth through years of captivity, and some had never come home. And from the moment of each one's capture, each had surrendered his or her future to the unknown. None had known when or if they would see freedom again.

It was my fourth day as a prisoner of war in Somalia. I knew I couldn't deal with my captivity in terms of years, but I had to mentally prepare myself for a long haul. So, as I stared at the crumbling ceiling of the Hotel Nowhere and listened to the furious buzzing of the black flies, I told myself that I would survive just one day at a time. I would not imagine my captivity as years of tortured waiting, because if I really believed that, I would probably die. My mind could not accept being in prison for that long, and those kinds of thoughts would break me.

Like any major challenge in life, you have to take it in bits and pieces. You don't try to tackle the whole thing at once. I remembered how I had reacted at the crash site when it was overrun and I had focused on surviving for just five minutes, and then making it through the next five. And so, as Day Four dawned and I ventured farther into that black tunnel of captivity, I needed a limited point of reference or that darkness would just overwhelm me.

You just need to make it to tomorrow, I told myself. *If you wake up tomorrow, you'll figure out how to survive tomorrow. Today, you've got to figure out how to survive today.*

And still, there was no way to know when it was all going to end. So, even though I was trying to convince myself not to worry about it, those images of endless years would continue to ambush my mind.

As the city began to slowly waken I slipped into its rhythm, taking stock of my injuries and moving carefully. A night of sleep might have helped the healing process, but my flat repose on the cement floor had also stiffened me up again. Blood would have coagulated at my wound sites, pockets of swelling grown tight and turgid. I shifted my leg a bit, raised my head, and rolled my shoulders forward. Yes, the pain was all still there. Dr. Kediye's aspirins might as well have been children's vitamins.

I looked around the room. The gritty floor was strewn with crusty food wrappers, bottle caps, and oily rags. Hundreds of flies dove at every morsel like scavengers after a battlefield massacre. Firimbi was there, asleep on his mat and still snoring, his heavy glasses folded and clutched in one hand. He was wearing the same loose shirt and trousers of the day before, and the day before that. He probably bathed only once a week, and from across the room I could smell his musk, but it was no longer offensive. In a land of no colognes or perfumed soap, your nose quickly adapts to the scents of the local skin, if not the local litter.

Firimbi was my full-time warder now, and he left the room only for very brief periods. He never carried a weapon, although I knew that the guards outside the room were well armed. Two of them were posted there, young nameless men who rarely entered my cell. Yet they seemed calm, deliberate, and professional, exhibiting none of the hyped-up aggression that had unnerved me before.

Firimbi snorted and woke up. He rolled over, looked at me, and blinked, as if he wished as much as I did that this predicament were no more than a dream. He didn't greet me, but put his glasses on, barked an order at the door, and stood up. One of the young guards entered, and Firimbi went out.

I saw it as my chance to make another "friend." I made a loud snoring sound, said "Firimbi," and made the sound again. The guard looked at me, and then he understood. He threw his head back and laughed hysterically. He called out to his partner; the second man entered, and I heard them exchange Firimbi's name and they both roared with laughter. I grinned at them. They probably didn't make fun of Firimbi very often, at least not in his presence.

The guards walked out and closed the door, still chuckling to each other. Establishing a connection with them was a good tactic, but it did little to decrease my pervasive sense of vulnerability. Once again I heard the laughter of playing children, the sounds of old engines cranking to life, the calls of women to their neighbors. But then the rattle of a submachine gun hammered somewhere close by, and I winced. I knew that these men wanted to keep me alive, but I also knew that the populace had ideas of its own. The civilians out there were still burying their dead, and if they knew that I was here among them, and alive, no one would be able to stop them from

swarming over this small enclave. That feeling of uncertainty and little faith in my protective envelope would continue throughout my
captivity. It was a constant source of tension, and it would remain
with me long after my release.

Yet the things that occupied my mind that morning were not my
wounds or chances for survival and freedom. I had been a special ops
pilot for years, and my mind tended to focus on the operational details of my profession. Automatically, I fell into the pattern of a sys-
tematic mental debrief, reviewing our mission preparation, mission
execution, and after-action results. What had we done well? What
had we done wrong? What could we have done differently?

The fates of my men from the crash site weighed heavily on me.
In particular, the images of Tommy and Bill, so badly injured and
helpless, caused me to reevaluate my decision-making after the crash.
Had I been thinking clearly, I could have told Randy and Gary, the
two Delta operators, to hide Tommy and Bill in the tail boom of
Super Six-Four.

The tail boom on our Blackhawk was different from that of a standard UH-60. There was a large panel cut out of the right side of the
boom, because we would place a lot of our avionics inside and there
was a big door on it with a key. The key would have been hanging
on the ignition ring or in our logbook. I thought that maybe we
could have saved our crew chiefs by pulling off a "Trojan Horse" and
hiding them in the boom. When the Somalis overran the chopper,
it was highly unlikely that they would have figured out someone was
still inside.

Then there was the issue of the caving ladders. Every Blackhawk
in the unit had one of these extraction devices curled up in its cargo
bay. The caving ladder was a simple, thirty-foot construction of metal
rungs and cables rolled up into a spool, meant to be deployed over
water if a pilot went down in the ocean. All of us wore extraction harnesses, and if a helo had come in over our crash site and unfurled a
caving ladder, certainly Ray and I could have been snap-linked to the

This picture, taken from the interrogation video while I was in captivity, is supposedly the first to simultaneously run on the covers of *Time, Newsweek,* and *U.S. News & World Report.*

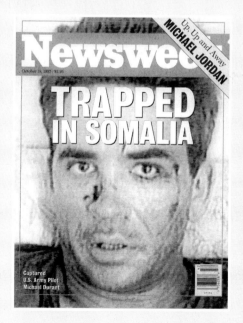

1979: A shot of the Army's newest eighteen-year-old soldier! My official graduation from basic training photo.

(COURTESY OF THE U.S. ARMY.)

Right after flight school, I attended the Blackhawk qualification course at Fort Rucker, in December 1983.

Flying the lead helicopter lining up for an air assault with the
101st Airborne at Fort Campbell, Kentucky, in 1986.

Our company commander, Maj. Mike Zonfrelli, pins an air medal for
the Panama operation on my uniform, with Donovan Briley at my side.

The Night Stalker DAP (Direct Action Penetrator) gun platoon poses for a photo with the newly developed armed Blackhawk. I'm sitting on top on the left, Cliff Wolcott is on top on the right, and Dan Jollota is on top in the center. Stan Wood is seated third from left.

Crew of Super Six-Four in Somalia, 1993. From left to right: Winn Mahuron, Tommy Field, Bill Cleveland, Ray Frank, and me.

In the cockpit of an MH-60 Blackhawk in Somalia with Dan Jollota on my left. (COURTESY OF GERRY IZZO.)

Ray Frank in front of the JOC in Somalia. (COURTESY OF GERRY IZZO.)

One of Super Six-Four's crew chiefs, Tommy Field. (Courtesy of Gerry Izzo.)

Super Six-Four's other crew chief, Bill Cleveland. (Courtesy of Gerry Izzo.)

Helicopters parked at Mogadishu Airport behind sandbag revetments. Note the runway to the left, and the ocean just beyond. (Courtesy of Gerry Izzo.)

Aerial photo of an open-air market in Mogadishu. (Photograph courtesy of the U.S. Agency for International Development [www.usaid.gov].)

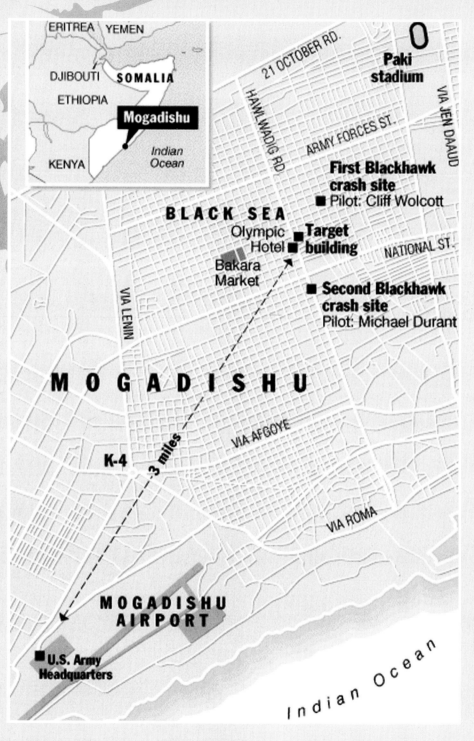

ERITREA   YEMEN

DJIBOUTI   **SOMALIA**

ETHIOPIA

Mogadishu

KENYA

Indian Ocean

21 OCTOBER RD.

Paki stadium

HAWLWADIG RD.

ARMY FORCES ST.

VIA JEN DAAUD

First Blackhawk crash site
■ Pilot: Cliff Wolcott

BLACK SEA

Olympic
Hotel

■ **Target building**

NATIONAL ST.

Bakara Market

■ **Second Blackhawk crash site**
Pilot: Michael Durant

VIA LENIN

M O G A D I S H U

VIA AFGOYE

K-4

-3 miles

VIA ROMA

**M O G A D I S H U
A I R P O R T**

■ **U.S. Army Headquarters**

Indian Ocean

Gary Gordon (left) and Randy Shughart (right), the Delta operators who, for their actions at Crash Site Two, were posthumously awarded the Medal of Honor. (COURTESY OF CARMEN GORDON AND STEPHANIE SHUGHART.)

The remains of Super Six-Four, a few days after the battle, as seen by an Army helicopter.

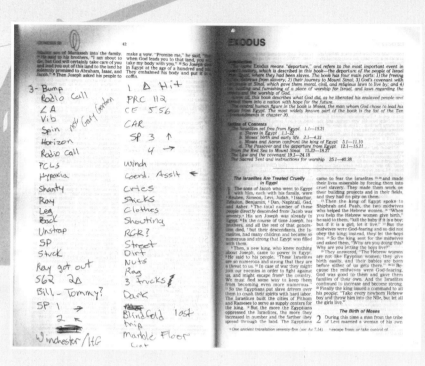

My coded timeline of events written in a U.S. Army Bible.

Members of Task Force Rangers carry me to the back of a waiting
C-141 transport just prior to leaving Somalia. (COURTESY OF THE U.S. ARMY.)

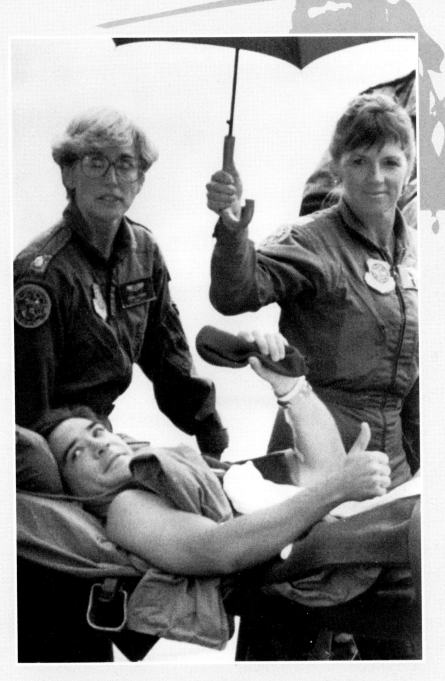

Giving the thumbs-up to the photographer while being sheltered from the rain by two nurses who accompanied me on the C-141 flight to Ramstein Air Force Base, Germany. (Courtesy of the U.S. Army.)

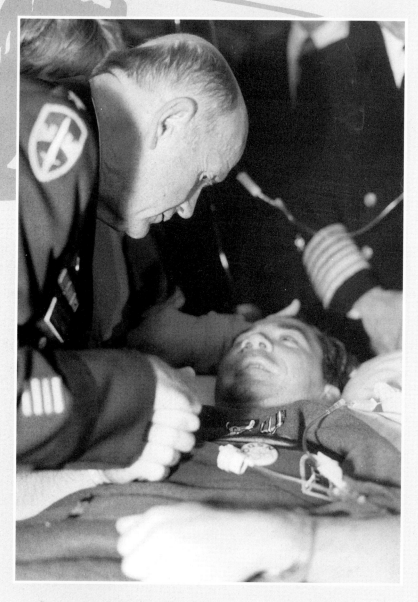

Gen. Gordon Sullivan, Chief of Staff of the Army at the time, pins the Purple Heart on me just after I touched down again on U.S. soil. (COURTESY OF THE U.S. ARMY.)

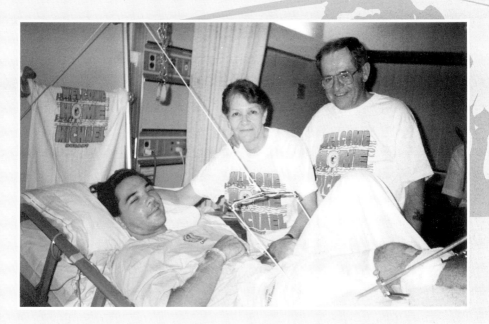

Recuperating at Blanchfield Army Community Hospital at Fort Campbell
under the watchful eyes of my parents.

All smiles for my first training flight in a Little Bird after regaining flight
status in the summer of 1996.

This sign for the topless club Cat West on the strip outside of
Fort Campbell says it all.

Giving a speech at a Veterans Administration hospital in the mid-1990s.

Crossing the finish line at the 1995 running of the Marine Corps Marathon in Washington, D.C., with a time of 3:37:10. NSDQ! (MarathonFoto.)

Driving my boat with my son Joey on my shoulders in the summer of 1994. The realization of a dream.

rungs and hauled out of there. Of course, with our injuries, we would probably have been screaming our heads off, but it was certainly a better option than death or capture. Why had no one in the unit thought of that? Was it because the ladders were regarded only as water-extraction devices, and in the heat of battle no one's mind ventured "outside the box"? Why hadn't I thought of it myself?

That's how it should have been done, I decided. *We should have hidden Tommy and Bill in the tail boom, because they were too badly injured for a hoist exfil. Then a helo should have dropped a caving ladder, and Ray and I and those two Delta men could have been extracted in a flash. At night, after the Somalis thought they had picked Super Six-Four clean, a Night Stalker assault could have been mounted to come back in and get our crew chiefs out. . . .*

But even though I forced myself into these painful analyses, I also knew that Monday morning quarterbacking works both ways; it might offer solutions for the next time, but it pours salt into the wounds of failure. For all I knew, the issue of using those caving ladders had come up in the JOC and been rejected due to the high risk of losing another hovering helo to RPGs. And as far as the tail boom shelter was concerned, hiding Tommy and Bill in there would probably have done no more than sealing them in their own coffin. After all, the entire fuselage of Super Six-Four had been punctured by hundreds of bullets.

Would've, could've, should've, Durant . . .

I knew that one part of me was performing a professional debrief of the mission, while another part was just conjuring up hopeless solutions out of desperation. I knew that all of these men were most likely dead, but I felt like the driver and only survivor of a fatal car crash. Over and over again I replayed it in my head, but of course I couldn't change it.

I was grateful when Firimbi and the guards returned, distracting me from my mental self-flagellations. By midmorning the African heat had already suffused the small room with humid steam, and

Aretha's incense burner was having little effect on the flies. The temperature seemed to cause my injuries to throb, and my slick skin was sticking to the straw mat she'd provided. The guards had brought me some sheets, large rectangles of soft pink cloth covered with loud floral patterns. They were thin, but they made a much finer mattress than the prickly straw and it felt a lot better to stretch out onto cotton.

Aretha showed up, wearing a Caribbean blue Somali sarong and offering a wide grin of pearl-white teeth. She presented me with a large wooden bowl and a plastic spoon. The bowl was brimming with pasta mixed with vegetables and had some type of soup bone thrown on top. I looked at the meaty shank.

"Gammell," Firimbi said, waving his fingers and urging me on to eat.

Camel, crocodile, whatever, I thought. I was hungry, and I nodded my thanks and dug in. The pasta was fantastic and the camel tasted like beef to me. I must have looked like a starving child as I wolfed it down, because Aretha waddled gleefully from the room and came back with a hunk of bread, and as I used it to soak up the sauce and stuffed myself, my guards watched me and grinned.

That bowl was enormous, like a family salad bowl, and there was no way I could finish the meal. I held it out toward Firimbi and the guards, offering them some.

"No, no." Firimbi wagged a finger and declined. He pointed at himself and his men. "One time. Eat one time."

I understood that the Somalis ate only one meal per day. To an American, that might be the definition of starvation, but to them it was the normal fare. I never saw them consume an actual meal, and the only thing they accepted from me was the hot sauce from the MREs, which they drank down like alcoholics snapping up airline cocktail bottles. They left me alone to work on my bowl, and pretty soon I had to put the uneaten half of it down. I lay back down from my elbow, letting the nourishment flow through me. I wasn't exactly feeling fat, dumb, and happy, but it wasn't a bad start to Day Four.

During the night I had topped off my Disney bowl with urine, and Firimbi came back in to carefully remove the waste. A few minutes later, he returned with the same bowl, now full of water, and a washcloth and sliver of soap.

"I hope you washed that damned thing out," I said to him through a halfhearted grin.

"Yes yes," he said, but I knew damn well that he hadn't understood a word.

Once again, he helped me wash up. He was methodical and thorough, taking care not to cause me any additional pain as he worked over my limbs. The task didn't appear to be subservient to him, just an assignment he had been given and intended to carry out well. Who knows? Maybe it was an honor for him to be entrusted with the care of a high-value prisoner of war. At any rate, it felt good to get myself clean, and I knew it was important because of my injuries. I just hoped I wasn't coating myself in my own bacteria.

Firimbi did demonstrate subservience when Minister Abdi suddenly arrived, trailing his entourage of bodyguards and once again sweeping into my cell like the Prince of Wales. As before, the Minister looked clean, alert, and freshly pressed. Since he was obviously a man of considerable power in these parts, I suppose I should have been glad to see him. But the truth is that anything or anyone who attracted attention to my "hideout" caused me conflicting emotions. If my comrades were tracking the moves of Mohamed Aidid's power brokers, this might be one way to pinpoint my location. On the other hand, the same could be said of those people who still wanted my head on a pike. It was almost as if I was a prisoner of the Somali National Alliance, but the SNA was a prisoner of the people.

"Good morning, Mr. Durant." Abdi folded his hands behind his back, his white safari shirt gleaming. His head didn't dip even a centimeter, and he exuded that air of arrogance.

"Sir," was all I said.

"I trust you are well?"

"My guards should be commended."

Firimbi was standing off in one corner, and I hoped he could understand my compliment. Abdi turned his head, cocked it slightly at Firimbi, and briefly closed his eyes. My roommate looked at me, and I could see the pleasure in his expression.

"I may have some good news for you, Mr. Durant." The minister focused on me again. "It appears that a representative of the Red Cross might be able to visit you."

God, that would be fantastic, I thought. *If a Red Cross worker witnesses me alive, it's one more step toward a survival guarantee.*

However, by this time I was on to Abdi's game. He was a professional politician, and he never gave up anything for free. I just looked at him as if waiting for the rest, and it came along soon enough.

"Would you like to be visited by the Red Cross?" he probed.

"Sure," I said as casually as possible, "if it's not too inconvenient."

He smiled at me. The man was a shark.

"And after that, perhaps you would speak to some journalists?"

"No, Sir. I would not."

He nodded pensively, though I saw the ire flash briefly in his eyes. A burst of AK-47 fire suddenly erupted outside from somewhere nearby. Abdi didn't even blink, and I'd be damned if I was going to blink first. He crossed his arms over his chest as he thought for a moment. He had all the time in the world.

"Your family now knows of your situation, Mr. Durant," he said.

A tight constriction gripped my throat. Images of Lorrie and Joey and my parents swept across my mind's eye, but I showed him nothing on my face.

"The video of you is still being shown every day on the news. You have become a media 'celebrity,' shall we say."

Once again my mind shot over every word I had said during that taped interrogation. But I was still satisfied with it and felt no remorse at anything I'd uttered. And as far as having my face splashed across television screens, I had found a way to deal with that exposure as well. If I ever got out of there, I could have a buzz cut, grow a mustache, and still go back to work.

Since I didn't visibly react or address any of Abdi's news, he apparently decided that he wasn't going to get much from me today. He turned to leave while his bodyguards snapped to, and then he turned back.

"I will have that radio delivered to you today."

"I'll be grateful for that, sir," I said, while giving no indication of what my gratitude might entail. Still, Abdi hadn't revealed anything about the path this event was taking, and I decided to pose a question and gauge the truth of his answer in his eyes. "Mr. Minister?" I asked. "When will I be allowed to see my family?"

My meaning was clear. *Are you going to release me or not?* But this time the Minister did not leave it in the hands of Allah.

"You will be released, Mr. Durant," he said, "when the United Nations releases the twenty-four Somalis who were captured by your task force." He raised a finger of his right hand, while sweeping the air with his left. "One prisoner for twenty-four. I think that is a fair exchange, don't you?"

And then he was gone, like some wicked wizard from a children's fairy tale.

Firimbi trotted out after his boss, leaving me to ponder Abdi's every word and nuance. One part of his revelation was encouraging. Conditions for my release had been established, which meant that somewhere, somehow, the SNA and the United Nations were holding discussions. On the other hand, a prisoner exchange was a complex matter, especially while hostilities were ongoing. And this wasn't like the end of a major conflict where each side signs off on a peace agreement and each country releases its warrior pawns. This was East Africa, with a culture akin to its Middle Eastern neighbors', where the techniques of negotiation were comparable to the argumentative shopping in the local *souks.* You laid an offer on the table, knowing it would be rejected, and then you stomped your feet and stormed out of the shop. When the proprietor ran after you, you would reluctantly return for more discussions, knowing all the while that your initial proposal was a gross exaggeration of what you'd eventually settle for.

In the past I had seen these sorts of things take a long, long time. America had wrangled with the Russians and the North Koreans for months or years over the release of a single man. The Israelis had bartered and blustered with their radical Arab enemies for a decade over the return of a single IDF corpse. When American hostages were being held in Tehran, we had secretly tried to bribe the Iranians with shipments of TOW missiles. On the surface, enemies maintained entrenched positions, while under the table hard cash deals were made.

But the United States regarded the Somali National Alliance as renegades and terrorists, and I knew that no such overt prisoner exchange would be arranged. And while I desperately wanted to get out of there, I also did not, under any circumstances, want to be the fulcrum for the bending of my country's honorable policies.

I decided it was going to be a long wait. Like a pilot who had parachuted into a cold deep ocean, I would have to conserve my energy and "tread water." I would have to slow the metabolism of my hope, not overreacting to any positive sign or despairing with any setback. Captivity is a mental struggle, with the demands on the mind as strong as any physical injury. I had both to deal with. If my captivity turned out to be short term, it would be a welcome surprise. And if it dragged on and on, I would be prepared.

But I was not alone in my captivity. Abdi's words still rang in my head.

Your family now knows of your situation, Mr. Durant.

In effect, the people who cared about me were also being held captive, and I could imagine what they were going through. I had seen it all before.

IT IS NOT EASY to be the wife of a special operator.

When a woman falls in love with any man in uniform, she knows she is inviting a difficult marital life. A man who is committed to the service of his country must first obey his orders; the needs of his family will always take second place. There will be long periods of separation, assignments to faraway and unattractive places, and the constant tension of an uncertain future. Still, the balance of military personnel are often able to set down roots, remaining assigned to one particular base for years at a time. The families of these people lead seminormal lives, develop social circles, and manage to keep their children in the same schools for extended periods. In times of peace, the larger percentage of military men and women go off to work in the morning and return at night.

But when a woman falls in love with a special operator, she knows she's in for a roller-coaster ride. Marry a SEAL, a Ranger, a Night Stalker, or any member of Special Forces, and you can forget about counting on celebrating birthdays, holidays, or anniversaries together. You might be in the throes of honeymoon bliss when his beeper goes off and he jumps up to leave. You might be clutching his hand in the final agonies of your first labor, when he kisses your sweat-soaked brow and walks out the door. Your mother might pass away and he won't make the funeral. *His* mother might die, and you will have to watch him kneel at her graveside, stricken with remorse, long after she's cold.

If you are a woman in danger of falling for one of these men, your family and friends may wisely warn you to cease and desist. But the heart is a blind hunter.

By October of 1993, Lorrie and I had been married for five years. The daughter of an army sergeant, she knew what she was getting into from the beginning, and the fact that I was assessing for the 160th did not dissuade either of us. The good thing about the unit was that we would be permanently stationed at Fort Campbell. Sure, we pilots and crews would be gone for long stretches of time, but our families could set down roots, build houses, and have children who wouldn't be moved around the world every other year. The only problem with being the wife of a Night Stalker was that the guys were always gone and the missions were always very high risk.

But for pilots like myself, it was all good. Our wives were always there, holding down the fort, keeping the house in shape, and taking care of the kids. The unit was exemplary in caring for their needs. There were support groups, social groups, and army psychologists. There were "coffees," where the wives got together and played poker, exchanged gossip about the post, bitched about the army, and blew off steam. We pilots were members of a very special club, and our wives were an integral part of that organization.

There was only one club that they never wanted to join, the Gold Star Wives Club. All of the members were widows.

Perhaps it is a selfish thing for a special operator to marry and have children. But after all, we're only human, and the love of a wife and family is an important part of what motivates us, an essential kernel of that American life we dedicate ourselves to protect. And no matter how many names of our friends are etched into the Night Stalker memorial wall, none of us really believes that we will leave behind a bereaved family.

But to the warrior goes the glory, while to the wife goes the pain. A special operator may be killed in combat and even suffer terribly at the precipice of his death, but then it's over for him. For his wife, the agony goes on forever.

My wife and I never spoke about my potential death, and certainly the idea of my becoming a prisoner of war never entered our minds. Such discussions were left to the wives' social engagements, and the subject was taboo in front of us men. Even the funeral of a comrade was only a brief window of opportunity to face the realities of the profession. Of course, we shed tears for our fallen comrades, because despite the tough-guy image, a deep-seated patriot has to have a well of tears somewhere. But such events turned quickly into inebriated reminiscences, full of laughter and jokes about the departed friend. We were jolly, cynical men on the outside. Yet despite our jovial "covers," our wives knew us well and had to deal with hard truths.

Throughout those years I was gone from home for long periods of time. We would be just moving into a new house and my beeper would go off. I'd have to report to base immediately and then a blackout period would ensue. I couldn't call home, and there would be no contact allowed from my wife or family. Of course, if trouble was brewing somewhere in the world and the news reports were intensifying, our wives would correctly speculate to one another about our deployment. But if we were engaged in some classified mission for weeks on end, even our safe return shed little light on the matter.

I'd suddenly arrive at home, sporting a deep tan and a couple of new scratches. After the customary romantic reunion, my wife would wade in without really expecting enlightenment.

"So where were you?"

"The Middle East."

"How was it?"

"Hot. What's for dinner?"

It was August of that year when our beepers went off for Operation Gothic Serpent, the special ops slice of Operation Restore Hope. Joey had been born the year before, and he was the light of our lives. I had never imagined feeling about another human being the way I felt for my son. His arrival hadn't changed my commitment to the unit or the mission, but it made our deployments doubly difficult. Throughout the summer, the situation in Somalia had been heating up and rumors were circulating, but you couldn't try to plan your life around speculations. We were building a new house, Joey's first birthday was coming up in one week, and my parents would be flying in from New Hampshire for the celebration. With the beep of a pager, all of that was put on hold.

I called in to work and was told to report immediately for deployment. My duffel was always packed and ready, and I had just enough time to wolf down a bowl of pasta and say my goodbyes. My wife cried. Her instincts told her this wasn't a training exercise.

As always, the ensuing blackout period was the hardest on the families. It was only some days after our deployment that a meeting was called by our commander's wife and a captain in the unit who hadn't deployed. In a room on base crowded with nervous women, the families were informed that we had relocated to Fort Bragg and would shortly deploy to Somalia. A young wife put her head on a table and began to cry, while the other, more veteran wives tried to comfort her.

"Everything will work out fine," they assured her. "Our husbands are very good at what they do."

"Yes," she responded between her sobs. "But how good is the enemy at what *they* do?"

When emotions had been calmed, the usual questions ensued.

"How long will they be gone?"

"Can the men call us?"

"Who do we call for a family emergency?"

The answers to most of these questions were standard. No one knew how long we would be gone. No calls could be made. The wives could not talk to their husbands on the phone. But as always, letters and packages would be permitted, and unit representatives would be available to deal with any family emergencies.

Joey's first birthday was celebrated without me. I had missed other anniversaries, birthdays, Christmases, and Valentine's Days, but not being there to see Joey blow out that single candle caused a painful stitch in my chest. Yet all over Fort Campbell other wives and families were enduring the same sense of deprivation. Wives could tell no one outside their circle where we were. They had to make up cover stories, claiming we were off training on some other post. They knew that the success of our mission depended on secrecy, and they held it close. That is one of the reasons why such wives' groups are so intimately bonded. They all have to keep the same secret, and no one outside their group can understand their private corner of hell.

During the next eight weeks our wives slipped into their mutual life-support routines. Without us there to occupy them, they got together frequently, setting up spontaneous poker games, suffering the endless waiting without news, and sharing their fears. When a Blackhawk from another unit serving in Somalia was shot down, badly injuring both pilots and killing everyone in the crew compartment, our unit decided that our wives deserved a morale boost. Satellite phone calls were arranged from the Task Force Ranger compound, and each of us had ten minutes to greedily absorb two months of homefront news from our wives. It was a boost for all of us. It was Saturday, October 2, 1993.

Perhaps the hardest things for our wives to attend were the notification meetings. These drills were designed to inform them about what to expect if the very worst happened. They had to fill out cards indicating who they would like to come to their houses for support. They were told that if any of us were wounded or killed, two officers wearing dress greens would appear at their houses. The days of notification by telegram were thankfully long gone. All of the women detested those macabre get-togethers, but they were a necessary evil of being a Night Stalker wife.

When men are killed or wounded during classified missions, it is often the media that break the news first. Special operations units are very wary of making erroneous assessments and perhaps mistakenly notifying a family of bad tidings. In the fog of battle initial reports are often confusing, and no one wants to announce a tragedy that hasn't been absolutely confirmed.

Well before midnight on that Sunday evening in America, my

family suspected that I might have been shot down in action. News channels were reporting that two army Blackhawks had gone down in Mogadishu, and the wives began frantically calling each other. The commander's wife as yet had no "hard information," but prior to that she had always been quick to announce it if everything was all right.

No one at Fort Campbell slept that night. Our unit had a policy of no notifications between the hours of 10:00 P.M. and 6:00 A.M., which seemed somewhat absurd to the wives. If their husbands were dead, disturbing their sleepless torments was a non-issue.

My wife's mother had come to the house to be with her daughter. My parents had already seen too much on CNN and were home in New Hampshire suffering the tortures of the damned. At exactly 6:00 A.M. on Monday morning, headlights washed across the windows of our house in Clarksville and tires crackled on the gravel. As Joey slept in his crib, Lorrie and her mother gripped each other, shaking uncontrollably as a pair of grim officers in dress greens rang the doorbell.

"Oh my God. Oh my God" was all Lorrie could say, over and over.

An officer removed his hat and performed his duty, the worst job that the army has to offer.

"Your husband, Michael Durant, was involved in a helicopter crash. His aircraft was shot down. He is listed as missing in action."

LYING THERE IN my cell on my fourth day of captivity, I could not know with certainty what was happening at home, but I could imagine it well. With the first breaking news reports on Monday, there would have been panic among the families of all combatants, as each wife, parent, and child held their breath for the inevitable arrivals of the somber notification officers. Then, it had been like the spinning of a gruesome roulette wheel, as some men's numbers came up and their families were forever shattered, while the healthy status of other men was relayed to bring ecstatic relief. Wives who had lost their husbands had crumbled into the arms of our friends, while other wives had been overcome with guilt for exhibiting relief.

For the first few days, the shoot-downs of Super Six-One and Super Six-Four would keep the loved ones of our crews in a cruel state of limbo. The families of Cliff and Donovan were notified almost immediately of their deaths. But all of us involved in the crash of Super Six-Four, including Randy Shughart and Gary Gordon, were listed as missing in action. Those horrible images of American corpses being dragged through the streets of Mogadishu served only as confirmation that men had been killed, and our wives huddled around television sets, trying to discern an identifying feature among those bloated and mutilated bodies. Clay Hutmacher, who was serving temporarily as the unit's liaison to the Air Force in Florida, flew back to Campbell to support my family. Convinced that I was dead, he cried on the flight, yet held his emotions in check from the moment he deplaned. But within twenty-four hours of my capture, my videotaped interrogation was appearing on the nightly news in the States. My family knew that I was captured, and alive, for now.

Your family now knows of your situation, Mr. Durant.

To me, Abdi's words were ominous and brought no relief at all. Did he mean that due to the broadcasts, my family was no doubt aware that I was alive and in captivity? Or did he mean that some Somali asset in the United States had made contact with them? Part of my training at SERE School had focused on all the methods of exploitation that might be used by an enemy. It was not unheard of to have the family of a captured serviceman be suddenly contacted by some mysterious stranger. That stranger could be serving an enemy power and, while pretending to be a sympathetic supporter, attempt to glean personal information that could be used against the captive. I knew that Lorrie and Joey were surrounded by the most professional military officers in the world and that no real harm would come to them, but I couldn't bear the idea of their exposure to more pain.

For that reason, I had claimed during my interrogations that I lived in New Hampshire. Part of that tactic was to throw the Somalis off the scent of Fort Campbell and the Night Stalkers, but another motive was to redirect any attempt at exploitation toward my parents. God bless them, I surely did not want them hurt in any way, but I somehow had faith that they would handle any such attempts with great strength. My father was a die-hard military man himself, and woe betide the Somali agent who tried to screw with him in his own backyard.

A civilian might wonder why I hadn't simply lied outright and claimed a residence in California. Well, one of the most basic rules about fashioning a credible cover story is that you have to stay close to the truth. You have no idea if you'll be held captive for three weeks or three years, and trying to remember the details of a fabrication can be difficult under conditions of torture and deprivation. I couldn't deny being a helicopter pilot, but I had spent enough time with the 101st to make my claim of serving there completely credible. I couldn't pretend to be a native of Alaska, because once news of my capture made headlines, some enterprising reporter was going to dig up the details of my life and publish them. Eventually, my captors would storm into my cell waving a copy of *People* magazine in my face, and the interrogations would begin all over again.

In truth, what was happening at the moment was that my captors were actually treating me fairly well, while the interrogations and harassments were being foisted upon my family by the news media. My house in Clarksville was surrounded night and day by reporters. When the bodies of my friends were returned to America and my wife traveled to their funerals, reporters would corner her in airport rest rooms. All of my friends and relatives handled those intrusions with grace and elegance.

I was later proud of their aplomb, but during those long days in Mogadishu, I feared for them all.

THE DAY PASSED SLOWLY, just another autumn afternoon in Africa. My leg swelled further in the heat and the pain in my back rippled in waves when I breathed. The doctor had not returned, and without pain medication or antibiotics, I knew that my condition would only deteriorate. The single window stayed shuttered and the door remained closed, and the cell was like a dinghy slowly sinking into a sea of flies. They kept on flowing inside, and with all the tasty morsels of trash around and the sweaty oozings from my wounds, they had no reason to leave.

For the most part, Firimbi sat across the way on his mat, reading the Koran. Occasionally he would glance at his watch, then maneuver his mat so it was angled toward Mecca. He'd arrange himself on his knees, bow his forehead to the mat, and murmur his prayers. I had been raised to respect all religions and all faiths, and I admired his dedication to Islam. Yet I knew that if the operators from the Task Force suddenly busted in here, they would take down anyone who wasn't me. I did not want to see Firimbi die, but in truth, I was willing to live with his death in exchange for my rescue. Still, it would be good if he was somewhere else when the event occurred.

At one point he fished in his trouser pocket and came up with a huge wad of Somali currency and began to count it. I looked at him and raised my hand as if to ward off an offer.

"No, really, that's unnecessary," I said. "I'll get combat pay for this."

Of course, he didn't understand the joke and just grunted as he focused on his accounting. He called out to his guards, they entered the room, and he gave them half the wad. I had no idea what that was all about.

Aretha came in carrying a large bedsheet. At this point my bloody and sweat-stained army T-shirt had been taken away, hopefully to be washed, and with the exception of my bandages I was completely naked. But my state of undress didn't seem to offend her any more than it would a hospital nurse. She draped the sheet over my body, apparently to keep the flies off of me. The sheet was dark gray, with purple and green stripes arranged in a tartan pattern.

"Thank you," I said. "Is this a donation from a Scottish member of the clan?"

She grinned, as always, and nodded and left. They were a tough audience for my feeble attempts at humor.

I lay there thinking, mostly about Joey. He was a beautiful boy, but like most babies, his features were still cherubic and unformed. I wondered what he would look like as a five-year-old, as a teenager, as an adult. If I lived, I swore to never miss another of his birthdays.

I will be there, I pledged to him silently. *No matter what I have to do, I will survive and come home. I will be there for all of it.*

And once again, my mind swam back to the crash site. I kept on wondering about my crew, where they were. I continued to try to figure out if there was a way they could have survived. Could they have crawled into the tail on their own? Could they have buried themselves under some debris? Could they have somehow hidden somewhere until the chaos was over with and then gotten out of there? But I figured that it wasn't likely. The only one who might have been able to do that was Ray. Tommy and Bill were too badly injured and Randy and Gary had gone down fighting. So Ray was really the only one I thought had a chance. But I am an eternal optimist, there's no question about it, and I refused to give up hope until there was just no doubt.

The sun had set and the children in the streets had all gone home when Abdi fulfilled his promise. Firimbi came in carrying a small multiband radio. It was brand new, and when he handed it to me, I looked at it as if it was some sort of fantasy treasure from *Raiders of the Lost Ark.* This was more than I could have hoped for, my first link to the outside world. I swallowed as I turned the volume to the lowest setting, held it to my ear, and switched it on. I was still concerned that the vengeful civilians might discover my location, and I wasn't about to blast out some rock and roll and start dancing.

The radio worked. *Outstanding!* I searched all the bands, finding the BBC, the Armed Forces Network, and Radio Mogadishu. I tuned back and forth between them, trying to hear any news about the situation. It didn't take long. News about my captivity and the battle was included in every broadcast. On AFN, an American major serving as a spokesman for UNOSOM was issuing a prepared statement at a press conference and taking questions from reporters.

"On Sunday, October third, at around four P.M.," he began with grave formality, "the U.S. Quick Reaction Force detained twenty-four suspected Aidid militia members in a search-and-seizure operation east of the Bakara Market. We believe there were several key militia members among them. Three of the twenty-four detainees died of wounds received during the operation, and one other detainee was wounded and is being treated. The key militia members we have detained were *not* among those who died or were wounded. I want to emphasize we were searching for the individuals we detained. We were *not* searching for Aidid. . . ."

Well, my first slice of news was that at least the mission had been a success. The statement had been crafted to tell the SNA that we had captured Omar Salad and Mohamed Hassan Awale, respectively Aidid's top political adviser and his chief spokesman.

I would not realize until much later that the Awale who had been captured was not the original target of intent. That target was Abdi "Qeybdid" Hassan Awale, the man I now knew as Minister Abdi. In effect, I had been trying to capture *him*, and he had captured *me* instead.

"As the operation was in progress," the major continued, "two U.S. Army UH-60 Blackhawk helicopters were lost due to ground fire. During this time ground troops evacuating the detainees came under fire and returned fire. About seventy Rangers surrounded one of the downed helicopters at dusk. They formed a perimeter to protect the wounded members of the crew while awaiting a medical evacuation, and they too came under fire. . . ."

I assumed that he was referring to Cliff's and Donovan's bird. I turned up the volume just a bit, straining to hear the outcome of that effort.

"A task force was organized, consisting of two U.S. Army infantry companies, twenty-four Malaysian armored personnel carriers, four Pakistani tanks, two Pakistani armored personnel carriers, a Ranger platoon, and a company of armored Humvees. The Task Force reached the downed aircraft at two-thirty Monday morning and evacuated the soldiers."

I realized that that had been the furious battle I'd witnessed on my first night of captivity. *Yes!* No matter what injuries Cliff and Don had sustained, I was now certain they had been rescued.

"Regrettably, there were a number of U.S. casualties in these engagements. As the Pentagon has already released, five U.S. soldiers have died. In addition, a number have been wounded. . . ."

It wasn't good news. The major's tone was funereal and cautious, and I knew that his announcement of casualty figures was preliminary. I had no doubt that the numbers of our dead and wounded would increase.

"I am waiting for further figures on U.S. casualties," he confirmed. "They were significant, and I don't have clearance nor the firm figures to release to you yet. We acknowledge that there are some U.S. soldiers missing. We don't know their status at this time. We can't confirm if they are dead or alive. . . . One would hope, though, that if these missing soldiers are in the hands of the Aidid militia, they would treat them with the same humanitarian needs in mind that we treat the SNA militia. That is, adequate medical treatment, and food and water and visits by the International Committee of the Red Cross. . . ."

That shed no light on the status of my crew. But being the eternal optimist, I hoped it meant that some of them might still be out there and alive, and our officers did not want to offer any information that might encourage the SNA to search for them. I could hear a reporter in the background asking a question.

"Major, it goes without saying that they do have a live prisoner and they're parading him on CNN. Isn't this going to make the political issue surrounding this whole operation very hot?"

"Undoubtedly," he answered.

Well, there wasn't too much I could do about that. It was up to the President to handle the political ramifications of my capture. It was up to me and my buds to get me out of it. Another question shot out from the crowd, but this one I was not prepared for.

"Major, can we get your reaction again to the U.S. soldiers— which four journalists eyewitnessed—almost naked American soldiers being dragged around?"

"Absolutely hideous," he answered. "I am shocked."

I was disgusted and infuriated to hear that confirmation, but I wasn't shocked. After all, I had already seen more inhumanity close at hand than most people could ever imagine, and Mohammed Gait had hinted at this early on, even though I didn't really believe him. I prayed that those soldiers who had been dragged through the streets weren't members of my crew. I prayed that they weren't really Americans at all.

I turned off the radio. Like a desperately thirsty man, I had anticipated drinking from its fountain of information and being satisfied. Instead, the news was essentially bleak and no one was discussing my release. I decided I would listen again in the morning.

It was already late in the evening when the two guards entered my cell, showing Firimbi a large bundle of something that looked like freshly picked weeds. I knew what it was and now understood why Firimbi had given them so much Somali cash. The bundle contained *khat*, fresh leaves from the *Catha edulis* tree. We had been briefed about *khat* before arriving in-country. Many of the locals chewed the leaves like tobacco, and its chemical properties were similar to those of amphetamines. The militia chewed handfuls of the stuff prior to combat, and it allegedly made them more aggressive. I hadn't ever tried it, but I had firsthand knowledge that it worked.

Firimbi and his guards laid the bundle on the floor and unwrapped it. One of the guards began separating the *khat* into three piles. Firimbi stopped him and pointed at me.

"You try *khat*," he said.

"No, thanks," I replied, shaking my head. "As soon as I get out of here, they're going to piss-test me."

"Good! You try!" Firimbi insisted, and as he spoke he looked at me and winked. I might not be the sharpest tool in the shed, but I knew what he was trying to do.

"Okay," I said.

Now the guards redivided the *khat* into four piles. Firimbi got one, I got one, and they each took their share and left the room.

As soon as the door closed, I took my pile and tossed it back to Firimbi. He grinned from ear to ear. Between the hot sauce and the *khat*, I knew I had won him over. If Firimbi had orders to kill me in the event of a rescue attempt, it was going to be a tough choice for him.

Firimbi and the guards chewed that *khat* all night. It didn't seem to make them wild or aggressive, but they sure enjoyed it. I asked him why they liked the weed so much. He stuck out a forearm and made a fist, which I understood to be a reference to sexual performance.

"You have child?" he asked me.

"One." I raised a finger. "You?"

He couldn't count in English, so he raised both hands, showing me all ten fingers. Then he raised one hand and showed me four more.

"Fourteen children?" I couldn't believe it, so I repeated his gesture with my hands. *"Fourteen?"*

He nodded vigorously and grinned. He had made his point about the *khat,* but I thought that maybe he should have spent all that money on condoms.

I came to wish that night that I had shared some of the drug. The pains of my wounds were building, and a mind-altering substance might have been better than no medicine at all. I hadn't seen my own face in days, but I could feel that it was swollen and stiff. My right cheek seemed to be partially paralyzed, and I had no feeling in my upper lip or teeth. An infection was settling in there, and if it raged in this heat, it was only a short trip to my brain.

At last, Firimbi fell asleep and snored once again like a lion. I wanted to snuff out the oil lantern flickering in the corner, but there was no way to reach it. The light seemed like a beacon to the flies, and they swarmed in through the window without end. I pulled the tartan sheet up over my head and lay there inhaling the stench of my own sweat.

If you guys are out there preparing a rescue mission, you'd better make it fast, I thought.

Otherwise, you're gonna be rescuing a corpse.

Chapter 8

THE WARRIOR ANGEL

October 7, 1993

ON THE FIFTH DAY of my captivity, room service was pretty weak.

Firimbi and his men had been up half the night chewing *khat*, and now they were paying the price. My personal caretaker was obviously hungover, big time. He lay there on his mat, alternating between snoring, moaning, and farting, which were pretty much the sorts of sound tracks and atmospheric scents I had come to expect in the Hotel Nowhere. The thin warble of a *muezzin* calling Moslems to prayer from a minaret did not wake him. Neither did the rising chatter of children playing in the courtyard. He didn't twitch when an AK-47 blasted out *k-k-kung k-k-kung* right outside. I realized that these people came out of their houses in the morning and casually tested their weapons, a habit as natural to them as a rooster crowing at dawn. Gunfire turned heads here about as much as car horns in Manhattan. But still, Firimbi was clearly smoked.

"Morning, Bwana," I said. He didn't move. I tried Spanish. *"Buenos días, dondiego de día."* Nothing. "That's all right. Don't bother making up the room. And I'll just go down to the lobby for the buffet."

Well, it didn't look like I was going to get cleaned up today—or fed, for that matter. I ran my fingertips through my two-day growth of beard and explored my face. The broken cheekbone was swollen and my lips were still numb. It felt like touching rubber. I pushed the tartan sheet down from my chest and flicked away the fat corpses of black flies. I must have been killing them in my sleep.

Lying very still on my back kept all the pain at a low ebb, so I didn't really want to move. But I had to urinate, so I pulled the Disney bowl close to my hip and braced my left elbow on the floor. I slipped my right hand beneath my broken leg and in one swift motion rolled onto my side. *Mia madre!* It hurt like hell, but the outgoing relief almost made up for it.

For breakfast, I settled on a half bottle of water and some crackers from one of the MREs, imagining they were a can of Budweiser and a slice of Papa Gino's. I don't normally drink beer or eat pizza for breakfast, but I certainly would have in Mogadishu if anyone had been delivering. I turned on the radio and held it up to my ear.

As most people who travel a lot have discovered, the BBC is usually pretty accurate with the news, so that was the station I turned to. The bone-dry voice of the announcer was recounting the events in Somalia of the past few days, and he even mentioned me by name, but other than that there was no real news. The best part about it was hearing the time: 6:00 A.M. I had lost my watch on Sunday and hadn't seen a clock since then. I am a very time-focused individual. Most special operators are that way.

I switched to the Armed Forces Network, but there were no big revelations there either. Our casualty figures were higher, just as I'd expected. "U.S. Army helicopter pilot Michael Durant is still being held prisoner, it is believed by members of the Somali National Alliance . . ."

Thanks, I know that.

"And five U.S. servicemen are still officially listed as missing in action."

All right. Missing In Action is still better than Killed In Action.

There was still a chance that some of them were alive out there, and my prayers for them went on almost like a subconscious litany.

After an hour, the AFN switched over to a direct broadcast feed from a local station out of Los Angeles. Listening to the mindless patter of an L.A. disc jockey was surreal, and after a while I turned it off. I didn't know how long the radio batteries would last, and who knew if there would be any more after these went dry?

Firimbi still didn't stir when Dr. Kediye showed up. I was glad to see him, because this time he was carrying his tackle box, plus some large packages with Red Cross markings on them and some sort of heavy wire-mesh material.

"Good morning, Mr. Durant." Kediye's voice was weak, his shoulders hunched, and his eyes sunken.

"Morning, Doc."

"And how are we feeling?" he asked. He obviously hadn't had a break in days, and he set to work like a worn-out old robot, laying out his instruments and gauze pads by rote.

"We're feeling stiff," I said.

"Yes. Well, I am going to make you a bit stiffer."

He removed my soiled bandages, cleaned my wounds, and applied fresh dressings. I was relieved when he didn't probe too deeply into my leg wound. Then he pulled large rolls of gauze from the Red Cross packets and held up that strange wire material. It looked sort of like the cheap metal shelving you can buy at Kmart.

"I am going to apply a splint to your broken leg. It should make you more comfortable."

"Whatever you say, Doc. That's why you get the big bucks."

I actually got a small smile out of him. He placed the "shelving" along the length of my right leg, then bent the bottom of it so it curled around my foot and back up the other side. Then he carefully wound the gauze rolls around it, from my toes to my thigh, covering every inch of my leg right up to my crotch, until it looked like a mummy's limb. He sat back on his heels and checked over his handiwork. It looked pretty good to both of us.

"Thanks, Doc."

"It will help, *Insh' Allah*," he said.

He packed up his wares, leaving me with another bottle of antibiotics and one of aspirin to replace the ones I'd lost.

"One of these every six hours," he instructed. "And take the aspirin as you would at home."

"Right now, I'd take the whole bottle," I said. "You don't have any morphine, I guess."

"I am sorry. As I told you before . . ."

"I know. This isn't California."

"Correct."

He trudged out with his gear. The poor bastard must have felt like the only veterinarian on Noah's Ark. But I sure felt better. My wounds were cleaned up again, and the fresh Betadine was probably already killing off the bacteria and whatever other foul stuff is contained in fly saliva. I had this new splint on my leg. The only thing about it I didn't like was that now I couldn't rotate my foot at all and my knee was completely immobilized. But maybe that immobility would keep the broken bones from shifting. I decided to test the splint's effectiveness, so I rolled my shoulders up a bit, grasped my leg, and shifted it to the right.

Holy Mother of God!

Only the subconscious warning of not giving away my location prevented me from yelling. The pain shot up from my broken femur, and I swear it stopped my heart for that moment. Sweat sprang from my face, and I crashed onto my back, just trying to breathe again without cursing out loud.

The doctor's splint was a frigging torture device. Instead of supporting my broken leg, the wire and gauze had added untold weight to the limb, and now the only "hinge" was at the site of my broken femur. If I moved in the slightest, my bones were going to grind against each other like the gears of a busted clutch.

"*Jeesuss!*" I hissed up at the ceiling. "*And this guy went to med school in California? If Joey ever wants to be a doctor, he's getting his education east of the frigging Mississippi.*"

I pounded the floor with my fist in frustration. Firimbi rolled over, belched, and kept on snoring.

THERE WERE HELICOPTERS in the air that day. But I didn't take much heart in that, because I knew that any rescue attempt would be executed by night. I figured it was probably just a "signature" flight.

All throughout that summer in Somalia, we had been running such flights regularly. A substantial element of the Task Force would take off and fly a circuit over the city. The objective was to reduce the probability of Mohamed Aidid's getting spooked when we finally launched an actual mission. When you think about it, if you're Public Enemy Number One and you're downtown when all of Task Force Ranger launches, what are you going to do? You're going to get the hell out of Dodge. But if they're flying every day and night, that tends to reduce the immediate sense of alarm and you let your guard down. Eventually, it had worked, and Aidid's people held their public rallies and planning sessions without regard to the helos overhead. But instead of going to ground, they had armed every militia household with RPGs and machine guns, and had set up teams of signalmen throughout the city. They were a wily and cunning enemy, and we had surely underestimated them.

I thought back to an incident in late September, when I'd had my first real taste of the unpredictability of East Africa. It was then that I learned how tables could turn here in an instant. The grateful civilian could quickly flip into thievery, and his patient benefactor could find his generosity savaged.

It was already late one afternoon when we took off from the airfield. I was Flight Lead of two Blackhawks on a low-level flight route to a remote area along the coast. The sun was sinking low toward the seam of sky and ocean, and the waters below shimmered with lances of light. The hot summer day was already cooling, and the winds had died down to languid breezes.

What a great day, I remember thinking. *As far as flying goes, this is as good as it gets.*

We weren't doing anything special on this flight, just transporting the Rangers out to the countryside so they could do some weapons training. The exercise was important, because they had to keep their skills sharp, but probably not as important as providing the soldiers an opportunity to escape the Task Force Ranger compound. We had been in-country for almost two months, and the mission we had come here to accomplish had thus far eluded us. For that reason, the compound that held roughly four hundred of us seemed to grow smaller every day. It was good to get away from there occasionally.

We were going to keep the two helicopters parked out in the rough countryside while the Rangers trained. That way, if a mission developed back at the airfield, we could get the rotor blades turning, load the troops, and the whole package could be back at the compound in fifteen minutes. We dropped them off about a half-mile from the coast and landed to their rear along a dirt road paralleling the ocean. We started the aircraft shutdown procedures and settled in for a few hours of boredom.

The flight back to the airfield would take place after sundown, so I decided to get out my night-vision goggles. I had been keeping them underneath my seat, where they were secure as long as the seat was adjusted all the way down. I pulled on the lever and raised the ballistic bucket. Now I had easy access to the NVGs, and Ray and I continued with our checklist.

Ray was a CW4, considerably older than I was and holding a rank above mine. Technically, he was my copilot, but in my mind I never thought of him that way. The only reason I was Flight Lead for these missions was that I had been a Night Stalker longer than Ray had. But our relationship was solid, and those details caused no problems for either of us. With the men of Super Six-Four, any in-flight situations were resolved *as a crew.*

Ray was an easygoing guy, with a boyish smile that belied his years on the job. I could remember only one time when we'd disagreed about some procedure, and it was so minor I let it ride. Hell, he was probably right anyhow. Ray had been flying helicopters since Vietnam, and his dress greens were festooned with combat ribbons; to disregard his wealth of knowledge and expertise would have been foolish. Just a couple of years back, he had survived a major crash, broken bones and multiple surgeries, and now he was flying again as if it had never happened. This was going to be his last real-world operation, but Ray Frank had earned his retirement long before that day. His time had come, but I knew he would miss it. He was a great guy, and we made a damn fine team.

Gerry, the pilot in command of the second Blackhawk, called over on the radio to say that he'd developed some kind of hydraulic system problem. It wasn't a major issue, but together we all decided that Gerry should take the bird back to the airfield and summon the maintenance team. If the firing exercise wrapped up before he could return, Super Six-Four would just have to fly the Rangers home in two rotations.

Ray and I completed a commo check with both the Rangers and the ops center on the handheld radio. Now it was just a matter of waiting, a skill I have never really mastered. Flying has been categorized as hours of boredom punctuated by moments of sheer terror. I think that statement's slightly exaggerated, but I considered the waiting part to be one of the least desirable aspects of the job. Still, the weather was nice here, as always, and hanging out wasn't exactly punishment. More important, this *wasn't* the airfield.

On previous excursions into the countryside, we had found the locals to be quite friendly. It was a very different environment from that in Mogadishu proper. By our standards the people out here were very poor, but they weren't starving and seemed relatively happy. The reason they liked us was clear: Some of the aircrews had been giving out bottled water, food, and other tidbits the Somalis apparently coveted. Our crew chiefs, Tommy and Bill, had done the same. Bill and Tommy were super guys, and the response was automatic for them. They gave what they had, because the Somalis had less.

At first, the country folk were very grateful and it seemed as though our generosity was a good thing. Each of the handfuls of locals we encountered returned home with something that was of little value to us, but for some of them, especially the children, these items were treasures. We gave them water bottles, MRE pouches, and packs of gum. Each time we visited the area, more Somalis would come to see the helicopters. Today, at least for the moment, there were not very many of them around. But it was only a matter of time. They would show, no question.

The four of us sat there—one helicopter, one crew, waiting for nightfall in the middle of the Somali countryside. We didn't talk about it, but I knew what we were all thinking about: home. I wondered what my son was doing at that exact moment, half a world away. I had to note the day of the week and then compute the time-zone conversion. I tried to imagine how much he had changed and what he might be thinking. *What do one-year-old boys think about?*

I wondered. I always hoped that somehow my thoughts would touch my little boy's heart, and that he would smile. I really missed him, and after that long, unexpected period of months away, I was ready to go home. But it wasn't time yet. We had a mission to accomplish. The moment passed quickly, and my thoughts drifted back to reality, Somalia, and Operation Gothic Serpent, the quest to capture Mohamed Aidid.

The locals did not disappoint us. They began to gather soon after we'd shut down, but to be honest, I was a bit annoyed by their presence. I hadn't eaten much that day and I wanted to take a few minutes to have dinner, but I felt awkward eating in front of them. Bill and Tommy had already given out what food and water they had to spare, but it wasn't enough. The older children were snatching items away from the younger ones. Some of the adults were trying to resolve the disputes, while others grabbed up goods for themselves. It was obvious that the Somali solution in that situation was to take whatever you could get and run.

The only place for me to partake of my meal in peace was on top of the helicopter, so I decided to climb up there with an MRE. At this point there were more than twenty Somalis around the aircraft, and I began to feel a bit uncomfortable with the situation. I had a good view from atop the aircraft, but there were just too many of them. Ray, Tommy, and Bill had their hands full watching the crowd from down below. The sun continued its now rapid descent off to the west. Just another day in Paradise.

A group of older Somalis began singing and dancing together on the left side of the aircraft. They were clapping their hands and seemed to be having a good time, but something in my instincts forced a thought into my mind: *diversion.* I turned and looked down to the right side of the bird. A pair of young men were standing near the doorless side of my cockpit, and I suddenly had the sinking feeling they had taken something from inside. One of them looked as if he had a bulge under his loose-fitting shirt. As I started to climb down, they nudged each other and began to sidle away.

"Ray, Tommy, Bill," I called out to my crew. "I think those guys might have ripped us off. Let's run a quick inventory."

As the men checked the loose gear inside the bird, I noticed the two Somalis beginning to run up a hill. I quickly searched the area around my seat. I didn't keep much in the cockpit with me and everything seemed to be in order, but I just *knew* something was missing.

I turned to look at the two Somalis as they crested the hill in the distance. Then they turned, one of them held a square object high over his head like a prize, and both of them danced and laughed in victory.

"My goggles!" I yelled in disbelief. "They took my goddamn night-vision goggles!"

"Oh, for Christ's sake," Ray spat.

"Damn!" said Bill. "For every good turn, a swift kick in the ass."

Those goggles were valued at several thousand dollars. Only losing a weapon could have been worse. I had to get them back.

I grabbed my weapon—the MP-5 locked down next to my seat the way my NVGs *should* have been—and started up the hill after them. They had at least a hundred-yard jump on me, and man could they run, even though they were wearing flip-flop shower shoes. I was wearing boots, but my rage was like rocket fuel and I sprinted up that hill like the cartoon Roadrunner.

I was absolutely *furious*. When we first arrived in Somalia I had actually felt sorry for these people—they obviously weren't responsible for their own plight and these poor folks deserved our help. But at that moment, all of those feelings vanished and I was instantly enraged with them, and at myself. I had let my guard down and they had stolen my NVGs! Worse still, the goggles were a sophisticated piece of night-vision technology. Without a power supply or proper helmet mount they might be useless, but for all I knew some Somali technician would be able to make them function. Then, one of these nights, a Somali sniper could be using my NVGs to pick off one of my own comrades.

I reached the top of the hill, cursing under my breath, but I could see I hadn't gained much ground on them, if any. I crossed the dirt road and raced after them, and I could just make out their outlines as they crested the next row of dunes out in front of me. I was never going to catch them, so I decided to shoot. I learned later that based on the Rules of Engagement I was justified in opening fire, but at the time I didn't give a damn if I was justified or not.

I fired two rounds at them, but the range was too far for the weapon and the bullets just kicked up sand behind their sprinting heels. They ran faster, and I took off after them again and fired a couple more rounds. Then another shot rang out, but not from *my* weapon, and I skidded to a stop and crouched low.

Great! One of them out here has a weapon, and now I've gotten myself into a goddamn gunfight.

But I turned as someone came pounding up behind me. It was Bill, gripping his M-9 in his hand. He paused and fired a couple more rounds from his pistol, which were about as effective as mine.

"Bill," I hissed at him. I was out of breath, not so much from the exertion of the run as from the adrenaline of my rage. "Get back to the bird and radio for some help." I pointed to a distant collection of huts in the desert. "I'm gonna circle around to the right and see if I can head them off."

"Roger that." He sprinted away.

I moved quickly and quietly, staying low, and after about a quarter mile hunkered down, hoping to ambush the thieves if they turned toward the small village. Some minutes passed, but the only people who came by were a family herding their goats. I waited in silent frustration and began to realize it was just hopeless. This was the thieves' backyard, and they could probably hide out in these wilds for days.

In the meantime, Gerry's bird had been repaired and was en route back to our landing zone. Ray called on the radio to inform the ops center of our situation, and Gerry heard the call and flew out over the dunes to try to help me. But by now it was completely dark, I had no radio, and I was so pissed off I didn't even try to signal them as they flew by. I walked back to the landing zone, trying to calm myself down.

Back at our bird, I was so red-faced and furious that Ray just watched me like a kid whose alcoholic father is on a binge. I got on the radio and explained to the commander at the ops center what had happened. I acknowledged it was all my fault. He agreed. I felt like an ass.

While the Rangers humped the half-mile back to the helos, a negotiator and a translator drove out to our location. They had been in this area before and had established a relationship with the locals. During a previous exercise, a farm animal had allegedly been killed by our gunfire and the owner had been paid a generous price for his loss. The payoff was an act of goodwill on our part, so the negotiator's foot was already in the door.

The two men drove down to the village, and the translator later told me that the negotiator did not mince words.

"The thieves are to return the American goggles *immediately*," he announced to the local elders. "If the goggles are not returned by tomorrow, a hut-by-hut search will be conducted until they are found. This despicable act could jeopardize the good relationship that has been established here."

The next day, an anonymous Somali brought my NVGs to the airfield entrance. There was no accompanying message and the case was gone, but the goggles were undamaged.

I was one lucky pilot. I was responsible for the security of those NVGs and I had failed, and I was angry and embarrassed. It was a hard pill to swallow, but so is every lesson learned well. From that day on, we no longer took security lightly out there in the countryside.

In the aftermath, one of the more talented members of Task Force Ranger sketched a rendition of the event, showing me running, gasping for air, and shooting wildly as two Somali children in flip-flops danced away in front of me. Since the goggles had been recovered I was able to laugh at the cartoon, but it made me think about how our meager attempts at giving comfort had resulted in this near-deadly misadventure. Our crews, motivated only by a desire to help, had given food to a few poor Somali children and unwittingly created a situation that ultimately led to open conflict. Those children had begun to squabble with one another over items they didn't even need. Their elders had begun to steal from us.

On a small scale, that experience paralleled the life cycle of the United Nations relief effort itself. Operation Restore Hope had initially been a gesture of goodwill by the people of the world, and the mission to save the starving populace had been deemed a success. Unfortunately, the additional supply of food also gave the warlords something else to fight over. The struggle for control of those supplies added fuel to the already volatile political cauldron, and we had become caught in the middle.

By the time the people of the United States and our political leaders would realize that the situation in Somalia was out of control, my friends had already shed their blood and given their lives trying to help resolve that dispute. Some of our most precious resources, our nation's sons, had been taken from us forever.

THAT RECOLLECTION SOURED my mood for most of the day, not that I'd been feeling carefree to begin with. Kediye's makeshift splint was damned medieval. What little mobility I'd had before was now completely restricted, and I felt like my leg was nailed to the floor. On top of that, I had begun to sweat into the tightly wound gauze, so every inch of my skin itched like mad.

California, I whispered in disdain. *He was probably over there studying some alternative lifestyle . . . like bondage and discipline.*

At the very first chance, I was going to get somebody to cut this damn thing off. But it didn't look as if Firimbi was going to be much help today. Finally, sometime during the afternoon, he groaned, sat up, and dropped his forehead into both his hands. I watched him with a knowing smirk as he very carefully rolled onto his knees, his head hanging down like a hunk of lead.

I guess you overdid it, pal, I thought. *But you'll get no sympathy from me. Been there, done that, got the T-shirt.*

He slowly raised his head and looked at the door. Then he staggered up and sprang for it, yanking it open as he stumbled outside. I heard his palms smack down onto the rail of the walkway's balcony and his painful retching as he vomited into the courtyard. I no longer regretted having declined my share of *khat*.

After a while Firimbi wavered back into my cell. If a Somali can look pale, then he looked pale. He was carrying what resembled a fluted glass milk bottle, topped off with a thick yellowish substance. He slowly lowered himself to the floor next to me and held out the bottle.

"Gammel milk," he said. "You try."

"That's okay." I raised my hand. "I'll pass."

"No, you try!" he insisted. "Medicine good."

"All right, what the hell." I shrugged. Maybe some Somali witch doctor had cooked up this stuff and it was good for whatever ails you.

I reached for the bottle, took a swig, and nearly gagged. The camel milk was warm, sour, and had curdled lumps floating in it. It was the most disgusting substance I had ever tasted, and I pushed the bottle back at him as I screwed up my face.

"*Christ!* It's all *yours*, Firimbi."

I couldn't believe it when he drank the entire thing down. He rubbed his stomach, made a bubbling sound, and said, "Good, good."

Whatever you say, man. Enjoy your Third World Alka-Seltzer.

He seemed somewhat with it again, so I pointed out my new splint to him and tried to tell him that it hurt like hell and I wanted to get it off. But he didn't understand and must have thought I was complimenting the doctor's talents. He nodded and grinned, gave the splint a big thumbs-up, lay back on his mat, and went right on snoring.

I blew out a sigh. *So this is what it's going to be like if I survive,* I thought. *These endless days with Firimbi, the guards, and Aretha. Not being able to really communicate, never seeing another American . . .*

As my time in captivity stretched into the unknown, so would each day seem to grow longer. They would move me, no doubt, again and again. Eventually, I would find myself speaking Somali. I would listen to the news from The World, yet gradually it would no longer register any significance. "After six months of captivity, U.S. Army helicopter pilot Michael Durant is still being held somewhere in Somalia. . . ."

I thought about Minister Abdi's hints about that possible prisoner exchange. But I couldn't let myself sink into that hope. I didn't know if these people had been trained in indoctrination techniques, where you would lift the prisoner's spirits and then let him crash hard, weakening his resolve. They might have been utilizing learned techniques, or they might have been operating on instinct. On the other hand, many of these Third World leaders had attended Russian or even Western military schools. They had been through institutions like the School of the Americas, where our own instructors taught them military and intelligence techniques, and then they turned bad on us and used our own tactics against us. It happened time and again. I seemed to remember that Mohamed Aidid himself had attended some high-level U.S. military courses. Strangely enough, his own son had emigrated to the States and joined the Marine Corps, and had recently been back in Somalia serving with U.S. forces.

The place was no Wonderland, but I sure as hell felt like Alice.

My injuries continued to sap a lot of my strength, and I had been dozing again when my eyes suddenly snapped open. The sound of a helicopter flying overhead was louder than before, and in addition to the familiar twirling of Blackhawk rotors, I heard something else. It sounded like some sort of broadcast, as if a large stereo speaker were mounted on one side.

It was probably a propaganda effort of some kind, I reasoned. The helo was flying in a large circular pattern and the transmission was difficult to discern, fading in and out with the wind and the changing position of the aircraft. I looked desperately around the room, wishing I had some way to signal them. Now, as the helo turned again, the thin sound of tolling church bells grew clearer.

Bonggg! . . . *Bongg!* . . . and then it faded out for a moment as the aircraft made a turn away from my location.

When I heard it again I raised my head. *What the hell is that?*

"I'm a rolling thunder, a pouring rain . . .
I'm comin' on like a hurricane.
My lightning's flashing across the sky . . .
You're only young but you're gonna die."

I sat straight up. My crushed spine sent jolts to my brain, but I didn't even feel it.

"I won't take no prisoners, won't spare no lives . . .
Nobody's putting up a fight.
I got my bell, I'm gonna take you to hell . . .
I'm gonna get you, Satan get you."

"Hell's Bells"? Somebody up there was playing "Hell's Bells"?! I rubbed my eyes, thinking I must have lost it. But the rock group AC/DC was one of my favorites, and this was sure as hell no accident!

"Hell's Bells,
Yeah, Hell's Bells.

You got me ringing Hell's Bells,
My temperature's high, Hell's Bells."

I was *not* dreaming. The Blackhawk made a roaring turn right above the Hotel Nowhere and AC/DC's earsplitting tune about challenging Satan and his forces of evil thundered into my cell and banged off the walls. Firimbi woke up with a start and sat up like an electrocuted Frankenstein, staring at the ceiling. He fumbled for his glasses and stumbled out the door, and I could hear the other guards chattering in excited tones. I caught a glimpse of them standing in the courtyard and pointing up at the sky, their expressions as dumbfounded as my own.

"I'll give you black sensations up and down your spine . . .
If you're into evil you're a friend of mine.
See my white light flashing as I split the night . . .
'Cause if good's on the left, then I'm stickin' to the right!"

I smacked my fist into my palm. The Night Stalkers were sending me a message, there was no doubt about it. I had no idea why they were playing that specific tune, but at the time I didn't care—it was music from heaven. Later, I would learn that it was all part of a plan. Suffice it to say that the concept was brilliant.

The Blackhawk moved off and the broadcast faded, but I had blasted out "Hell's Bells" in my bunk at the compound often enough and I knew the words by heart.

"I won't take no prisoners, won't spare no lives . . .
Nobody's puttin' up a fight.
I got my bell, I'm gonna take you to hell . . .
I'm gonna get you, Satan get you."

I hear you, boys, I thought with an incredible surge of excitement. *I hear you! I don't know what you're trying to tell me, but I'll think about it over and over until I get it!*

I wondered who was flying that bird up there. It could've been any one of our guys, maybe Stan or Dan or Gerry. Hell, maybe Cliff had only busted an ankle in his crash and was up there flying around with Donovan, his leg in a short cast, searching everywhere for me. The sound of the rotors grew louder again as the helo made a close pass, and then I heard the voice of some warrior angel, calling out to me from that speaker, so loud and clear.

"Mike Durant . . . Mike Durant . . ."

Oh Lord in Heaven, I couldn't believe it. My heart started to pound and the tears just sprang from my eyes.

"Mike Durant . . . Mike Durant . . ."

It was Dan's voice. I'd know that voice *anywhere*. My good friend Dan Jollota was up there, calling out to me, searching desperately for me. He knew that he was flying above a hornet's nest of RPGs and could get himself shot down at any second, but he just didn't give a damn.

"Mike Durant . . . We will not leave without you!"

I swallowed hard, my streaming eyes following the sweet drone of that helo's rotors, my ears every syllable of Dan's oath.

I know you won't, Dan. I tried to reach out to him by telepathy. *I know you won't!*

The broadcast and the Blackhawk faded away. I listened hard for a good long minute, but they were gone. Yet I knew that they'd be back. They wouldn't give up. Soon enough, they would find me. Soon enough, it would all be over.

It was quiet again. The children played and mothers called them home. There was no gunfire. I looked over at the small window of my cell. The orange rays of the setting sun were slanting in through the shutters, and in my mind I could still hear Dan's voice and promise.

"We will not leave without you."

My spirit was soaring, but I quickly wiped the wetness from my cheeks and settled down. I wasn't going to allow the Somalis to witness the heights of my new hope.

As the sun continued to set on that day, I experienced a wave of powerful feelings. But there was one thing I no longer felt at all. . . .

Alone.

Chapter 9

PANAMA

December 1989

THE FIRST SNOWS OF THAT WINTER were just falling on Tennessee when I threw away my tickets for a Caribbean vacation. General Manuel Antonio Noriega, the dictator of Panama, had just screwed up my Christmas. But in truth, I didn't mind it at all.

His Christmas was going to be a whole lot worse.

The "Panamanian Pineapple" had been asking for it for years. Noriega had risen through the ranks of power as an intelligence officer under the tutelage of his mentor, General Omar Torrijos, who had ruled the country with an iron fist. Then, in 1983, the protégé had demonstrated his gratitude by helping to arrange the death of Torrijos in a plane crash. Noriega quickly took control of the government and the Panamanian Defence Force, reining in the national police, customs, and intelligence services. Yet although the people of Panama were clearly unhappy with the substitution of one dictator for another, the acne-scarred Napoleon of Central America made it clear that he would brook no opposition. Public demonstrations against him were met with PDF gunfire and the leaders of democratically inclined political parties were forced into hiding. And finally, as if to rub salt into the people's wounds and thumb his nose at the world, Noriega invited Colombia's Medellín drug cartels to sup at the table of his dictatorship.

To say that the United States was "concerned" would be a gross understatement. We had built the canal that connected the Atlantic and Pacific oceans across Panama's isthmus, and joint American-Panamanian military cooperation had kept that critical trade route open throughout many of the century's upheavals. Still, over the years the people of Panama had eventually grown to resent our power and presence, so we had agreed to a timetable of gradual withdrawal. Yet even while we were preparing to relinquish many of our military bases, Noriega repeatedly fanned the flames of anti-Americanism.

Many of the Panamanians were not buying Noriega's line. They did not view the United States as an "imperialist devil" and understood that America's military, diplomatic, and commercial contributions helped maintain Panama's economic stability. They saw Noriega for what he was, a ruthless dictator who executed his opponents, dealt openly in the drug trade, and used his army and police to suppress the democratic dreams of the people. He regularly ordered torture, interrogations, and rapes as convincers, all the while building his power base and amassing troops and weapons. He invited Cuba and Nicaragua to provide weapons and instructors for his "Dignity Battalions" and accepted millions in bribes from Libya to set up bases for terrorist trainees. By 1988, he was organizing mobs to attack the U.S. embassy and openly harassing the many American citizens living in Panama.

So, long before my beeper went off for Operation Just Cause, U.S. Armed Services leadership had begun its contingency planning. While Noriega literally rattled his saber, railing against America and

banging his machete on his podium, plans were drawn up at the
Pentagon for simultaneous military strikes all across Panama. The objective of the mission would be to dethrone Noriega and his cronies,
eliminate the corrupt and oppressive elements of the PDF, and return power to the people and their duly elected officials. But the operations had to be surgical and precise. Many of Panama's military
bases served as dual residences, with American and local forces living and working side by side. Many Americans in Panama had in-
termarried with the local population, and wholesale destruction of
civilian areas would not be tolerated.

The use of heavy artillery, armor assaults, or a massive bombing
campaign was out. The use of special operations forces was in.

Having served for two years in Panama as a radio intercept operator, I knew the people and the place very well. The Panamanians
were warm, hospitable folks. But they were not Third World or un-
sophisticated, and their will would not be easily bent. Some of them
would welcome our incursion and the subsequent change in government. Some of them would fight back hard.

On Sunday, December 17, I was packing up bathing suits and
suntan lotion at my house in Clarksville when my pager beeped and
hummed. At the time, Clay Hutmacher had become my platoon
leader, but he was already more than that. Clay lived right above Lorrie and me in our two-family house, so we had spent a lot of time together on and off base. He was my boss, but he was also my friend.
I called in to Fort Campbell and he picked up on the first ring.

"Hutmacher."

"Durant."

"Come on in."

"Roger that."

I did not experience even a twinge of surprise, and I quickly
switched my vacation suitcase for my combat duffel. Like many special operators I was a news junkie, watching and listening for inter-

national flare-ups the way stockbrokers scan for ticks in the market. I knew that Manuel Noriega had already pushed the United States over the edge.

On Saturday night, four young American officers had been driving downtown in Panama City, in search of the perfect pizza. Outside La Commandancia, Noriega's military headquarters, they had been stopped at a PDF roadblock. When members of the Policia Nacionale began beating on the car with batons and hauling on the door handles, the young Americans concluded that they were about to disappear into one of Noriega's notorious dungeons—forever. The driver hit the gas pedal and the Panamanians opened fire, killing Marine First Lieutenant Robert Paz.

It hadn't ended there. An American Navy lieutenant, Adam Curtis, had witnessed the shooting incident along with his wife. Both of them were dragged off to the Commandancia for interrogations. While Mrs. Curtis was forced to "assume the position" against a prison cell wall and repeatedly threatened with rape, her husband was gagged, pistol-whipped, and kicked in the groin right in front of her. This had gone on for four hours, until the battered young couple was released to collapse into a public street.

Noriega's message had been clearly received in Washington: "Come and get me, *gringos*."

All right, so I'd have a warm-weather vacation of a different kind. My wife wasn't home, so I left her a note and started driving for the Kentucky border.

The snow was already coming down in sheets by the time I arrived at Fort Campbell. The runways were covered in billowing waves of white while army plows and sand trucks tried to hold back the deluge. Our crew chiefs were slogging through the blizzard, preparing our birds for loading onto huge C-5A transports, but the jet wings were sagging under thousands of pounds of ice. The airfield was socked in and no one was going anywhere yet.

I reported to an empty hangar over at the 160th. The helos had already been disassembled and were being hauled up into the C-5As, but pilots and crews were few and far between. Lots of the guys had already been on holiday leave for days and were now en route back from family homes in distant states, but the huge storm system had smacked into the entire Atlantic coast. The crews were coming back in, but slowly. With commercial flights grounded, some of them were jumping on trains or hitching rides with policemen. Once there, all of us would be under total opsec blackout. No one could call home and no calls would be received. If you lived three blocks from the base and had forgotten some critical item at your house, it didn't matter, you weren't going there. No one was going to risk some guy whispering to his wife as he kissed her goodbye, "It's Panama, honey."

Cliff Wolcott showed up, covered with snow and jumpy as hell. We had completed the testing and approval phases on his "baby," the Direct Action Penetrator. His Blackhawk, all decked out with fixed forward M130 miniguns and rocket pods, was already cargo-loaded and ready to go, but the airfield was completely shut down. No incoming flights, no outgoing flights.

"When's H-hour?" he asked me as I sat in a leather armchair, tapping the soles of my wet boots together.

"Oh-one-hundred, Wednesday morning," I said.

"*Jeezuss.*" Donovan Briley had just barreled into the ready room, slapping his wet gloves together and looking at his watch. "It's almost *Monday.* That gives us only twenty-four hours to get down south, assemble, and crank them up!"

"No sweat," I said. "Don't forget, the entire East Coast is getting hammered just like us. Nobody else is launching either."

"Oh yeah?" Wolcott fumed, tossing his gear down and punching his fists to his hips. "There's no snow in *Florida.* With our luck, they'll give our mission to the friggin' Air Force."

"Don't worry about it." Clay Hutmacher had appeared carrying piles of maps and aerial recon photographs. "Nobody's pulling off this operation without the Night Stalkers. Almost everybody's here. Briefing in thirty minutes."

He turned to leave the room, then spun back and looked at me.

"You're the only one who should be worried, Durant."

I stared at him. *Oh, no. Don't tell me they're leaving me here for some goddamn reason.* Clay pointed at Donovan Briley.

"Briley's going to be your copilot."

Cliff laughed and Donovan grinned at me.

"Ain't you one lucky s.o.b., Lone Ranger," said Donovan.

I smiled back at him. We had seldom been teamed up in a cockpit before and I didn't know him that well yet, but at that point I would have flown with Elmer Fudd. This was going to be my first war.

As it turned out, Clay had been right. Operation Just Cause was not going to come off without the Night Stalkers. It seemed that every helo, pilot, crewman, and soldier in the 160th was involved in the operation in some way and the various elements of the unit would be going into action simultaneously all across Panama. Night Stalkers would be making gun runs, supporting massive airborne assaults, and inserting Special Forces teams. A total of twenty Little Birds, nineteen Blackhawks, and seven Chinooks would be involved in operations. Nearly four hundred and fifty 160th personnel would take part. If you called our unit at Fort Campbell on the night of the twentieth, the phone would probably have just keep on ringing.

We had all spent a nerve-racking night back at Campbell, praying for a break in the weather, but before dawn on Monday the C-5s had finally been de-iced and we had taken off for Panama. Now, less than a day after arriving in-country, Donovan and I were sitting in an extremely heavy Blackhawk on the runway at Howard Air Force

Base just southwest of Panama City. It was almost midnight as we waited for the launch order.

"Bull, this is all pretty unbelievable," I said as I peered through my NVGs, watching a flotilla of helicopters assembling on the tarmac. "Don't you think?"

"Yeah, I guess so," Donovan mumbled without looking at me. "Just got a few more waypoints to program in here."

I translated his response as "Don't bother me with small talk while I'm programming the navigation systems," so I kept my peace for a while and let him work. No one in the unit did as much programming as Donovan. If he wasn't actually flying the helicopter, he was inputting systems data inside the cockpit. "Bull" was the consummate planner, tackling every mission as if it were the Normandy Invasion. And he didn't do it to impress anyone, but only because he believed that was how things ought to be done.

I already realized that we were going to be the perfect pair. Donovan was the "detail guy," while I was the "big picture" type. I dealt with the systems only when I thought it was necessary, while Donovan had a real passion for those technicalities. Yet no pilot could dispute that his approach was sound; situations in the air are much easier to handle if you take the time to plan for them on the ground. Outside the cockpit he could be an outrageous jester, but once he slid into that ballistic seat he was a hard-core professional and a real pleasure to fly with.

Still, the circumstances *were* pretty unbelievable. Instead of rushing around at home doing last-minute Christmas shopping in brightly lit malls, we were sitting on a blacked-out airfield in Panama, feeling the thunder of aircraft engines humming through the tarmac. Just hours before, we had been trudging through calf-deep snow to our ice-bound transports, and now we were sweating in the heat of a jungle night, about to go into combat.

What a difference a day makes, I thought.

Donovan and I had barely deplaned from our C-5A in Panama when we had rolled right into the mission briefings. Other elements of the 160th had made it down before the blizzard hit back home, so we were well behind the curve and had a lot of catching up to do. It was like a scene out of a Hollywood war movie as hundreds of men and women crowded into Hangar 3 at Howard. Huge maps were pegged up on briefing boards, and our mission commander stabbed at an arrowhead-shaped patch of land along Panama's southern coastline and about fifty miles southwest.

"This is Rio Hato," he said. "As you know, it is a combined military airfield and infantry base, housing the NCO Academy and currently occupied by the 6th and 7th Companies of the PDF. Those personnel are highly trained and will be operating a myriad of weaponry, from AK-47s and .50-caliber HMGs, to Russian ZSU and ZPU antiaircraft batteries." He moved the pointer downward to the coastline. "Here, at the southern approach to the airfield, lies Manuel Noriega's 'Farralon' beach house. We do not know if anyone is at home there, but if so, they won't be getting much sleep tonight." He looked at his watch. "At this time, seventeen C-130s have already launched from Fort Benning, carrying elements of two battalions from the 75th Ranger Regiment. At H-hour plus 3 minutes, the Rangers will execute an airborne assault on Rio Hato."

Heads turned and eyes widened all around, but you could have heard a pin drop inside that hangar. *Seventeen C-130s.* Two of those big birds would be carrying jeeps and motorcycles to be dropped by parachute, but the remaining fifteen would each have sixty-five Rangers crammed into their cargo holds. With nearly a thousand Rangers parachuting from the sky, it would be the largest combat airborne drop since Vietnam.

"It is expected that the PDF will put up some stiff resistance," he continued. "Therefore, our mission will be to prepare the drop zone and suppress that resistance. At H-hour, Air Force F-117 Stealths will drop 2,000-pound bombs adjacent to the PDF barracks." That also raised eyebrows. The Stealth fighter-bombers were still so secret that none of us had ever seen one. "Subsequently, 160th Little Bird gunships and AH-64 Apaches will engage PDF antiaircraft batteries and continue to do so throughout the airborne assault. AC-130 Spectre gunships will also be on station for ground support."

Things had moved super fast after that, with the briefing breaking up into smaller versions for detailed preparations. It was already Tuesday evening and the Rangers were on the way. Donovan and I were tagged with a FARP mission and would be flying in a Blackhawk loaded with rockets, ammunition, and fuel to support the Little Birds at the target. It wasn't the most glamorous assignment, but it was a combat role in a real-world mission, and we were just fine with that. On the other hand, Cliff Wolcott would be left stomping around the hangar and cursing. Even though his DAP had made it down in time for the mission, its usage as a gun platform had been superseded by the injection of Apaches into the mission. The AH-64s were brand new and their debut was a political decision. But the reasoning didn't matter to Cliff. He was duly pissed off.

Now I was handling the part of any mission that grinds my mental gears: waiting. I kept glancing at the clock on the instrument panel. It was already past midnight and our helicopters were still assembling on the long, dark tarmac. Through my NVGs, everything before me had taken on that mossy green, electric hue. There were no lights glowing anywhere on the field, but the night-vision goggles exposed the glow of a score of turbine engines, covering the area like small fires.

With our helmets on and NVGs pulled down, Donovan and I looked like alien insects as we pivoted our heads around. But at least we could see. In the back of our Blackhawk, our crew chiefs, Sergeants Brandenberg and Gornto, waited in total darkness, along with three company armorers and a Ranger staff officer. Those men could barely move, being crammed into the cargo hold along with two fuel pumps, flexible hoses, seventy-six 2.75-inch high-explosive rockets, crates of minigun ammo, and 4,436 pounds of JP-5 fuel. To them, it would be like riding off to war on an overweight truck bomb.

I watched as four Little Bird guns lined up for takeoff. Two Apaches were supposed to line up next and then our Blackhawk would bring up the rear, but the new AH-64 gunships were nowhere in sight. Donovan and I looked around the airfield and spotted one Apache running on the ramp off to our right. It taxied out and moved to the other end of the airfield, exactly where it was *not* supposed to be.

"Well, what do you think about that?" I asked Bull.

"I think they don't know what the hell they're doing," he grunted.

The remainder of the helicopter task force was waiting for our element to get the hell out of the way. Those running behind us had other missions to execute in various parts of the country. If it was all going to work, everyone had to take off on time. Radio calls were supposed to be kept to a minimum, but someone had to straighten out those Apache pilots. I decided to make the call.

"White Wolf, you are lined up facing the wrong direction, on the wrong end of the runway."

I actually felt sorry for those guys. They had been thrust into the middle of our mission briefing, and by the looks on their faces, their heads were spinning. Their pair of birds was already down to just one, as their wingman had developed a power problem during run-up and had to abort.

"Your flight is waiting to your rear," I added. "You need to turn around and line up behind them."

My call was followed by a brief moment of silence and then the Apache pilot answered.

"This is White Wolf. Roger." The gunship lifted up to a hover, and I could just imagine that pilot blushing deep crimson.

"Get with the program, boys," Donovan commented, but only on the internal intercom.

The Apache passed in front of us and slipped into position while

I continued our forward roll along the taxiway. It was time for us to pull in behind the flight, so I applied some power to lift the aircraft off the ground. But because Donovan and I had been given our mission at the last minute, we hadn't had time for performance planning and we weren't sure how much the aircraft actually weighed. This Blackhawk was an Alpha model, one of the heaviest ever flown, loaded to the roof with ammo, rockets, fuel, and personnel.

The bird was damn heavy and it wasn't responding, so I gave it more power. The launch order was hissing in our helmets and our flight was moving out.

I cranked the power up higher. The engines whined and the helo struggled up, and then I gave it everything we had and we moved off toward the flight of waiting aircraft.

"I think we broke the wire strikes," Donovan said.

The wire strikes were a series of blades mounted forward of the helo and designed to slice through any power lines encountered during a low-level assault.

"Fortunes of war," I answered. "Just keep your eyes peeled for clotheslines."

"Roger that," he replied, and I could hear his smile in my headset.

This was it. We were on our way to a war and there was no turning back. Sure, secret missions were often aborted, sometimes at the very last minute, but I knew that wasn't going to happen tonight. Operation Just Cause was launching with thousands of men and machines, a military tidal wave that would be nearly impossible to stop. Only Manuel Noriega himself, whose exact whereabouts were presently unknown, could do that. And he would have to appear on national television, drop to his knees, and surrender, *right now*. It wasn't damn likely.

I'm by no means a warmonger, but anyone who serves long and trains hard wants the chance to use his skills against a living, breathing enemy. This would be my first real opportunity, and Donovan's as well. There were a lot of "freshmen" on our team who had only done their jobs in a training environment. But we had the best equipment in the world and had honed our expertise. We were ready, able, and more than willing.

We lumbered into position behind our waiting flight of five, the Little Birds hovering now like deadly wasps at the edge of a picnic. The lead Little Bird turned into the direction of takeoff, and as the Apache in front of us rose, we nursed our flying gas station into the dark sky behind them.

Just please don't let us lose an engine, I prayed to some nebulous God of War as we cleared land and turned right over the Gulf of Panama. I wasn't worried about going down in the water. I was worried about being benched for the game.

Our small flight poured on the power now and we swept quickly into the night, running less than fifty feet above a gently swelling sea. The helos before us were in total blackout, but through my NVGs I could see the rims of shimmering heat in their exhausts and their silhouettes against the flickering pinpoints of stars. There were few clouds in the sky, which was fine for us but even better for the Rangers. Hanging below their parachutes and temporarily helpless, they would be hard to discern from the ground without a ceiling of clouds above. But at any rate, they would not be exposed to ground fire for long. The Rangers would be jumping from an altitude of only five hundred feet. They had all left their reserve parachutes at Fort Benning. If any of their main chutes failed, they would not have enough time to deploy a reserve.

We were less than twenty minutes from target now, and as I watched the seconds tick away on our digital clock, I thought about those young Rangers, flying toward their destinies at Rio Hato. Most of them had surely never been in combat before, and while Donovan and I were certainly pumped for our first taste of warfare, I could only imagine what those young warriors might be thinking. Yet I knew their minds, because all of us were linked by that one inexplicable personality trait, a dormant gene awakened by the theme of a quote from Isaiah that had become part of the Night Stalker creed:

"Then I heard the voice of the Lord saying, *Whom shall I send? And who will go for us?* And I said, *Here I am. Send me . . .*"

"This guy's riding high." Donovan's voice snapped me from my brief philosophizing and I peered forward at the slim form of the Apache. The AH-64 had drifted up to two hundred feet above sea level and was lagging at least two miles behind the Little Birds.

"Damn," I said. "I'm gonna have to break radio silence again."

"Better you than me, boss," said Donovan.

I keyed my mike switch. "White Wolf, bring your altitude down to fifty feet and close it up on the AH-6s."

The pilot didn't respond, but he nosed the Apache down and sped away to catch up with the flock.

"He doesn't like you much," said Donovan.

"I'll live."

"Maybe you will. Maybe you won't."

I smiled and turned the controls over to Donovan while I ran through a checklist. As pilot in command I was responsible for many more tasks than just flying the helo: managing the overall flight, monitoring radio traffic, navigating on the map, balancing airspeed versus time-to-target, and interfacing with the folks in the back. But I had no reservations about letting Donovan fly the machine. He was not only a fanatic about mission preparation, but a damn good stick as well.

It was clear to me now that under the pressure of impending combat, you could count on Donovan Briley. I had secretly been wondering about that when Clay teamed us up for the mission, because I hadn't flown much with Donovan before. He was such an incorrigible joker that it was hard to imagine him getting down to business. Guys in the unit laughed about his strange habits, such as taking out his bicycle at midnight and riding it up and down the runways at Fort

Campbell. Donovan himself got the biggest laughs by making fun of his own Native American heritage and allegedly backwoods up-bringing. He loved telling stories about his friend "Billy Battles," a tobacco-chewing, overall-wearing country boy with a raging libido and a penchant for practical jokes. Eventually, we would all come to the conclusion that Donovan Briley was, in fact, the hero of his Billy Battles legends.

But that was clearly the "other" Donovan. Now, just a minute before H-hour, he was deadly quiet and about as serious as a heart attack.

"Boss," he said evenly, "we are one minute from the hold point."

"Roger that," I said as I took the flight controls back and dipped the nose a bit. We were flying almost due north now, approaching the southern coastline from the gulf. The thin strip of beach grew thicker in the distance, and I could see the black runways of Rio Hato and the clusters of PDF buildings and barracks on the base. Groves of waving palms bristled up on all sides, and to the north of the air-field the mountain peaks of Sofre jutted up like black camel humps.

Our holding point was a small island just off the coast, and as it loomed before the cockpit, I selected a visual reference point to ori-ent on just to the east of the cluster of sand and trees. As we began to circle in a figure-eight pattern, Donovan looked down to the left, scanning the island through his NVGs. Intel might have failed to pick up on any PDF gunners posted down there, and we didn't need a surprise SAM-7 fired up our ass.

"Crew chiefs, man your guns," I said over internal.

"Roger, Sir," they answered.

"I am arming," I said as I flicked the switch to provide juice to their miniguns. "Brandenberg, keep an eye on that island."

"If anyone spits at us, Sir," the chief answered, "he's toast."

"Thirty seconds," said Bull.

We watched the digital clock as it ticked toward oh-one-hundred. We squinted at the small silhouettes of the Little Birds and the

Apache, holding their own pattern just to the west. We peered up at the sky, looking for any sign of the mysterious Stealths. An AC-130 Spectre gunship was supposed to be orbiting overhead, but there was no sign of that either. We looked at the calm and eerily silent landscape of Rio Hato. Five seconds to H-hour. Four. Three. Two. One . . .

Suddenly four huge explosions impacted across the airfield, blossoming up into sharp fingers of white light. The Stealths were worthy of their name—none of us had even seen them. And they were right on time.

"Wow," said Donovan. "One point for the Air Force."

"No hitting the snooze bar on that wake-up call, boys," I said. "Time to get up."

But for a few seconds, it seemed as though nothing was happening. There was no visible activity on the ground. Then the huge flight of C-130s roared in from the sea. It was an absolutely awesome sight as that train of massive cargo craft passed so close, heading for the airfield. We could see the black slits of their open jump doors and then the Rangers begin to stream from their birds, hundreds of them burdened with heavy combat sacks full of weapons, ammunition, and explosives, their bodies jerking and swaying as their canopies snapped open.

Then the Panamanians opened up with everything they had. As the Rangers started hitting the ground, hundreds of green tracers from AK-47s started raking across the drop zone. A ZSU-2 double-barreled antiaircraft gun began firing up at the C-130s, its heavy 23mm shells lancing past the wings of the lumbering birds. But in the midst of a jump run those cargo planes could not take evasive action, and they just kept on disgorging their Rangers. I knew they *had* to be taking hits from that gun.

"Damn," I hissed into my mike. "Where the hell's White Wolf?"

"Here he comes," said Donovan.

The Apache skidded to a hover at the far side of the island and let loose with his 30mm chain gun, firing at the PDF barracks on the northwest and northeast sides of the strip.

Get that goddamn ZSU! I thought in terrible frustration. I couldn't stand watching those Rangers getting hammered by that gun. Then it seemed almost like the Apache pilot had heard my mental scream, and he turned his gun on the antiaircraft battery. A line of 30mm high-explosive rounds impacted close to the ZSU, and then, inexplicably, stopped. The Panamanian antiaircraft gun went right on firing.

"Charger, this is White Wolf," the Apache pilot called the Air Mission Commander on the radio. "We've got a weapon system malfunction."

"Roger that, White Wolf," the AMC replied. "Break it off and RTB."

I couldn't believe it when the Apache suddenly banked right and headed up the coast, returning to base.

"Shit," Bull cursed.

Half the Rangers were on the ground now, but half of their flight was still in the air. The C-130s were grinding along like freight trains, and we just knew they were taking impacts from that gun. Our Little Birds were already engaged, zipping around the airfield and chewing up the PDF troops, who were firing at the Rangers as they struggled out of their parachutes and charged into the assault.

"Bull," I said. "*We're* gonna take out that goddamn gun."

"Roger that," he agreed. "But you better run it by the major."

He was right. The Ranger major in the back of our bird was the ranking officer on board. He wasn't in charge of our helicopter, but only he could make the decision to supersede our FARP mission and engage that gun. But I was sure he would want to do it, because they were *his* Rangers who were taking all that fire. I was wrong.

"Negative, Durant," he responded to my request. "We've got a FARP mission to execute, and those Little Birds are going to need our support."

"But, Sir, the Panamanians probably don't even have night vision down there." I tried to reason with him. "We can get in close and hose them with the miniguns before they even know we're there."

"And with all this shit on board," he replied, "we could take one round, get blown to hell, and leave your birds high and dry. That's a negative."

I sat there and fumed. Even if our fuel tanks took a round, they were self-sealing and I didn't think they'd explode. The rocket warheads weren't armed and their motors required electrical priming to set them off. But who knows? Maybe that major was right and I was just being a hotheaded combat pilot. Maybe we'd just get ourselves shot down and leave those Little Birds without fuel, rockets, or ammo. I looked over at Bull. With our NVGs on it was impossible to read each other's expressions, but I could tell by the slow shake of his helmet that he was telling me to let it go. I thought about it for a minute, made the wrong decision, and heeded his advice.

Then Bull slapped me on the arm and called out an aircraft at twelve o'clock high. The AC-130 Spectre had come in low, bracing one flank of the airfield as he fired his 105mm howitzer at the ZSU. His heavy shells pounded the position and the antiaircraft gun stopped firing.

Thank God, I thought.

"Charger Two-Five, this is Charger." The AMC was calling us on the radio. "Execute your mission."

"Charger Two-Five, Roger."

We were going in. I rolled out of holding and headed for the coastline. It was my responsibility to get us to the refuel and rearm point, but Donovan was just as capable a navigator and I turned the map work over to him. We skimmed low over shallow waves and went feet dry over the beach, hitting our checkpoint dead-on.

"Come left six degrees," Donovan said.

I made the turn.

"Right there."

He oriented me to a large field just four hundred meters east of Rio Hato, and as I brought the helo in it seemed like the battle was raging right there in front of our cockpit. We were less than half a klick from the airfield. Wicked lines of tracers were punching out from Ranger positions into the barracks buildings, ricocheting from hard points and winging off into the night. The heavier tracers from PDF guns were spitting every which way. Grenades were exploding in small mushrooms of yellow-white light, and the rockets from Ranger Light Anti-Tank weapons were whooshing across the base and punching down doors. A PDF fuel truck was sitting there in the middle of the base, vomiting streams of flames across the tarmac.

"Jesus," said Donovan as we landed in a cloud of loose grit and sand.

"It's the frigging Fourth of July," I said as the dust cleared and I pushed my NVGs up over my helmet.

But I knew that both of us were thinking the same thing. We were setting up a FARP at the edge of a firefight, without ground security, which was definitely *not* standard operating procedure. Normally under combat conditions a security team would fly in on another helo, or be waiting in position when you landed your flying ammo dump. But tonight there were so many ops going on that the unit didn't have enough assets for that.

"If any of those Panamanians break and run . . . ," Donovan began.

"They're going to run this way," I finished.

We were going to be extremely vulnerable as we set up to refuel and rearm the Little Birds. Even a squad of Panamanians would be able to overrun us. I felt like the driver of a getaway car during a bank robbery.

"I'm gonna keep the APU running," I said. The auxiliary power unit would allow us to shoot the miniguns and get the aircraft off the ground quickly if we had to. Even if we were in the midst of refueling, we could cut the main line and get the hell out of Dodge. We'd have to leave the pump and lines behind, but it was better than losing the aircraft and the crew.

"Roger that," said Donovan as he disengaged from his seat. "I'll hustle the men." He was going to supervise the chiefs as they set up the pump and fuel lines and make sure the company armorers hauled all the rockets and ammo out of the helo.

"You can put the major on the right gun," I said. Donovan grinned at me as he unhooked his harness. Neither of us knew that Ranger major well. He would be manning the minigun on the right side of the aircraft, facing east, where no threat was likely to appear.

"When I'm done," said Donovan, "I'll take the left."

"I'll be right here," I said.

I settled in to monitor the instruments and fuel gauges. Once Donovan was back on the bird and manning the left minigun, we'd have the best security we could hope for. If a horde of Panamanians came across that field, the last thing they'd see would be Donovan's squint behind that gun.

It didn't take long for Donovan and the crew chiefs to set up. The combination of the main fuel tanks and the internal Robertson tanks in the back held over four and a half thousand pounds of JP-5. We would refuel the Little Birds from the mains first and then draw from the Robertsons. A fifty-foot main line was hooked up to the pump, and from there two more fifty-foot lines snaked out to the Little Bird landing zones. The crew chiefs set out infrared chem lights so the Night Stalkers would see where to set down. The company armorers started unloading the rockets and minigun ammo and hauling them to a safe distance from our Blackhawk.

Rio Hato continued to roll and thunder under the onslaught of the ground battle. The gunfire and explosions were nonstop and intense, and I knew I was witnessing what few people ever get a chance to see: a classic airborne assault from start to finish. And this was just one of a number of such missions that were going down at that very hour all across the country. Yet even though many 160th personnel were involved in those missions, everything was compartmentalized and held very close. My comrades did not know the nature of my mission, and I didn't know the natures of theirs.

Almost at that very moment, an incredible rescue operation was taking place at the Commandancia in Panama City. For some months, a CIA operative named Kurt Muse had been held inside the compound at the Modelo Prison. Muse was closely guarded, 24/7, and his guards had orders to execute him if a rescue attempt was made. As the battle began to rage outside his prison walls, I am sure he expected to die.

While an AC-130 Spectre blasted the Commandancia from overhead, 160th AH-6s and MH-6s swept in over the rooftops. The Little Bird guns took out four .50-caliber machine guns firing at them from surrounding emplacements, while the Little Bird assaults dropped off a six-man team on the roof of Muse's prison. The operators charged down through the darkened stairwells, taking out stunned PDF guards as they sprinted. On the second floor they blew Muse's cell door, quickly dressed the stunned spy in a flak jacket and Kevlar helmet, and had him back up on the roof within six minutes of landing.

But the mission wasn't over, not nearly. As the two MH-6s came back in for the pickup, heavy fire raked them from a nearby cell block. Major Rick Bowman, at the controls of one of the Little Birds, took a round that smashed his elbow. His partner reached over, locked Bowman's shoulder harness so he wouldn't fall out, took over the helo, and landed on the roof, picking up two of the rescue force. The remaining four operators piled Muse into the second Little Bird and they lifted off.

It still wasn't over. The second Little Bird was now overloaded and unable to gain altitude. A skid caught a power line and the helo smacked down hard into the street. But true to form, Night Stalkers Don't Quit. The pilots nursed the bird over to a parking lot, where they would have a running start, and they cranked the power up and took off. They made it up to about thirty feet when machine-gun fire peppered the helo, taking it down for good. The Little Bird crashed on its side. Miraculously, Kurt Muse was unhurt. His rescuers had cushioned their precious cargo with their own bodies. But now, three of the operators had been injured in the crash and one had suffered a bullet wound in the leg.

The operators ignored their own wounds and formed a perimeter around Muse and the pilots. Within seconds they were engaged in a fierce firefight, holding back repeated assaults from PDF troops. And they kept on fighting until an element of light armored vehicles from one of our mechanized infantry battalions showed up. From there they fought their way out of the Commandancia to a local junior high school, where a 160th Blackhawk picked them up and flew them back to the field hospital at Howard Air Force Base.

Two more of our pilots, Fred Horsley and George Kunkle, were at that moment engaged in their own struggle for survival. They had been making a gun run on the PDF headquarters at the Commandancia when their Little Bird was also brought down by ground fire. Horsley and Kunkle crash-landed the helo, *inside* the compound, where it slid up against the security fence as its rotor blades disintegrated. While every Panamanian in the compound opened up on them, they threw their survival vests on the top of the razor wire and vaulted themselves over to the other side.

For two hours, Horsley and Kunkle were pinned down beneath the portico entranceway of a building. When a lone PDF soldier came crawling by in the grass, they took him prisoner and hightailed it toward a passing element of the same mechanized infantry unit that had just picked up the rescue force, *their* pilots, and Kurt Muse. The Special Forces soldiers manning the LAVs saw Horsley and Kunkle approaching at a sprint with their captive and challenged them with the password.

The two Night Stalkers had just endured a violent crash and three hours of combat, and they could barely remember their own names, let alone some obscure password.

"We're goddamn Americans!" they shouted. Apparently, that did the trick.

Night Stalker helos were also conducting assaults at Colon and Albrook Army Airfield, and two nine-man teams of 160th soldiers were even parachuting into Torrijos-Tocumen Airport and Rio Hato. These were the incredibly courageous men of our Airborne Platoon, whose mission was to jump into the night from C-141s, following twelve-foot pallets called "Big Willies," loaded up with additional rockets, minigun ammo, fuel, and refueling gear for the helos. While the Big Willies descended under triple-canopy cargo chutes, the airborne teams followed them right down into the middle of those heavy firefights.

Our men were engaged in combat all across Panama when I finally received the radio call that Little Birds were coming into our LZ. They landed and started taking on fuel, while the firefight at Rio Hato ballooned into a full-course battle. Donovan and the major were manning the miniguns, but our crew chiefs were out there alone in the dark—and I didn't like it.

The Little Bird pilots called over on the radio to say that none of them had yet fired rockets, so they wouldn't be needing our stash of 2.75-inchers. They also still had plenty of 7.62mm ammo. But their fuel tanks were bone dry, and I watched as our fuel-level indicator continued its seemingly endless descent. Then something nasty winked at me from the console. It was a main module chip light, coming from the transmission underneath the main rotor system. It meant that the transmission was probably overstressed, parts were failing, and the metal debris in the oil was being picked up by magnetic indicators. Under most conditions you wouldn't fly the bird with that chip light glowing. You'd just shut it down and leave it until a maintenance crew showed up. But that wasn't going to happen out here, not tonight.

Donovan was in back wearing one of the crew chiefs' headsets, and I keyed my mike switch.

"Bull, we've got a main module chip light up here."

With the exception of the gunfire and explosions raging outside, there was silence in my headset for a second.

"Mmmm," Donovan grunted. "That's not good."

"No shit. But we're not leaving this bird here, no matter what."

I glanced at the fuel gauge and my eyes popped. The Little Birds were sucking us dry. I had already calculated the cutoff point, beyond which we would not have enough fuel to make it back to the airfield. We needed at least seven hundred pounds to make that thirty-five-minute flight, and we were quickly dropping past the eight hundred mark.

"Bull, get out there and shut down that pump!" I snapped.

I twisted my head around, watching him dive from the cargo bay. His dark silhouette was on the run, but the gauge was still going down. Seven-fifty . . . seven hundred . . . I unhooked my harness and leaned out the door.

"Stop fueling!" I waved my arms at the crew chiefs. "Stop!"

The pump shut down. In half a minute, the Little Birds were airborne and heading back into battle. Donovan showed up at the cockpit.

"How bad is it, boss?" he asked.

"Six hundred."

"Shit."

We didn't have enough fuel to make it back. We would flame out and crash before reaching Howard. But there was still an untold number of pounds left in the fuel lines outside, and a procedure for transferring it back into the helo.

"Reverse the pump," I said, "and we'll see what we've got."

"You got it," said Bull.

"And Bull, tell the men to load the rockets and ammo back on board."

He looked at me and frowned.

"You don't want to leave it here for the Little Birds?"

"They've got only enough fuel to fire off the rockets and ammo they have. After that, they'll have to RTB anyway to fuel up. I'm not leaving this stuff here for the enemy."

"You know, Durant?" He grinned. "You're smarter than you look."

Our crew chiefs reversed the pump and we transferred enough fuel back out of the lines to break the seven-hundred-pound mark. The armorers didn't look too happy with me as they reloaded thousands of pounds of rockets and ammo back into the bird. I'll bet they're still cursing my name.

The battle at Rio Hato was finally dying down when we took off for Howard, both Donovan and I keeping our eyes on that chip light and hoping we'd make the airfield with the engines still running. We kept it over the water but close to the shoreline, and when the Air Force base came into view we had about two hundred pounds of fuel left, barely enough for ten more minutes. Initially, the air controller did not want to admit us into his airspace. All right, there was a war on and he was being cautious, but what were the odds that Noriega had managed to launch a single-helicopter assault on Howard?

"Listen up," I snapped at him over the radio. "We're fuel critical and we're coming in."

We set it down at about 0330, and it was then that the exhaustion swept over us. Donovan and I hadn't been to sleep in a day and a half. We wrote up a terse report: "Aircraft has a chip light. It's full of rockets and out of gas."

There was no one home to debrief our mission, so we engaged in our own private version of post-op analysis as we half stumbled across the tarmac and slid into a pair of empty bunks in the base barracks. We agreed that most of the decisions we had made were sound, although running a FARP without security in the middle of a firefight was not a procedure we'd care to repeat. And we had been extremely lucky to make it back to the base on little more than fumes, and with that chip light glowing like a death knell. But I was still pissed off at that Ranger major for rejecting my request to take out that ZSU. As it would turn out, thirteen of the C-130s had taken hits from that gun, and some of them had landed on flat tires and spewing jet fuel.

"I don't know, Bull," I said as I closed my eyes and felt the cloak of sleep descending on me. "Maybe that major was right. Maybe we would have just bought the farm."

"Negative," Donovan mumbled as he pulled a blanket up over his head. "*You* were right. That major was a pussy."

In the morning, we awoke to the bitter news that two of our friends, Sonny Owens and John Hunter, were dead. Four Little Bird guns had conducted a raid on a beach house near Colón, where high-ranking members of the PDF were holed up. Sonny and John had taken heavy ground fire and had crashed in the Canal. It was the first time, but not the last, that I would wake up after a mission to the news that my comrades had been killed in action.

Cliff Wolcott never did get to fly the Direct Action Penetrator in Panama. But sometimes fate has a way of paying off its debts.

Over the next two weeks, operations in Panama wound down quickly. I was sent back to Fort Campbell to train some new pilots, but Cliff remained behind to participate in the hunt for Manuel Noriega. The dictator had proved himself to be very elusive. One by one, his "kingpins" were picked up, along with their huge stashes of drugs, multimillions in cash, and their weird accoutrements of voodoo witchcraft and rancid pornography. But Noriega himself was nowhere to be found, and over at the 160th the dragnet for him came to be known as "The Hunt for Elvis."

At last, the monsignor of the Papal Nunciatore, the Vatican's embassy in Panama City, admitted that the dictator had taken refuge there. The ornate buildings were surrounded by our troops, but our government was not about to conduct a raid into a diplomatically immune and holy enclave. As the days passed, many thousands of Panamanians thronged outside the compound, decrying their former dictator and threatening him with the fate of Mussolini, which would mean a bloody lynching. When the United States suggested to Noriega, via his mistress, that it might just withdraw its troops from the dispute, he came out.

Cliff Wolcott flew a Blackhawk into a nearby soccer field, carrying a team of special operators. Noriega emerged from the Nunciatore, wearing his general's uniform and carrying a Bible and a toothbrush. Two huge operators flex-cuffed him and hauled him up into the helo. The final objective of Operation Just Cause had been accomplished, and I just know that Cliff was grinning from ear to ear as he flew that Blackhawk back to Howard Air Force Base.

In effect, "Elvis" had captured Elvis.

Chapter 10

WHISPERS FROM THE WORLD

October 8, 1993

WHEN THE SOMALIS BROUGHT ME A BED, I knew something was up.

Ever since Minister Abdi had sent me the radio, I had been waking up in the morning just before 6:00. At that hour, the BBC and the local Armed Forces Network made their first news broadcasts, and like a commuter who can't afford to miss his morning train, my internal clock had taken over to rouse me in time. I had begun to look forward to that short span of solitude, between the last of Firimbi's snores and the first bursts of gunfire, when I could listen in peace to the whispers from the World.

But this morning Firimbi was not on his mat, and even before he rushed back into the room herding two of his younger guards, I could tell that something unusual was going on. There were low whispers outside, pattering sandals on the balcony, and the clatter of heavy objects. Then the two young Somalis came in, carrying large paper bags and a broom, with Firimbi close behind. He shut the door quietly and began snapping out orders like an impatient father with a couple of lazy teenagers.

They started cleaning the place up, gathering every piece of trash, tossing my discarded MRE wrappers and clumped, soiled bandages into the bags. They swept the whole floor, raising dervishes of dust that made me squint and cough, until their pile of food morsels and fly corpses was large enough to be scooped out the door and into the courtyard.

I raised myself up on my elbows and watched, trying hard not to speculate yet unable to stop. *This behavior is definitely not standard operating procedure,* I thought. *But don't get your hopes up, Durant.*

Firimbi hissed an order to someone outside and another pair of guards joined the first. They flanked me on both sides and reached down for my mat. I looked up at Firimbi and jabbed my finger at my splint.

"*Dolor,*" I warned him. "*Doh-lohr,*" I said again.

For a day I'd been trying to tell him the damned thing was useless, except that it caused me more pain. Dr. Kediye's best effort was just pissing me off, and every time I moved now that busted femur rang bells in my whole body. But either Firimbi didn't understand, or he didn't want to insult Kediye, or he thought *I* didn't appreciate the wonders of modern medicine. So he always just nodded and ignored my complaints.

"Yes, yes," he said now as he urged the guards on. But he must have warned his gunmen to be mindful of the leg, because they gripped my mat and carefully slid me from my corner of the room to the other side.

The wooden bed arrived in pieces. It looked like something from a Sears catalogue, with a polished ornate headboard and smooth dowel supports. Watching four Somali *mooryan* assemble this thing was almost comical, like some skit out of *Saturday Night Live.* But when they brought in the mattress, dressed it up with my flowered cotton sheets, and came up with a pillow, it wasn't funny anymore.

Why are they doing all this? I asked myself. Yet at this point there was only one answer. *They're getting ready to release me.* And still, I forced that thought down. *No, don't go there. Not yet . . .*

When they lifted me up and moved me onto the bed, the pain hardly registered, because my heart was already hammering in anticipation. The guards added a nightstand and placed my remaining MREs, the radio, the aspirins, and the antibiotics on it. Firimbi brought in a yellow plastic bottle and my dog bowl filled with water. Then he proceeded to give me a full-up "whore's bath," from toes to nose, including shampooing my hair in the bowl and drying me off with a towel.

If this keeps up, I thought, *I'm gonna have to change my review of the Hotel Nowhere from a minus-three-star to a minus-one.*

And then the whole thing started to get almost silly as Aretha showed up with some kind of an aerosol can. She started waddling back and forth, "crop-dusting" the room with the thick scent of roses, while one of the guards produced a tin of bath powder and a can of deodorant. He dusted me from neck to crotch and sprayed me with his "Somali Right Guard" until I smelled like a French hooker.

Yet another guard appeared, carrying a folded set of blue hospital pajamas and a thick woolen robe. But it was already eighty degrees in there and I was sweating again from the jolts of pain, so I raised my hand and declined the Hugh Hefner outfit as politely as I could. Instead, they draped my tartan sheet over my nude form, covering me from the waist down. And as a final gesture, Aretha presented me with a "gift." It was a Somali flyswatter, a large square pennant made from woven straw and sewn to a two-foot wooden stick. She stuck it in my hand and grinned, as if she had just put the finishing touch on a wedding cake.

Firimbi snapped his fingers and they all left the room.

This has got to be a release, I decided, no longer able to suppress the obvious. *It's got to be!* That's all I could imagine at that point. *This is what they do before they let you go, make you look all pretty so they can say, "See how well we treated him!"*

I couldn't believe it. There had been no warning that this was coming. But that's how things happened in this part of the world. One minute you were flying along and the next minute you were shot. One minute you were a POW and the next minute not. There was just no other explanation for this whole dog-and-pony show.

The door opened. A woman walked into the room, followed by two Somalis. But I didn't really notice the men as I blinked and stared at her. She had shoulder-length blond hair and deep-blue eyes. She was slim, maybe in her midthirties, and wore a khaki-colored safari shirt, blue jeans, and sneakers. Her face glowed with a deep tan and her smile was stunning as she seemed to float toward me.

I thought I was dreaming. This creature didn't look like just a woman to me. She looked like an angel. But as she reached out her hand and grasped mine, I could feel that she was very real.

"Hello, Michael," she said in a soft Scandinavian accent. "I am Suzanne Hofstetter. I am from the International Committee of the Red Cross."

"Hello," I whispered. It was hard to find my voice.

She looked at me, and she must have seen the hope in my eyes. She cocked her head and covered our clasped hands with her other.

"No, you are not being released. Not today." Her tone was apologetic, although still soothing and optimistic. "But hopefully that day will come, very soon."

My hope took a nosedive, but having this incredible angel of mercy standing there gave me something to hold on to. The poor woman must have been in pain, I was still gripping her hand so hard. Yet she didn't show it.

"I'm afraid I didn't bring you very much," she said as she turned and glanced at the Somalis. I looked at them too, realizing they were men I'd never seen before. "They simply came to my hotel and told me to come with them to see you," she explained. "I had already prepared some things for you, just in case, but unfortunately the box is back at our office." She shrugged and smiled. "Perhaps we can have it sent over later."

"Thank you," I said.

To be honest, I was trying to hold myself together. I didn't care what she had or hadn't brought with her—just her presence there was a gift from God. There was so much compassion in her eyes that just looking at her made the tears well up in mine.

She told me how things were being perceived on the outside— what the rest of the world was saying about the situation in Somalia and how the story of the battle and my captivity was front-page news all over. I told her that I knew about some of that because I had been given a radio. She raised an eyebrow, seeming to store that bit of surprise information for later.

"And how is your physical condition?" she asked.

"The Little Colonel is doing very well," one of the Somalis interjected. His English was perfect and nearly unaccented, as if he'd been educated in the States.

Suzanne glanced back at him and smiled, but it was almost like the expression of a patient attorney who'd been interrupted by a fool. She turned back to me.

"Little Colonel? And why do they call you that?"

"They couldn't figure out what a warrant officer is," I explained. "So I guess they calculated my age and decided on a rank, lieutenant colonel. Maybe 'little' is easier to pronounce than 'lieutenant.' "

"I see." Her easy grin was patient and kind. "So how are they treating you?"

I was honest with her and told her that the treatment was okay and that a doctor was visiting regularly. But I also realized that her escorts spoke English well and I'd have to be very careful. I wanted her to know that the medical care was primitive and that my injuries required serious attention.

"But under these conditions," I said, "I'm concerned about my long-term chances for survival."

"Yes." She looked at my leg and the bandage on my arm. "I understand your concern." Then she bent forward a little, looking at my face. Her brows knit slightly, as if she were a plastic surgeon examining the errors of a colleague. She leaned back again, but I was still holding her hand. "Well, I can tell you that everything that could possibly be done to get you released is being done," she said. "And now that the Red Cross is involved, the Somalis know that they are fully accountable for you."

That message wasn't for me. It was for her two escorts.

"Suzanne?" I said. "Do you have any news about my friends who were shot down with me?"

"No, I really don't." She shrugged slightly. But I knew that if very bad things had happened to them, she was not about to discuss it in this forum.

"Do you have any idea how my family's doing?" I probed.

"I'm sorry." She shook her head sadly. "I'm afraid not." And then she brightened as she proposed, "Would you like to write a letter to them?"

I gripped her hand even harder and came up on my elbows. "Yes."

She turned to her escorts for their assent. I couldn't see her eyes, but I saw them both nod. She reached into her shoulder pouch.

"I had only two blank Red Cross forms with me when they came," she said. "Here, let me help you." She laid the leather pouch over my lap and smoothed a Red Cross letter form over it.

"We must go soon," said one of the Somalis. "It is not safe for you here, Miss Hofstetter."

Suzanne ignored him, but it struck me that this woman had not only compassion but great courage. It was amazing that she would venture out into the Mog like this in the middle of the day. The place was still seething with gunfire, and she would make a damn fine target. She handed me a pen. The Red Cross form was in English and Somali, and I began filling out the "Sender" heading. I stopped myself.

What should I write? How should I write? What tone should I use? I tried to think back to SERE School, where they had instructed us on how to write letters while in captivity. I knew the letter would be read by many people outside my own family, and I figured the Somalis right there in the room would read it as soon as I was done. So I couldn't say, "Dear Family . . . The place is lightly defended . . . at least five guards . . . AK-47s . . . Tell the boys to come and get me!" And besides, even if I could come up with some seemingly innocuous code, I really had no information to divulge. I didn't know where I was, and I really didn't know how many Somalis were in the hotel. For all I knew, they had an entire company outside and an anti-aircraft battery.

I decided to keep it personal and mostly informative, so that at least my family would worry less. This is what I wrote, word for word:

Dear Lorrie & Joey.

I know you must be worried about how I am doing. They are treating me well. The Somali doctor comes every day and cleans my injuries. The people taking care of me also are treating me well. They get whatever kind of food I ask for but there is no pizza available unfortunately. I want nothing more in the world than to be with you and Joey again. I see his face and I pray that this will all turn out OK. Please tell everyone else in the family that I hear their prayers and things will work out OK. Nothing else matters more to me than to see my family again. I think I will. I really do. You stay positive and be strong and give Joey more hugs and kisses for his Dad that misses him so.

I broke my leg (compound fracture right femer) and injured my back in the crash. I think my nose is broken but it does not hurt. I have a superficial gunshot wound in my left arm. The leg and back are the only real problems but as I said the medical care has been very good. I hope to see you soon and I pray for the others who are missing. Ray, Bill, Tommy and anyone else.

I love you.

I signed my full signature, *Michael Durant*, a particular scribble that would assure anyone reading the letter that I had in fact written it. When I was done, I was in tears. To think that this document would soon be in the hands of my family was just overwhelming.

In fact, a copy of that letter would be faxed to the Pentagon that very evening. My own comrades at the airfield, along with intelligence officers in the Mog and all over the Washington, D.C., area, would be poring over it and consulting with one another. My reference to pizza was just a lighthearted comment to let everyone know that I was doing all right, but since it was common knowledge that spaghetti is my favorite, it left a few people scratching their heads. "What the hell is he trying to tell us?" they wondered. "Is he located near a pizza bakery? Is there even *one* pizza place in the Mog?" And I had also, unintentionally, misspelled femur as "femer." That one made everyone nuts. But in fact, I'd only done what I'd been taught to do. I'd kept it simple and innocuous. That way, if I wound up in captivity for a long time, they'd let me write more letters. And eventually, I'd figure out *exactly* where I was and somehow help facilitate a rescue.

Suzanne retrieved the letter and passed it to the Somalis without being asked. That was the standard procedure for the ICRC. They looked it over, and the senior man said, "Just fine."

"I'd like to write one to my friends at the airfield," I said. I was sure they wouldn't allow it, but I gave it a shot. "If that's all right."

They stared at me while I inwardly held my breath. The head Somali looked at his watch.

"All right," he said. "But quickly, please."

I couldn't believe it. I remembered that when Nick Rowe had been in captivity, it had taken *years* before the Vietcong let him write letters home. And then they'd torn them all up because he refused to include laudatory comments about the righteous ways of Communism.

Suzanne handed me her last letter form. I had to think fast. I had no idea that so much information about the mission and its participants had already been broadcast and printed, that there were hardly any secrets left for me to reveal. On CNN, the words "160th Special Operations Aviation Regiment" had actually flashed on the screen next to my image. All I knew was that I had to be very careful.

I addressed it to "Hooter Brothers and Friends." That was the nickname of our company. I kept it short, telling them that I was doing all right and that I was hearing their comments from the air. I told them to pray for Ray, Tommy, Bill, and "anyone else," to let them know that those two Delta men had been with me and might still be out there somewhere. "Don't drink my bottle of Jack without me!" I wrote. All of my buds knew that my bottle of whiskey was only supposed to be opened upon the capture of Mohamed Aidid, so it was my way of telling them that I was still in the game and they should carry on with that mission. Again, I signed my full name, no rank, and added the unit motto, "NSDQ!," for Night Stalkers Don't Quit!

The Somalis quickly reviewed the letter and seemed satisfied with its contents. However, before delivering it, the International Committee of the Red Cross decided that "NSDQ" had to be some kind of encoded message. Their reputation as a neutral organization had to be maintained, so they crossed that out. But the obscured capitals still remained legible, and back at the airfield my comrades blew that letter up to poster size and hung it up in the JOC.

It was time for Suzanne to leave. She had been with me for about an hour, but it seemed like only five minutes. I didn't want her to go, but I also didn't want her to be exposed to danger any longer than necessary.

"Thank you so much," I said as I gripped her hand again. "For the visit, and for the letters."

"I promise to get that box of comfort items to you as soon as possible, Michael," she said. "And I hope to visit again soon."

I forced a smile. "If you do, can you bring me a pizza?"

She laughed, even though she'd probably seen plenty of false bravado before. And then she was gone.

My head was spinning. I hadn't been released, but I was overcome with emotion. Happiness, sadness, hope, and despair, all rolled into one. I was suddenly very optimistic, sure that the Somalis would do everything they could now to ensure my safety. They were now under the scrutiny of a neutral humanitarian agency. And Mohamed Aidid was no fool. He knew very well where any additional aid would come from if things in Somalia ever got straightened out. It would be a public relations disaster for the SNA to kill me. Yes, my future looked good, but the fate of the other five of my comrades did not. I wished I could still do something for them, but it was over. We had fought until we could fight no more. I was beginning to accept the fact that they were all dead. . . .

I wasn't alone with my thoughts for more than a minute when I heard the chatter of more strange voices outside the room. *Now what?* I thought as without warning three more people entered. One was another Somali I'd never seen, and the other two were Caucasian men. They were wearing the "mufti" of Europeans in the Mog—safari shirts and cargo pants—and one had a heavy camera bag on his shoulder and the other a tape recorder. It didn't take a rocket scientist to tell they were journalists.

My hackles rose immediately. Abdi had asked me if I would speak to some journalists and I'd blatantly refused, but here they were anyway. It was clear that the Somalis regarded Suzanne's visit as a gesture of goodwill, and I was expected to return one in kind. At any other time I would probably have gone stone silent at the appearance of reporters, but Suzanne had just left and I was still in an emotionally charged state. My defenses were down, and maybe the Somalis had anticipated just that.

The two men introduced themselves as Mark and Paul. Mark spoke with a French accent and said he worked for a paper out of Paris. Paul was Canadian and wrote for the *Toronto Star*. They were very friendly, upbeat, and unassuming, but being a suspicious character regarding all forms of media, I assumed that friendliness was a technique of their stock-in-trade.

"We'd like to speak to you, *Monsieur* Durant," said Mark. "We will be recording the conversation and take a few notes, if that is all right."

I didn't say anything yet, but if my look of suspicion could have killed, they would have dropped right there.

"You don't have to answer any questions you don't want to, Mike," Paul said casually, as if it really didn't matter to him one way or the other. "It's all up to you. But maybe it would be a good thing to do."

They waited, while I thought fast. *Would* it be a good thing to do? Under most circumstances I would have said, "Hell no." But throwing them out, figuratively of course, might not be the best course of action. It was pretty clear to me now that I was the only survivor of Crash Site Two and that no one from the Task Force knew what had happened there. This might be a way to get all that information back to them, and maybe the details of my capture and imprisonment might offer some helpful hints I couldn't yet imagine. I pointed at the tape recorder as Paul's finger hovered over the Record button, stopping him.

"Okay," I said. "But no questions about my mission or my unit."

He shot me a thumbs-up and switched it on.

I relayed everything I could remember from the time of the crash until that very morning. But even as I spoke, I was censoring myself, intentionally leaving some details unclear. I didn't want the Somalis to know how many men had been at the crash site. I figured they would have given up their search by now unless they couldn't account for all the personnel. I didn't know that the civilian mob had taken the bodies and the SNA couldn't account for them anyway.

"You were very badly injured, *Monsieur* Durant," said Mark. "How did you get out of the cockpit?"

"An American pulled me out," I answered. "I don't know who it was."

I told them about the riot. I didn't tell them about being beaten with a severed limb, but I pulled no punches either about the rest of the savagery during my capture. I relayed every detail about being moved and the cells I'd been in. Maybe some sharp intel analyst would be able to put the pieces of this puzzle together somehow. I complimented my captors when they deserved it and took them to task when they didn't.

In the middle of all this, I suddenly asked the journalists what I looked like, because the way Suzanne had looked at me had piqued my curiosity. I hadn't seen myself since Sunday before the mission. One of them left the room and came back with a small mirror, the kind you find in the cosmetic pouch of a suitcase. Paul held it up in front of my face.

I was shocked. My face looked like a couple of thugs had worked me over with a blackjack. Everything was swollen, my eyes were black, there were blotches of blood in my eyeballs. There was a long, curving slash from my left eye to the corner of my mouth, probably from pieces of the cockpit glass that had imploded on impact. I handed the mirror back.

"I look like Rocky," I said. Everyone had a friendly chuckle at that.

There's a technique journalists use when they're looking for a sound bite—that single phrase, the one that's going to sell papers. Interrogators use it too. You get the guy talking, about anything at all, and then you slip in that one question. I got sucker punched.

"So, what do you think about the mission in Somalia?" Mark asked.

"Americans are good people by nature," I responded. "We normally want to help when we see people in need. We *did* try to help. Something has gone wrong here . . ."

My voice trailed off and I stopped talking. *Aw, shit.* I mentally pounded myself on the forehead. *Man, you just made your first mistake.* As soon as that last phrase left my mouth, I knew I shouldn't have said it. It was exactly the kind of thing we soldiers had to avoid. It didn't matter whether I agreed with the policy or not; it was my job to carry it out and shut up about it.

With the video interrogation, I thought I'd hit a grand slam. It had been textbook. I had said exactly the right things and I was proud of my performance. But now I'd let myself get ambushed and I'd crossed the line. *Something has gone wrong here? Christ!* As it would turn out, not a single soul from our military or government would ever take me to task for that statement, but they didn't have to. I beat myself up about it for a long time, and it would be my greatest regret about the entire period of my captivity.

The journalists switched off their recorder. With my utterance of that careless phrase, they knew they had their "money shot." They took a few photographs. One of those black-and-white pictures appeared in the October 18, 1993, issue of *Time* magazine. You can see me lying there, my jaw set and my eyes averted, stone cold and pissed off at myself. Mark and Paul packed up, thanked me, wished me well, and left. I hardly noticed.

In an instant, the joy of Suzanne's visit had been completely erased. My morale took a nosedive and I fell into a chasm of gloom. I judged myself so harshly that the impact of it was far worse than not being released.

To a civilian, it might seem like my self-flagellation was over the top. But I was a special operations officer, and I was devastated.

MY COMRADES BACK at the airfield did not judge me. Instead, they threw me a radio party.

By midmorning Suzanne had already walked out of my prison, and by noon she was at the Task Force Ranger compound, delivering my letters and the news of my condition. Naturally, the special ops and intel officers were hoping to "debrief" her thoroughly and find out my exact location, but I'm sure they knew they wouldn't get very far. She was sympathetic and courteous, but very professional, and she was not about to breach the rules of neutrality for anyone. If she helped them find me and then a rescue was launched and people were killed in the process, no ICRC representative would be visiting another prisoner of war for a very long time.

She did describe my physical condition in detail, and she even commented that what she had witnessed appeared to be a version of the "Stockholm Syndrome," but in reverse. The Stockholm Syndrome refers to a strange phenomenon that occurs with some people when they're held hostage under great stress and begin to sympathize with their captors, at times even joining their enemy's cause.

"The Somalis have certainly been trying to influence Michael," she said. "But it appears to me that the captive has instead won over his captors."

She politely declined to offer more information than that. She accepted a few "donations" for me from the unit, items she could add to the Red Cross box, and she bid my comrades farewell. She was a very bright and worldly woman, and no doubt she expected to be tracked by CIA or Army Intelligence assets. But the Somalis were no fools either, and that's probably why neither she nor any other Red

Cross representative was "invited" to visit me again. Just before she left the compound, she added one bit of crucial information.

"And one more thing," she said. "The Somalis have given Michael a radio."

In the early afternoon I finally pulled myself out of my depressive state and turned on the radio. I figured there was no sense in ruminating further about my gaff with the reporters. *From now on, Durant,* I told myself, *you just keep your mouth shut. And if you say anything at all, it'll be the Big Four.* I figured I'd listen to some music and distract myself, so I tuned to the Armed Forces Network.

I was absolutely *stunned.* Requests for me were *pouring in* from all over the Mog! Guys from my own unit were calling into the DJ and dedicating songs to me. They didn't identify themselves by name, but they used code words that only I would understand.

"This one's for Mike Durant from the Hooter Brothers!"

I assumed that was a request from Herb Rodriguez, my company commander.

"This one's for Mike Durant from Thunderstruck!"

That had to be from the guys in the DAP platoon, because Thunderstruck was the nickname of one of our birds.

They played all kinds of stuff, from Willie Nelson to Meat Loaf, and every time I heard my name and another song came on, my smile just flowed across my face. Instantly, I had a whole new outlook. It was just an incredible feeling knowing that the guys were there, reaching out to me and ready to execute a rescue mission at a moment's notice.

"This one's for Mike Durant from First Flight!"

I grinned from ear to ear. Back in July I had been flying a load of SEALs somewhere on a training mission, and while I normally never goofed around on the radio, I had this song stuck in my head and I kept singing the chorus. I'd never really paid much mind to the lyrics, but now as the DJ played "Rooster" by Alice in Chains, it seemed like every line had been written just for me.

"Ain't found a way to kill me yet,
Eyes burn with stingin' sweat,
Seems every path leads me to nowhere.

Wife and kids household pet,
Army green was no safe bet,
The bullets scream to me from somewhere.

Here they come to snuff the rooster, oh yeah,
Yeah, here come the rooster yeah,
You know he ain't gonna die,
No no no, you know he ain't gonna die!

Walkin' tall machine gun man,
They spit on me in my homeland,
Gloria sent me pictures of my boy.

Got my pills 'gainst mosquito death,
My buddy's breathin' his dyin' breath,
Oh God please won't you help me make it through.

Here they come to snuff the rooster, oh yeah,
Yeah, here come the rooster yeah,
You know he ain't gonna die,
No no no, you know he ain't gonna die!"

The impact of hearing that song was a soaring morale boost for me. My buds must have known exactly what they were doing. That afternoon, they requested it over and over again, and every time I heard those words "he ain't gonna die," I really felt that way. No matter what, I was *not* going to give up.

"Ain't found a way to kill me yet . . ."

But by late afternoon, it seemed that the Somalis were still working on that. Firimbi came into the room wearing a dour expression and searching for some way to tell me the bad news.

"You must move," he said.

"Oh, come on." I shook my head. "No, you've got to be kidding me."

"Yes." He started pacing around the room, obviously frustrated. "Red Cross," he said, *"e giornalisti."*

He waved his arms and mimed a big commotion everywhere, and unfortunately I understood what he was trying to say. The visits had drawn a lot of attention to my prison, and the Somalis were obviously concerned that Suzanne or the reporters might divulge my whereabouts to my comrades. But damn, I knew I wouldn't survive another ride in that car again. With Kediye's splint on my leg, I wouldn't even be able to partially curl up in the back like I had before.

"No way," I said. "We're not doing that *again*."

"I sorry," Firimbi said. "You move."

"Okay, okay," I said as I raised my hands. Then I wagged a finger at him vigorously. "But no auto, no auto. Truck, Firimbi. Get the *truck*."

He shrugged hard. That word wasn't in his vocabulary.

I placed my hands on an imaginary steering wheel and made a *vroom-vroom* sound. I smoothed my palm back and forth in the air, trying to describe a flat surface. I lay down flat and bounced a little, as if I were riding in a flatbed. I looked at him hopefully. He was staring at me with his head cocked like a dumbfounded collie.

"Camión!" I finally blurted out the Spanish word for truck, hoping like hell that it was close to the Italian.

"Ahhh." He nodded at last.

He left the room, but I wasn't very optimistic. The first truck I'd been moved in had probably belonged to some other faction, and I doubted that these guys all shared a fleet of vehicles. I waited a long time for his return, all the while dreading the move. As long as I remained still the pain was tolerable, but I couldn't imagine surviving another trip like the last one. I prayed they'd find some other way. I prayed they'd change their minds. It was like a surgeon had told me he was going to have to remove my appendix without anesthetic.

I tried to take my mind off it. I forced myself to eat something and kept listening to the radio. The AFN was talking about the United States sending over a carrier battle group and that M-1 tanks were being brought in to beef up the Task Force. A show of force was all well and good, but I was full of dread about my impending move.

Been there, done that, hated the whole goddamn thing.

There were lots of children playing outside that day. I could hear their laughter intermittently, sometimes right out there in the court-yard, but they had never been allowed to look into or enter my room. Yet now, as evening fell, Aretha showed up at the door with four or five very small children. They hid behind her skirts and peered out at me with wide eyes and shy smiles, as if they knew they were doing something naughty. Aretha slowly waved at me and smiled, as if she were seeing a son off to college. I waved back at them all, and then they were gone. So much for a change of heart about my move. Everyone knew I was leaving.

With dark, gunfire erupted outside in the streets. I went extremely tense and wary, thinking that a rival clan or some angry civilians had discovered my location. I tried to stay calm, but I thought it was jus-tifiable paranoia.

Even paranoids have enemies, Durant, I told myself. *Especially you.*

Firimbi returned, looking more grim than before. It was difficult to understand him, but he was trying to tell me that there would be no truck. He mimed the courtyard gates opening, then the width of a truck body unable to get through. We would have to go in the car.

"Please don't put me in the backseat of that damn car again," I said, knowing my pleas wouldn't matter or be understood. "I'd rather risk being killed here in my sleep."

But it was no good. Three of the young guards entered and flanked the bed. Firimbi was clearly doing everything he could to instruct them, but they had no idea what they were doing. They lifted me up, and the splint bent sharply upward right at my fracture site. I cried out in pain, and they set me back down. I begged them not to move me, but my pleas fell on deaf ears. The guards looked at one another. Firimbi snapped at them and they grabbed for me again, this time without hesitation.

"Oh Christ!" I yelled out as they hauled me toward the door. I thought I was going to pass out as they reversed the routine, out of my cell, along the balcony, down into the courtyard. And there it was, that goddamn coffin on wheels waiting for me.

Firimbi got in the backseat and his men slid me in, but now I couldn't bend my knee to relieve the pressure and all I saw were bright lights and flashes of fire behind my eyes. His face swam into view, looking very troubled at the fact that I was suffering. I was hyperventilating again, the sweat pouring off my face, and he tried to comfort me, muttering encouragements. He was probably trying to tell me that it wouldn't be far to go, and he fanned my face with the flyswatter. Then he covered me with a blanket. I don't think he cared what I might see during that ride. He didn't want anyone outside to see *me*. He barked orders at the driver and we took off.

I thought I was going to die right then and there. I had begun to come to grips with the day-to-day pain, but now it was as fierce as it had been just after the crash. But I balled my fists and bit my lip as the car rolled and bumped for an endless quarter hour. *You haven't come this far to give up now, Durant,* I told myself. *You've got too much left to do to die here in this shithole.*

"Ain't found a way to kill me yet . . ." I sang it to myself over and over through my gnashing teeth.

The car drove through another metal gate and the Somalis pulled me out into another sort of compound. They carried me, one on each leg and one on each arm, and it was like being drawn and quartered. But even through my grimace I snatched a sense of the place — the special operator inside me still functioned while the wounded human swallowed screams. This building seemed more isolated than all the rest, something like a private home, a single-story "ranch house." We moved beneath a portico, down a long interior hallway, and into a room on the right.

They put me down on another hard floor against the far wall, beneath a pair of windows and across from the open doorway. It was a larger space than the last. The ceiling was ornate, with some kind of decorated pattern, as if a wealthy Somali had once lived there. But now there was absolutely nothing in that room: no pictures, no lighting, all the electrical plates ripped out. It was empty and desolate, and everything I'd accumulated at the previous location was gone. I had no bed, no food, no water, no medicine, no radio. But all I cared about was the incredible pain that wasn't subsiding now, even as I lay still.

The trip in the car had aced it. That splint had to come off. The fire in my thigh was incredibly intense, and I didn't even have the aspirin now for a "placebo effect."

Firimbi squatted down beside me. I must have looked bad, because he looked pretty worried. I gripped his forearm, hard.

"You've got to get the doctor," I said. My voice was dry and raspy. "Dr. Kediye. Right now. This goddamn thing has *got* to come off."

I must have been fairly convincing, because he hustled out of the place.

Without his oil lantern it was pitch dark. I lay there for a long time, not moving, just breathing and waiting. It must have been one o'clock in the morning when Kediye finally trudged in with a lamp and his tackle box. This time, no formalities were exchanged.

"Take this thing off my leg, Doc."

"It is really not a good idea," he warned.

"Yes, it *is* a good idea," I answered. "You've got to get this thing off me right *now*."

He sighed and rummaged in his box, coming up with a pair of those surgical scissors that have a flat bottom so you can slip them between a bandage and a limb. I could already feel the impending relief as he sliced through the thick gauze from my hip to my toes. My entire leg felt like it had just taken a huge breath after a near-drowning. He folded up the wreckage of the splint while I looked at it like it was a freshly killed rattlesnake. He glanced around the empty room.

"Where are your medications?" he asked.

"They left them all behind."

"I will bring them to you," he said as he packed up and left.

Right, I thought. *And don't forget the buxom nurse twins and the beer keg.*

I was not in good spirits. The whole day had been an emotional and physical roller-coaster ride. The pain didn't recede very much because the femur had been traumatized again, but it certainly was easier to make myself comfortable.

Firimbi finally came back in and set up his sleeping mat across the room. He looked somewhat sheepish, avoiding my eyes. I had nothing but the blanket from the move, but I didn't really care at that point. I was wasted and knew that I'd sleep through anything.

He started talking about a cease-fire. It wasn't easy to understand what he meant, but he said, "Radio Mogadishu." That was Aidid's propaganda station. "Mohamed Aidid no shoot. America no shoot. U.N. no shoot." Okay, they were somehow coming to cease-fire terms. "Mohamed Aidid say make peace, make peace."

"Yeah," I said, "but those politicians all sound the same no matter what language they're speaking, don't they? Blah, blah, blah, right?"

"Yes," he said, having no idea that I was spewing sarcasm.

Still, it wasn't bad news. A cease-fire would certainly be better for me than open warfare. And I certainly didn't want to see any more of my comrades dying for this "cause."

We both settled down into silence. Then I felt, more than heard, a familiar rumbling of big engines in the air. All of a sudden a 105mm cannon opened up somewhere, its shells cracking out huge explosions not too far off.

Firimbi sat up on his mat and pointed up at the ceiling.

"AC!" he yelled. "AC!"

He was right. It was an AC-130 Spectre gunship, probably firing north of the city into the test-fire area. *Wham!* There it was again. Another guard ran into the room, obviously very distraught as he chattered at Firimbi and also said, "AC!"

So the AC-130s were back again. They had been taken out of the country before Task Force Ranger arrived, but earlier in the summer there had been a lot of coverage about their attacks on Aidid's strong points and weapons caches. They had been very effective back then and probably would have been so during the battle of October 3. I wondered who the fool was who had pulled them out in July, and made a mental note to someday get his phone number.

"AC no good," Firimbi grumbled.

Well, it sounds real good to me, I thought. But I managed to calm the guards down, explaining to them that the gunship was only test-firing its weapons. And I was sure that that was true, but it was also clearly a show of force. Maybe it wasn't a sound tactic if a cease-fire was really about to go into effect, but the flying battle cruiser was a devastating weapon and the message was clear: "The boys are back in town."

Firimbi and his guards settled down and eventually all went to sleep. It wasn't long before I succumbed to my exhaustion as well.

But in the middle of the night, the Spectre returned. It wasn't test-firing now, but walking its big shells closer and closer to my new prison. I could hear those Hercules engines roaring and the chunks of cement shrapnel raining on the roof as those 105mm shells pounded nearby.

You're getting too close, boys, I warned that crew mentally. *You better change that damn trajectory.*

Another shell ripped into the courtyard right outside! The walls shook and parts of the ceiling came down. I twisted on the floor and tried to take cover as I heard the rushing scream of the next shell heading directly for my cell.

Wham!

I woke up in a cold sweat. It was dead silent except for Firimbi, snoring peacefully on his mat. I searched my body for fresh gaping wounds, then lay flat back and sucked air. The whole thing had been nothing but a nightmare.

I guess I was a little stressed out.

I thought I had been killed by friendly fire.

Chapter 11

THE BIBLE

October 9, 1993

ON MY SEVENTH DAY as a prisoner of war, I found religion.

It has often been said that there are no atheists in foxholes, meaning that even a nonbeliever will begin to pray when faced with his own mortality. But I had never been a Catholic of convenience who only prayed when times were tough. Admittedly, as a boy I'd attended church regularly with my family, while as an adult and full-time army helicopter pilot I had allowed that tradition to lapse. Yet my absence from the pews hadn't broken my bond with the Lord. At times I would offer my Sunday prayers from the cockpit, or say a silent Grace over an MRE between missions, or ask a chaplain for a quick blessing as I ran to my helo. It didn't require the threat of death for me to recall the sacraments. So when I say that I found religion, I mean it literally.

Sometime during the night Suzanne Hofstetter's Red Cross box had been delivered, apparently by Dr. Kediye while I slept. I had drifted off to sleep after my Spectre Gunship nightmare, and in the morning awoke to the dim light of my new prison. Maybe the place had once been the *hacienda* of some upper-crust Somali, but I found it wanting. The room was completely barren, and with the exception of my flyswatter, none of the items I'd accumulated over the past week had made the trip. Most important, my radio was gone, severing my contact with the World. I began to wonder if the "Bed Bath & Beyond" treatment had been nothing but a show put on by the Somalis for Suzanne. Yet as the light improved, I spotted that solitary box, so I dragged it over and started to explore.

It wasn't exactly a treasure trove, but there were some useful items inside. There was a disposable razor and a can of shaving cream, a real toothbrush and a tube of toothpaste. Good stuff. At least I wouldn't have to dry shave or brush my teeth with a stick. There were three paperback novels, their cracked spines and well-worn pages making me briefly wonder if some other prisoner had already read them all. Next came a tablet of writing paper, two pens, one recently issued MRE, and a bottle of water.

Okay, it's payback time, I thought. *I'm gonna eat this damn MRE and write a scathing review for some gourmet magazine.*

I found a fresh roll of toilet paper, which seemed an appropriate follow-up to the MRE. There was also a small first-aid kit inside, but nothing much was in it. I cocked my head quizzically at a bottle of Flintstones children's vitamins, and squinted at the label on a bottle of antibiotics. I wanted to start taking the medication right away, but then I realized that Kediye had already put me on some kind of antibiotics and mixing them up together in my gut might not be a good idea. I did swallow two tablets from a bottle of Tylenol, even though I knew it would have about as much effect as taking M&M's for a cardiac arrest.

In the bottom of the box were two small wooden crosses on beaded neck chains, next to a pack of playing cards.

We're getting some mixed messages here, I mused. *Say your rosary and pray for a straight flush?*

The very last item was a U.S. Army Bible. It was about the size of a small paperback, its cover and binding in desert camouflage colors.

It was then I realized that some of these items had come *directly* from Task Force Ranger. I knew that Suzanne had already visited the airfield, so the guys had probably donated some "gifts" for the box. *Wait a minute,* I thought with excitement as I started to go through the box all over again. *I'll bet I missed something!* Firimbi had left the room, but I didn't know when he'd be back, so I had to work fast. *Could they have slipped in some sort of a weapon?* I flipped through the paperback books and the Bible, turning them over and fanning the pages, looking for a thin blade or a razor. I tore open the pack of playing cards and thumbed through the entire deck. Nothing. I opened the vitamin bottle and poured all the rainbow-colored pellets into my hand, then did the same with the Tylenol. *Nada.* The MRE packet looked factory-sealed, but I ripped it open anyway and found . . . Meals, Ready-to-Eat.

Like some kid disappointed with his Christmas stocking, I turned the whole Red Cross box upside down and shook it. The toilet paper rolled across the floor. *That's probably from Cliff,* I decided. *Trying to tell me I'm full of crap.*

I stopped moving, bracing the empty box in midair.

Hold on!

I went through the whole thing all over again, searching all the objects for some kind of device. *Maybe there's a miniature signal flare in here, or a nail file at least!* I took the pens apart, found nothing, and reassembled them. I even opened up the antibiotics again and held every capsule up to the light from the window. But there was nothing in that box but comfort items. Then I remembered how thoroughly the Somalis had searched me, over and over again, and I realized that they had done the very same thing with that box.

Nothing that might be used effectively as a weapon, and certainly no high-tech electronic widget, had remained.

Somewhat sobered, I repacked everything just as one of the younger guards passed the open door. He was walking from the courtyard to one of the rooms at the back, carrying three AK-47s. The guards obviously distributed the weapons at night, when a rescue would be likely to occur. During the day, they kept them out of sight. These guys were no dummies.

I sighed and lay back down flat. All that exertion and excitement had brought the pains back clear and sharp. My palms were slippery with sweat. I smeared them across my soiled transport blanket as I tried to think if I'd missed something. In time, I decided, I would scan every page of the Bible and the paperbacks and examine every card in the deck. In truth, I doubted that my comrades would have had enough time to jot a secret message to me somewhere, but at least the search would keep me occupied.

Firimbi returned with my Disney bowl, and this time it was filled with hot water. Shaving with lather was outstanding, and using a real toothbrush and toothpaste was even better. Unfortunately, the donated toilet paper was also calling out to me. My intestines were churning, as I hadn't relieved myself since being captured. I somehow made Firimbi understand, and he rinsed out the bowl and helped me maneuver it underneath my butt. I'll skip the gory details, but let's just say the man earned his combat pay that morning.

"Thanks," I said to him as he was taking the bowl from the room, holding it at arm's length. "And you can keep the Donald Duck souvenir. I'm not shaving in that thing again unless *you* do it first."

"Yes, yes," he said as he left.

By early morning, my new prison was incredibly hot. The air hardly stirred, and I reasoned we had relocated farther away from the sea. There were no children playing outside and the sounds of car engines and horns were distant. There were no sounds of helicopters overhead. If in the past week my buds had made any progress in their search for me, now they would have to start all over again.

But the flies were as thick as a biblical plague. They settled on me in clusters, and even Firimbi cursed at their relentless dive-bombing. *The Task Force needs to recruit and tame a squadron of these damned things,* I thought. *They seem to be able to find me wherever I am.* It was too hot to keep the blanket on me, so Firimbi gave me the straw swatter and I just lay there naked, trying to fend them off.

A young Somali girl entered the room to sweep up. She was pretty, with her long ebony hair piled up on top of her head, wearing a green sarong and with tin jewelry jangling from her wrists. She smiled shyly as she swept the floor, keeping her eyes cast down. But she glanced at me once and almost giggled as I waved at her. I guess I was hard to ignore, sort of like a severed horse head on the dining room table. Soon after, she mopped the floor with something that smelled like kerosene. Half the flies left. The other half thought the fuel was dessert.

Throughout my captivity I had been reciting silent prayers regularly—for my comrades, my family, and myself. So, since I had no radio anymore, I figured that it might be a good time to read the Bible. I couldn't remember the last time I'd done that, so I began at the beginning. Firimbi always seemed to be reading something, and today it was his copy of the Koran, so he smiled and nodded at me approvingly as I took up The Good Book.

I had reached the end of Genesis when I realized that the rest of that page was nearly blank. I thumbed through all the pages and discovered a pattern. Almost every chapter ended with a similar blank page. The idea came to me quickly. The Somalis were very religious and seemed to respect that tendency in any man. If they ever released me, it was likely that the one item they'd let me keep would be that Bible. I knew that one of the first things that would happen upon my release would be a *very* thorough debriefing by the Army. If I could secretly write in those blank pages, recording everything that had happened, I would have a detailed record of all the events!

Just do it in code, Durant, I coached myself. *So if the Somalis take it away from you, at least they won't understand it.*

Of course, my captors could torture me for the translation, but I figured I could bluff my way through that. I was not sure how the Lord would feel about my desecration of His Book, but I knew that the Army would be more than pleased. So, being a mere servant of both, I decided to let them sort that out later.

As soon as Firimbi left the room again, I rummaged through the Red Cross box for one of the pens and found the blank page across from the first chapter of Exodus. "The Israelites Are Treated Cruelly in Egypt," read the heading. That seemed like an appropriate place to start, and I began to write my recollections in columns of my own private code, beginning with the moment Super Six-Four had been hit by the RPG.

3–Bump	(*3rd of October—RPG impact*)
Radio Call	
L A	(*Decrease in Altitude*)
Vib	
Spin	
Horizon	
Radio Call	
PCLs	(*Power Control Levers*)
Hypoxia	
Shanty	
Ray	
Leg	
Back	
Unstrap	
SP	(*Skinny Popper*)
Stuck	

Ray got out
S62 2Δ   (*Super 62 drops 2 Delta Operators*)
Bill—Tommy?
SP 1 →   (*I fired to the right*)
SP 2 ←   (*I fired to the left*)
Winchester/HG   (*Out of ammo/Hand Grenade*)

I wrote each item down carefully, making sure not to miss any important detail and keeping it all in chronological order. When I was done with that first column I was satisfied with it. Within days I would fill ten blank Bible pages with codes that only I would understand—or in the event of my death, my comrades could probably decipher. If my condition deteriorated beyond recovery, I hoped that at least my corpse would be turned back over to the airfield, my hands folded over the Bible on my chest. Not a bad legacy. I could live with that.

I heard Firimbi coming down the hallway, and I tucked the pen under my leg and turned the page. I didn't have to pretend to be interested in Exodus—I was reading it word for word. My ruse worked like a charm. Whenever the Somalis were with me, I would read. As soon as they were gone, I would write. And from that moment on, that Bible never left my side.

Little by little, the items from my previous holding cell began to arrive. The guards brought in the bed, assembled it, made it up, and carefully moved me off the floor. They gave me back my tartan sheet, which made it easier for the pretty house girl to glance at me without blushing. I wondered, hopefully, if they were setting me up for another Red Cross visit. But on the other hand, that might be followed by another parade of journalists.

This time, if you guys show up here, I warned those anonymous reporters silently, *you're gonna find nothing but a pissed-off mute.*

I began to feel a little better about my situation again. After all, I had been visited by the Red Cross and I knew my family was all

right. I had food, water, and medical treatment—albeit more sym-
bolic than effective. The hostile treatment was over and I was probably about as comfortable as I could be without morphine and an air
conditioner. But once again, I made a conscious decision to prepare
myself mentally for the long haul.

These situations are never resolved quickly, I thought. *You can create a psychological roller coaster in your mind that'll devastate you.
Just plan on staying for a long time, Durant, and anything else will
be gravy.*

That day just crawled along. There were no visitors, few distrac-
tions, and for a man accustomed to constant action, it was like being
banished to a Third World library. But when I thought about my lost
comrades, I didn't have to remind myself to be thankful just to be
alive. The pain from the last move was still pretty severe, but the Doc
never showed up. I figured he was riled at me because I'd insulted
his California medical education by rejecting his splint, and had
kept him up all night to boot. But in the late afternoon, Firimbi
brought the radio back. I hadn't realized how much I'd come to depend on that small square box until I saw it again, and I reached for
it like a drowning man for a life preserver. Right away I tuned to the
Armed Forces Network.

It was the top of the hour, and the first thing the DJ did was throw
a request for me on the platter. It was AC/DC's "Thunderstruck," and
I just lay there and grinned as I listened. Then there was a news
break and confirmation that the cease-fire was holding, but I just
thirsted after the next request. The guys were ordering up all kinds
of stuff for me, claiming these were my favorite songs. The DJ played
"Baby Got Back," which cracked me up, because it was a song that
Donovan had been singing over and over again during a recent training mission before our deployment. Firimbi raised his head from his
book and looked at me over the tops of his glasses as if I'd finally lost
it. The guys kept on calling in requests. Some of them were songs I
really liked and some of them were bogus. But I figured if you let

Donovan Briley, Stan Wood, Cliff Wolcott, and Dan Jollota get together, they'd come up with all kinds of crazy-assed stuff. I don't know who ordered up a rap song called "Whoops, There It·Is!," but I just laughed and thought, *Okay, bro, I'm down with that.*

With sunset, I ate one packet of boneless chicken from the MRE and downed a bottle of water. A guard passed by the open door, now carrying those AK-47s to the front of the house and the courtyard. I heard the distinctive sounds of the weapons' actions slamming home and ammunition being chambered. Although my "relationship" with the Somalis had stabilized, they were still maintaining a defensive posture, ready to battle any rival clan or fight off a rescue attempt. And I realized then that the door to my cell wasn't just open, there *was no door* at all—and I didn't much like that fact.

A well-armed mob could still rush this place and finish me off, I thought. Then I looked up at the window just above the left side of my bed. *Or even that coward who shot me before might show up here and put another round in me.*

There was nothing I could do about any of that anyway. I'd been up since dawn, reading and writing in my Bible, thinking and plotting. I was wiped out and decided to make an early night of it.

I was still concerned about being killed, but I didn't lose any sleep over it.

MY WIFE SPOKE to me at dawn.

I had woken up and turned on the radio, hoping to hear some more encouraging news and maybe some rock and roll to start the day off right. The pains from my leg and back, which didn't seem to keep me awake at night, gathered force the minute I opened my eyes. I wondered how it was that the human brain could shut down the nervous system during sleep, temporarily anesthetizing a wounded man, but seemed incapable of doing the same while he was awake. At any rate, I lay there with my eyes closed, the radio tight to my ear, hardly taking in the voice of the AFN's female DJ until she started talking about me.

"It's been a week since the U.S. helicopter pilot was captured during an all-day battle with supporters of Aidid. Michael Durant is being held by Aidid's forces. Red Cross representatives who have examined Durant say he is recovering from his broken leg and a bullet wound. On Friday the Red Cross delivered a letter to Durant's wife in the United States. She chose to answer him on camera on CNN, in hopes that her husband would hear her reply."

My eyes snapped open and I blinked hard, thinking I might still be asleep and dreaming. But no, it was Lorrie's voice, her light southern accent clear as a bell, and as I listened the emotions flowed through my veins and thudded in my chest.

"I'm making this statement in hopes that it will reach my husband. I want him to know that Joey and I are doing well. I received your letter from the Red Cross, Mike. I was very happy to hear that you are okay and that you're being treated well. Clay and the rest of the family are taking great care of us. Everyone is praying for you. I know you can hear my prayers and the prayers of your brothers. . . ."

As she took a breath, my own breathing was quick and shallow, my ears burning as I listened with every pore.

"Everything with the new house is moving along fine. We'll be living in our dream home soon. I hope they're taking care of you and feeding you right. I'll have a big pizza waiting for you soon. Joey is waiting for you to get back before he starts walking. He wants his father to see his first steps. Take care of yourself. Don't worry about us. We'll be fine. And remember, babe, as you've always told me—NSDQ . . . Night Stalkers Don't Quit. Take care of yourself. I love you very much, with all my heart."

To say that I was moved by hearing my wife's voice would be a paltry description. It felt like every fiber of my being was suddenly electrified. As soon as she started to speak, I knew that everything was going to be all right. My family was fine and strong. One of my best friends, Clay Hutmacher, was with them, a rock they could lean on. The only part of the message that had sounded strange to me was that one sentence including "Night Stalkers Don't Quit." I never said that at home and my wife certainly didn't, so I knew that the guys at the airfield had received my message and had asked her to relay that back to me. I felt as if we'd all gotten one over on my captors, and I was flying high.

The DJ cut right back in when Lorrie was done, but compared to my wife's voice her drone sounded cold and lifeless.

"The U.S. death toll from last Sunday's battle stands at seventeen, with one soldier still unaccounted for. Red Cross officials estimate seven hundred Somalis were killed or wounded . . ."

The Somali casualty figures stunned me. I tried to picture the enormity of the firefight that had claimed so many of the enemy. Yet again it was the casual reciting of our own dead that really struck home. I knew that some of those anonymous seventeen were the members of my crew, and most likely the two Delta men who had fought so valiantly to save my life. A wave of sorrow came over me, laced with the bitterness of guilt. I had just heard my wife's voice, but those men would never hear the voices or laughter of their loved ones again. Yet one soldier was still unaccounted for. There was still one thin ray of hope.

Who are you, man? I wondered. *Where are you?*

I focused on the radio again, listening for further details. But either they hadn't listed the names of the dead or I had missed it. I wished that I could hear my wife's message one more time. And within half an hour, the station broadcast it again and it had nearly the same effect as the first time. Firimbi had woken up, sensing my excitement, and I managed to explain to him that it was my wife sending a message to me. He grinned broadly and seemed genuinely pleased, and I truly believed that he wanted to see me go home. Our fight was over. There was no hatred for me or any other American in him.

Then I heard the distant sound of a Blackhawk. It was circling somewhere, though not directly overhead. And there again was Dan's voice, transmitting through a speaker, his words fading in and out. He was talking to me, telling me that Clay was with my family and my parents were there too. The message faded away into music, like the last scene of a great movie that you never want to end.

Firimbi was sitting on his mat, looking up at the ceiling and the invisible sky beyond. He knew my friends were talking to me and he glanced over at me, smiled, and returned to reading the Koran. I knew then that he was truly a compassionate human being, and I also knew that things would have been very different for me if some other Somali had been in charge of my care and security.

The air in the room seemed considerably cooler that day. Perhaps the wind was blowing from a slightly different direction. I shaved and brushed my teeth without breaking into a sweat immediately afterward. The noises outside were muted and I sensed that this compound was somewhat isolated, which in turn made me feel more secure. I turned the radio up a bit and felt my mood brighten a notch. I was beginning to think that I might make it out of this bizarre situation after all.

Dr. Kediye arrived, apparently having gotten over my snubbing of his medical improvisations. He was wearing clean clothes and looked as though he had gotten his first decent night of sleep in a week. Given the Somali casualty figures I'd heard on the radio, I was surprised the poor guy was still standing. He had brought another small box from the Red Cross, and I understood that he was serving as their go-between. It held nothing more than a fresh MRE, a bottle of water, and a carton of orange juice, but just swigging that sweet liquid was like getting the full breakfast course at the International House of Pancakes.

"Thanks, Doc," I said as he examined me.

"I do not know what is wrong with your back, Mr. Durant." He shrugged apologetically.

"Beats the hell out of me."

"I would like to take you downtown for an X ray, but I do not know if that will be possible."

"That's all right, Doc. It's already better," I lied.

Try to move me again and I'll strangle you, I thought.

But I mentally eased up on Kediye that day. Maybe he lacked the medical skills I was accustomed to, but his fees were reasonable and he made house calls. He was caring and dedicated and a good old-fashioned country doctor, the sort of physician you don't find too often these days.

He changed all my dressings again and seemed satisfied that nothing appeared to be festering. The Tylenol I'd received from the Red Cross was more effective than any medication he had to offer, so he told me to just keep taking it. He left, promising to return tomorrow.

Throughout that day and into the evening, it seemed that all of the characters in my Mogadishu drama made an appearance, one after the other. And there was a new face as well. He was a large Somali, and when he marched into my room, Firimbi and the guards reacted as they did whenever Minister Abdi arrived: spines stiff and very respectful. He was the first one I saw who was wearing some sort of uniform—summer khakis with some kind of ranks on his epaulettes. His demeanor was very calm, and he spoke English well.

"I am Colonel Kalif," he said. "I am the commander of SNA forces in this area."

Well, I understand rank structure, and to me this meant that he was now in charge of my captivity. I wasn't about to salute him, but I offered him a respectful nod.

"And how are you, Colonel Durant?" he asked.

"I'm doing well," I said. *And thanks for the promotion,* I thought.

He looked around the room and nodded with approval, then gestured at Firimbi.

"This man, Abdullahi Hassan Mohamed Firimbi," he said. "He

is a very good man. He is a well-respected man. General Aidid thinks very highly of Firimbi, and that is why he was chosen to care for you."

"It was a fine choice," I said.

Firimbi's eyes flicked from me to the colonel. He was probably hoping I wasn't ratting him out for getting high on *khat* and vomiting all over the previous prison. Colonel Kalif said something to Firimbi that elicited a smile, so I figured I'd done all right by him.

"Good luck," he said to me, and then he left.

After nightfall, Minister Abdi arrived, and I realized that despite his controlled outward appearance he was very cautious and moved around now only in the dark. There might be a cease-fire in effect, but those kinds of arrangements could collapse with a gunshot and he was still a major target for the Task Force.

Yet he was the same as always: calm, deliberate, well dressed, and in charge. He said he was there to make sure that I was all right, and he asked me if there was anything I needed. There was no point in reiterating my desire to go home, so I told him the arrangements were fine. He already knew what I wanted the most, and I knew that his people were still using me for leverage.

"There appears to be a real possibility, Mr. Durant," he said, "that you will be released very soon. Such a release would be unconditional, a goodwill gesture on the part of General Aidid."

Since when is Aidid in the goodwill business? I wondered facetiously. I had taken to "filtering" the Minister's statements, laced as they were with propaganda. But on the other hand, his word was usually good and his information came from the top. He had promised me medical attention and had delivered. He had said the Red Cross would visit me, and they showed. He had offered me a radio, and the result was right there in my hand. I had no idea what might prod the SNA warlord into releasing me, but no doubt there were negotiations and bartering going on under the table. Yet, as always, I waited for Abdi's other shoe to drop. But this time there was no other shoe.

"You will be able to see your wife and son again." He smiled slightly. "I assume that is the only thing you do want."

"At this point," I said, "I need nothing else."

He left without asking for anything, and thankfully without trying to indoctrinate me again. The news was all good and the atmosphere was steadily improving, rising like the mercury in a thermometer after a thaw. Yet still, I refused to allow myself to be sucked in by self-deception.

Remember, Durant, I told myself. *The fortunes of war can turn in an instant.*

And indeed they did, within the hour.

Firimbi was out of the room and a single lamp was burning in the corner when I first heard the helos. Initially, I thought it was just another signature flight, but when you've spent your entire adult life listening to rotors, it gets so you can discern the size of an element, its altitude, speed, and direction. This was a *large* flight of helicopters, a mix of Blackhawks and Little Birds. It was Task Force Ranger, no doubt about it, and they were bearing down on my location. It was so loud that I thought the Little Birds were landing around the perimeter.

At any moment, I expected to hear flash bang grenades and the voices of American soldiers shouting battle orders to one another. I braced myself for the inevitable staccato bursts of gunfire and the screams of the mortally wounded. *How come the Somalis haven't opened up yet?* I wondered. *They will, any second now!* I kicked myself mentally for having lazed around instead of coming up with a plan of action. Now I had to devise one in an instant.

What're you gonna do if they can't find you? I asked myself.

Shout out "Ranger! Ranger!" at the top of your lungs, I decided. That would be the most commonsense, recognizable signal.

What if one of the guards sticks an AK through the window and tries to off you before the boys make it in here?

It wouldn't be easy to defend against that, but there were open shutters on the inside of the window.

You're gonna reach up and slam the shutter, trap the barrel, and yank the damn gun inside!

And then there was Firimbi. He was a soldier after all, and maybe he had a pistol I'd never seen and strict orders to use it. He would have to come in close to execute me, I hoped.

And when he does, Durant, you're gonna just jabber at him and plead and whine, and then slam him in the nuts with your elbow. Maybe that'll buy you ten or fifteen seconds.

I didn't really believe that he'd kill me, but I knew that when Delta showed up, he'd be a dead man. I was hoping he'd choose the better part of valor and run like a rabbit.

The tin roofs of the nearby buildings were actually rattling from rotor wash when the flight thundered directly overhead and roared away, leaving me sweating and breathless. I lay there for half a minute, my muscles tensed and rigid as steel. But the helos were gone.

Talk about foreplay without a payoff!

But for some reason, I wasn't disappointed. The overflight had been a wake-up call, a reminder to keep my head in the game and stay prepared. And I was certain that my buds were getting very close now to finding me.

By the time Firimbi rushed into the room, looking both shaken *and* stirred, I was lying there reading my Bible. He jabbered excitedly, gesturing skyward and shaking his head, as if I'd repaid his kindness by calling in an air strike. But I just looked at him over the top of The Good Book and shrugged innocently. As soon as he went out, I took up my pen and made a note on a blank page.

"The helos know."

I'd certainly had enough excitement for one day, so I settled in for a night of sleep. Tomorrow, I was going to start working on some serious methods to signal my location. Maybe my release was imminent and maybe not, but I knew that until I was being carried through the gates of the airfield and into the Task Force compound, my comrades would consider my rescue fair game. Yet at the moment, all I longed for were a couple of months at home with my family, playing with Joey and mowing the grass until I'd be thoroughly bored out of my mind.

I was still keyed up, so I tried to will myself to relax. I closed my eyes and summoned up images of the most desirable vacation spots I'd ever visited. There were clear streams in New Hampshire, blessed with placid silence and full of fat trout. There were beaches in the Caribbean, where gentle waves lapped at white beaches and cold beers were delivered by bronzed angels. There were many beautiful images I could take with me to my rest.

But of all the places in the world I could dream of, I returned instead to memories of Iraq.

Chapter 12

IRAQ

February 1991

A SCUD MISSILE LAUNCHER loomed in my gunsight, and I knew I had it dead to rights.

The air war component of Operation Desert Storm was already thundering all across Iraq, with Allied fighters, bombers, and cruise missiles striking command-and-control centers, antiaircraft emplacements, bridges, and bunkers. The Coalition ground forces were swelling to maximum strength throughout the Saudi Kingdom and the Persian Gulf, hunching their shoulders and poising to strike across the enemy's borders on three fronts. But Saddam Hussein had already thrown down a trump card, hurling his SCUDs at the population centers of Israel and Saudi Arabia.

The old Soviet SS-1 mobile missiles were highly inaccurate and undependable, and as tactical weapons they would have virtually no impact on our massive forces. Yet Saddam's motive for using them was terror, not tactics. Much as Hitler had ordered the V-2 rocket assaults on London during World War II when the war was all but lost for him, the Iraqi dictator had thrust his SCUDs into this war as demoralizers. In order to increase the 300-kilometer range of their missiles, the Iraqis had been forced to reduce the 1,000-kilogram warheads and weld additional fuel tanks to the liquid rockets. But their improvisations were now proving highly effective and the SCUDs could "reach out and touch someone." In some bizarre twist of fate, the homegrown modifications not only extended the range but also made them more difficult for our Patriot missiles to destroy, because the damn things broke into pieces in flight. Some of our soldiers stationed in Saudi had already been wounded by the incoming warheads, and one direct hit on a hangar in Dahran would soon claim twenty-eight American lives and nearly a hundred wounded. In Israel, the missiles were raining down nightly like a meteor shower, smashing buildings, wounding civilians, and sending hundreds of thousands of Israelis into their sealed rooms to don their gas masks.

Saddam Hussein was probably dancing a jig in his underground bunker. He hadn't deployed chemical or biological warheads yet, but he certainly had that capability and everyone knew it. He was hoping that the Israelis would strike back at Iraq, because once that happened the Arab members of the Allied Coalition would have no other political choice but to withdraw from the field. The Israelis were straining at the leash, and President Bush (Senior) didn't know how long he could hold them back. Operation Desert Storm was in danger of coming apart at the seams.

For lots of good reasons, we *had* to get those SCUDs.

It was a coal-black night over the western Iraqi desert, and my wingman and I were flying into the kill box at Shab al Hiri. We had taken off from a small airfield called Arar, situated in northern Saudi Arabia just a stone's throw from the Iraqi border and three hundred miles east of the Kingdom of Jordan. Arar was a civilian airport that had seen better days. It had only a single terminal and a few modest hangars, but the runway was a decent size and the surrounding terrain was comfortably flat. Select elements of the 160th were stationed there now, including Blackhawks, Little Birds, and Chinooks, along with our pilots and crews. There were medics and Para Jumpers on 24/7 standby, ready to scramble for Search and Rescues, and a team of operators for special-tactics missions. The command-and-control officers from Joint Special Operations Task Force had established a JOC. All the helo crews slept side by side on army cots in the "welcome" hall of the terminal, like bums in a bus station, but no one complained. The accommodations were pretty good for a combat zone.

This war had been ramping up since the Iraqis had invaded Kuwait in August, and those of us who had been invited were pleased to be there. But no one was happier about it than Cliff Wolcott. His innovative concept, the Direct Action Penetrator configuration of the Blackhawk—which had missed the party in Panama—was finally going to see some action. However, while Charlie Company and its DAPs had drawn the assignment to provide four of the gunships for SCUD hunting, they didn't have enough qualified pilots for this operation. So five of us from Delta Company—myself, Cliff, Clay Hutmacher, Eddie Mull, and Stan Wood—had been called upon to complete the package.

We had hit the ground running, having deployed to Arar from Dahran with our helos. Almost immediately, we went into action. About two hundred miles to our northwest, close to the Syrian border, the Iraqis were launching their SCUDs from the vast expanses of the western desert. During the day they would camouflage the missiles beneath netting or hide them in secret tunnels, under bridges, or in dry riverbeds called wadis, and in those thousands of square miles of mottled, barren terrain it was nearly impossible to find them. At night, they would roll them out on mobile Transporter Erector Launchers (TELs), fuel up their liquid propellant engines, launch, and head for the hills. It was a classic shoot-and-scoot technique, and the entire process from rollout to launch took only about ten minutes.

Locating a live SCUD was like finding the proverbial needle in the haystack, and destroying one *before* it was launched required excellent intelligence information, constant overhead surveillance, and immediate response from Allied assets in the area. *Everyone* was looking for them: space-based reconnaissance satellites, U2 and SR-71 spy planes, unmanned drones called UAVs, and deep-penetration teams from Britain's Special Air Service and U.S. Special Operations forces. Our DAP mission to locate the SCUDs was termed "armed reconnaissance," which is just a polite military phrase for "find 'em and kill 'em."

It was the first week of February and late one night when my copilot and I had geared up for a mission. Maybe back in the States the groundhog had already stuck his nose outside and announced an early spring, but here in the Middle East it was still cold as hell. The desert could be like a deceptive sponge, soaking up the rays of sun during the day and shimmering with warmth until you had to strip down to your T-shirt and shorts. But as soon as the sun set it was like the hand of God had squeezed all the heat from the rocks and sand, leaving a frigid wasteland with an atmosphere to match.

Lance Hill and I would be flying one Blackhawk in tandem with another DAP on an armed reconnaissance and escort mission, while Wolcott, Wood, Hutmacher, and Mull would remain behind with the other two birds on ready status. The missions could be fairly grueling, sometimes as long as six hours, and we had been rotating the teams on alternate nights. But so far we'd spotted nothing out there but Bedouin tents and camels.

As Lance and I hustled out the door of the terminal toward our helo, Cliff caught me by the elbow of my flight suit.

"If you see one out there," he said with that sly grin of his, "hold your fire. . . . It's *mine*."

"Yeah, right," I scoffed as I pulled away.

Up until that point, no Direct Action Penetrator had ever fired a shot in anger, and Cliff obviously wanted to be the one to break that cherry. Quite honestly, he deserved the privilege, but if we located a SCUD, I sure as hell wasn't going to hesitate for the sake of fairness.

"I'm telling you, Durant," he warned with a dead-serious scowl, even though he was half joking. "Don't you shoot the first load from my baby!"

"Roger that," I yelled back to him as I jogged for our bird. "If we spot a SCUD, I'll just take a picture of it and say *bang bang.*"

Cliff laughed, but I knew he was secretly hoping we'd have an engine failure during run-up.

We took off from Arar, looking to stir up some trouble wherever we could find it, while providing armed escort for a flight of CH-47 Chinooks. The night was black as a crow's feathers, and even under NVGs it blended into the desert landscape of undulating sand and shallow wadis. We kept the altitude at no more than a hundred feet as we swept due west, staying inside Saudi territory and just a mile from the Iraqi border. Every night we were changing our points of ingress and egress to avoid becoming predictable, and now we flew straight for twenty minutes and then banked hard to the right, rushing over the enemy's revetments and emplacements at 120 knots. For the entire stretch of the mission we'd be nearly hugging the ground and keeping the speed up, making it very difficult for mobile anti-aircraft batteries or even shoulder-fired missiles to lock onto our darting shadows as we roared overhead.

Once again, our Blackhawks were loaded to the maximum with fuel, wing-mounted 2.75-inch rocket pods, and thousands of rounds of minigun ammo. The 7.62mm miniguns were fixed forward on the DAPs, their trigger mechanisms directly linked to the switches on our pilots' sticks. The aiming devices for the six-barreled miniguns were AIM-1 infrared laser beams, and the half-dollar-sized green dots they threw on the target could only be seen using NVGs. Tracers for night-vision missions like these were also infrared, slotted into the ammunition carriers at a ratio of one tracer for every fourteen standard rounds. But at the rate those guns fired, the spaced tracers would look like stuttering beams of green.

In order to engage a SCUD or other significant ground target with a DAP, you would execute a technique called "running fire." Essentially, this meant aiming the whole helicopter at the enemy missile while you charged straight at it and opened up.

The entire inside of the DAP's cabin was filled with auxiliary internal fuel tanks and the crew chiefs barely had room to sit. In fact, as the huge rubber fuel blivets drained, the chiefs would have to wrestle with them to keep from being smothered in neoprene blubber. As we rode on into the night, lines of green Triple-A fire reached up from concentrated population areas and Iraqi military installations, trying to strike Coalition airplanes and helicopters from the sky. But we had plotted our legs carefully, and our plan worked well in skirting around those large fixed sites.

The Iraqi guns and missiles were hazardous, but the desert was potentially more lethal. It spread out before the cockpit in a quilt of soft-focus features, with very few indicators of changes in terrain height. Racing along at a hundred feet over the deck, you had to stay intensely focused and keep one eyeball on the radar altimeter, because if you were off your game for even a second the ground could suddenly rise up and bite you in the face. It was sort of like playing "Sudden Death Nintendo," where you couldn't afford to lose—not even once.

After about two hours, the Chinooks had reached their designated landing zone. We set up an overhead cap, keeping an eye out for potential threats to the vulnerable big birds as they landed and discharged their special ops cargo. I looked down at the enormous dust clouds kicked up by the massive helos as they touched down on the desert floor. And I was thinking how glad I was to be up here in the clear night sky instead of down there wrestling with that brown monster, when the Satcom crackled in my headset.

"Zulu Three-Two, this is Charlie Four-Seven."

It was Lieutenant Colonel Doug Brown, Battalion Commander of the 1st Battalion of the 160th, making contact from the JOC at Arar.

"Roger, Four-Seven," I answered. "Go ahead."

"I have a mission change for you, Three-Two," he said. Colonel Brown's voice was usually cold as ice water, but on this night he actually sounded a little keyed up. "Copy these coordinates."

"Roger that," I said, and as Lance continued the lazy orbit over the activities below, I repeated the coordinates back to Brown.

"You are cleared direct to the target, Three-Two," the Colonel ordered. "Target is a possible . . ." *Crackle-crackle-crackle.*

His transmission had broken up on the last word.

"Four-Seven," I said. "Say again all after coordinates."

"Roger that," Brown answered. "I say again. It is a possible . . ." *Crackle-crackle-crackle.*

Goddamn Satcom! I fumed. I keyed the mike button once more.

"Four-Seven, you are breaking up. Please spell all after . . ."

"Sierra! Charlie! Uniform! Delta!" Brown growled.

I was writing the letters of the phonetic alphabet as he spoke and had only gotten as far as "Uniform" when I realized the target was a SCUD. "Copy, the target is a SCUD," I replied, and after quickly entering the coordinates into our aircraft navigation system, I told Lance to roll out on a course direct to the objective. Our wingman did not have an operational Satcom, so I radioed the details to them as I led us down the route. I was Tactical Lead now, and I took the aircraft controls back from Lance and called on my wingman to pick up a combat spread, providing more visual coverage of the area before us. We raced "right on the deck" over flat desert wastes and the rocky mouths of twisting wadis.

Suddenly the wide, pale strip of the Damascus–Baghdad highway zipped beneath our cockpit, and then a high, multistrand power line loomed right in front of us. I pulled the bird up sharply, dove over it close to one of the massive towers, and looked straight out in front of the aircraft as we dropped back down. And there it was—the proverbial ten-point buck in the form of a TEL launcher, filling the windshield at twelve o'clock, its flank exposed from left to right and its fat missile just sitting there on the long multiwheeled trailer.

I reacted on pure instinct. We were so close that I didn't feel comfortable shooting rockets, because we might be engulfed by our own explosions. Anybody who knows me would understand that we had to be *very* close for me to make that call. So I opened up with the miniguns, strafing the missile and its carrier with hundreds of rounds of 7.62mm. *Sorry about that, Cliff!* I thought—with just a shred of remorse—as the barrels on both flanks of the cockpit spat flame and buzzed like chain saws, their heavy bullets punching into the missile's skin and the trailer. But it happened so fast that before I knew it, I was banking hard to avoid any ricochets and descending even closer to the desert floor, trying to find cover in the desolate expanse. We came around hard for another pass. I could see our wingman roaring in over the target, peppering it with his own miniguns as I rolled in behind him for my second run.

But on this run I took my time, lining it up, making sure that we'd hammer that SCUD from its aft engines to its nose cone and have plenty of time to get off at least one pair of high-explosive rockets. I glanced down at the Forward-Looking Infrared picture as Lance tracked the SCUD through our turn, then shifted my focus back to my NVGs, placed our AIM-1 dots on the target, and slowly pressed the fire button as I whispered, *This Bud's for you, Saddam. . . .*

Nothing happened. The guns didn't fire. I pressed the fire button again.

Nothing.

What the . . . ? Then I hit the rocket switch, and still nothing.

We had missed that pass completely, and I broke hard again off the target to try to sort things out. As we rolled back around, I could see our wingman as he kept on having a go at it, his miniguns firing smoothly like they were brand new out of the box. I knew I'd pushed the correct firing switches, so I assumed that Lance hadn't armed the weapons properly. In my most tactful voice I said, "Lance, it's only one fucking switch. Put it to arm and leave it there."

He cycled the switch and said, "You're armed."

All right, I said to myself. *Let's try this again.*

And again, the weapons would not fire. We began to troubleshoot the system. I figured that maybe my "fun" switches had failed for some reason, so I turned it over to Lance and told him to nail that SCUD to the desert floor. As we came in low and fast again, *he* fired.

Nothing.

"Mine are dead too!"

Dead in the water! The guns wouldn't work. I couldn't believe it. Every swinging pilot in the Free World was desperately searching for one of these targets, and here we had found one and now we couldn't fire on it! I felt like an impotent man at an orgy. I was absolutely livid. Our wingman was having a party out there and we couldn't shoot another single round, so I told Lance to pull off to the east to stay out of the way and bring it to a hover. There might have been Iraqi troops crawling all over the place and they could have opened up on us at any second, but I didn't see anybody. I pulled out a screwdriver and started working furiously, yanking the gun control box out of the console, trying desperately to find the problem. I removed all the cannon plug connectors off the back of the box and tried to dislodge any sand that might have gotten in there to spoil my show. We checked every circuit breaker, connector, and switch in the front and back of the aircraft. Then I pushed the damn gun control box back into the console, took over the controls, lined up again on the SCUD, and pulled the trigger.

Nothing.

"Goddamn sonuvabitch!" I cursed.

But there was clearly nothing to be done. We'd have to return to base and get the maintenance crews to troubleshoot the damn system. I was infuriated, but after a while I calmed myself down, reasoning that we'd get plenty more chances at SCUDs. I made a call on the Satcom that we had engaged a SCUD TEL, but the fact that there were no secondary explosions and no support vehicles left us all wondering exactly what we'd found. By the time we returned to Arar, I was almost levelheaded again. Of course, as soon as we landed, we alerted the maintenance crews to the fact that we'd had a gun malfunction and the word spread pretty quickly. As I made my way back to the JOC, Cliff, Stan, and Clay were waiting for me outside the terminal like a pack of grinning hyenas.

"Heard you had a little gun problem," Cliff said.

"Yeah, yeah." I walked past them into the building, still steaming.

"You sure you remember which buttons to push?" Clay called.

"It's that little red one," Stan added.

"Yeah, the one I showed you a picture of on your first day of gunnery training, assholes," I answered.

Man, were they having a good time at my expense. But it was already near dawn, we'd been flying for six hours, and I was smoked, so I muttered a few oaths and crawled into my rack. When I got up the next day I skipped breakfast and went right out to the maintenance hangar, carrying a cup of coffee. And of course they were all out there, standing around my Blackhawk and looking at me with shit-eating grins. Even my crew chief was having a hard time suppressing a smirk.

"We checked it out, Sir," he said. "Guns work just fine."

I threw up my hands before they could all work me over.

"All right, all right," I said. "I don't know what the hell happened out there, but it wasn't procedures, that's for sure." No one said anything as I jabbed a finger at them. "But next time, I'm gonna *nail* one of those bastards."

"Not before *I* do," said Cliff. He was *so* enjoying this.

The waiting for the next mission was interminable, but we finally took off again on the following night. This mission was a little different. We were out there on pure armed reconnaissance, looking for action. And again, we rolled in on a TEL launcher, watching the SCUD's form grow fat in our NVGs, locking dead onto it, double-checking our arming procedures. I pressed the trigger, knowing those miniguns were going to work just perfectly and spew thousands of rounds into that missile . . .

Nothing.

I nearly punched my Nomex glove right through the windscreen. I cursed and sputtered. I switched controls with Lance and prayed that he'd have more luck. But neither the guns nor the rockets would fire, and we were left circling around the target like some toothless, prehistoric reptile while *again* our wingman went to town on an Iraqi missile. I was beyond outrage as we just sat there and watched.

"I'm a goddamn kamikaze!" I fumed out loud. "I'm gonna crash this frigging helicopter right into that target!"

"Uh, Sir?" One of my crew chiefs spoke to me in the tone of a concerned psychologist. "There's folks in the back here, you know."

Of course, I wasn't serious about a suicide run, but I guess I shook the crew chiefs up a little. Still, they were motivated professionals and I doubt that's what spurred them on into discovering the gun problem, although they certainly went to work the next morning with enthusiastic vigor. In spite of the incredible hazing I was getting from my pilot comrades, the chiefs didn't really believe that I'd screwed anything up. They also realized that the guns seemed to work fine when the aircraft was cold, so they pushed it into one of the hangars, applied electrical power to the systems, and just watched and waited.

After two hours, the gunnery system overheated and the triggers wouldn't function. A simple electronic component had failed, nothing more sophisticated than a single transistor. The chiefs piled into a Humvee, drove into downtown Arar, found a local Saudi version of Radio Shack, and bought the component.

From that moment on, the weapons worked fine. I was ready to go SCUD hunting in earnest.

LIKE MOST AMERICANS, I watched the beginning of Operation Desert Storm on television.

But that certainly wasn't what I had expected to be doing on the night of January 17, 1991—sitting there in my living room in Clarksville, Tennessee, staring at the TV screen. I leaned forward in my armchair, downing my third beer and shaking my head as hundreds of antiaircraft batteries in Baghdad loosed off thousands of Triple-A rounds at our aircraft. For a special operations pilot who should have been at the point of the spear, I felt like I'd just had my wings clipped. At that very moment I was supposed to be flying a Blackhawk on a lightning raid into the heart of Kuwait City. But I was sitting on the bench, because only a few weeks before, what would have been our most hazardous mission to date had been canceled.

In the early-morning hours of August 2, 1990, nearly a thousand tanks of the Iraqi Republican Guard had punched across the Kuwaiti border in a *blitzkrieg* invasion reminiscent of Germany's attack on Poland in 1939. Within minutes of the start of the armored assault, companies of Iraqi commandos were leaping from helicopters onto the rooftops of Kuwait City. By dawn, most of the Kuwaiti Army had been defeated, its officers and men killed or captured, its survivors fleeing across the southern borders into Saudi Arabia. The Iraqi incursion had been so rapid and unexpected that many foreign nationals were trapped inside the Kuwaiti capital—among them half the staff of the American Embassy, which was cut off and surrounded.

In Washington, U.S. government leaders gasped as images of Tehran and the 1980 American hostage crisis leapt to their minds. But the Army leadership wasn't having flashbacks to the tragedy of

Desert One. United States Special Operations Command had been preparing for this for years.

The Night Stalkers had become an integral element of any hostage-rescue mission. We had proved that capability in Panama with the rescue of Kurt Muse, and in between Just Cause and Desert Storm we were constantly honing our ability to suppress hostile resistance at a given target, deliver a special tactics package, support that mission, and get everyone out. On a personal level, I had taken it upon myself to raise the level of our Blackhawk pilots' performance another notch. Watching the Little Bird pilots harangue one another over the smallest mistakes during post-op debriefs was often not a pleasant experience, but there was something to be emulated there. It might be emotionally scarring, but it was therapeutically wise, a way to force a pilot to strive to do better and never make the same mistake twice.

This is what our newly created Blackhawk gun platoon needs to do, I decided. *Stop being so polite to each other and tell it like it is.*

At that time we were fielding the first DAPs, and if you were going to fly a gun platform there was absolutely no room for error. When you shoot very close to your own personnel on the ground, you've got to be extremely disciplined and precise, because if you make a mistake, people are going to die. I was determined that we would be on a par with the Little Bird gun pilots: shoot as well as they did, execute the mission as precisely, and be just as brutal in the debriefs. I was going to note every mistake that any of us made and take appropriate action. In short, I became a real pain in the ass, but for good reasons.

Yet in spite of my sometimes obsessive personality, the other men around me were A-types as well, and no grudges were held in the pursuit of perfection. The intensely bonded brotherhood that would one day deploy to Somalia was already taking shape. I had returned early from Panama to train Stan Wood, who had just graduated from Green Platoon. Stan's background was similar to mine. He hailed from a small town in Pennsylvania and had enlisted into the Rangers right out of high school. But he aspired to fly helicopters, and after four years of humping infantry gear he had made it into flight school and worked his way up to the Night Stalkers. Due to the fact that most of our personnel were still down in Panama, our instruction time together was one-on-one and our friendship had begun. Stan was a good stick and a cool character, unflappable as a rodeo cowboy, and the guy could just flat-out navigate with a map like nobody I'd ever seen.

Dan Jollota came aboard at about the same time, just a few months later. He didn't have the Clark Gable mustache Stan had at the time, but he definitely had the movie star's ears. He was physically tall and looked like he was made of steel, but he was friendly by nature, loyal to the bone, and intensely focused in the cockpit. Dan was a team builder. He had started his army career as a military policeman, then volunteered for Special Forces, and had spent three years as a member of the Golden Knights, the Army's highly elite parachute demonstration team. He had so many HALO jumps under his belt that he had lost count after twenty-five hundred. Like most of us, Dan was always looking for the next rung on the ladder and had gone to flight school in 1986. By 1990, he was a Night Stalker. He hailed from California, which I tried not to hold against him.

A few months after Stan and Dan got to the unit, we rolled right into our next contingency. The mission to rescue the Americans surrounded and cut off in our embassy in Kuwait City was when it all finally came together for USSOCOM. This was going to be the other end of Desert One, when American forces had been ill-prepared and ill-equipped to perform that mission. This time we were going to get it right.

The American personnel in the embassy compound were surrounded by Republican Guard troops, Saddam Hussein's Secret Police, and an Iraqi armored division. The mission would require simultaneous strikes across Kuwait City to prevent the Iraqis from assaulting the compound at H-hour. F-117A Stealth Fighters and F-15E Strike Eagles would be launching from Saudi bases to knock out air defenses and electrical power, plunging select city sectors into darkness.

The assault force would consist of thirty helos launching from a Navy amphibious assault ship in the Persian Gulf called an LPH. The ship was a vintage aircraft carrier, the flat top now used for helo support. No helicopter squadron of our size had ever been launched from an LPH. As planning progressed, it was decided that half of our helos would take off from the ship and circle on station, while the other half was brought up from below decks. There the rotors would be unfolded and assembled and the second wave would launch, while the first came back in for refueling. After that, the entire air squadron would assemble over the Gulf and move out.

All kinds of assets were involved. There were special mission units, Rangers, SEALs, and Air Force Special Tactics Personnel. On the ground in Kuwait City, infiltrated intelligence personnel would relay updates. Just before H-hour, an encrypted signal would be transmitted to the embassy, telling all the personnel to move to a secure area.

Cliff and I would be flying the DAPs for this mission, he in the first bird over the beach and me in the second, and we'd hit the target just as the air war began. We would have no customers on board our two attack aircraft, just fuel, ammunition, and rockets armed with high explosives and antipersonnel "flechettes" — 2,200 one-inch-long steel darts per warhead. My primary target was to take out the Iraqi guard barracks along the north wall of the embassy compound, wiping out the Iraqis before they could turn on our people. We rehearsed it and rehearsed it. We practiced the carrier liftoff from an LPH off the coast of Florida, then assaulted a full-scale mock-up of the embassy that had been built in a secret location just inland from the Atlantic. But we couldn't use live ammunition outside of a designated military range facility. We saved that for the final rehearsal at Fort Bragg in early December.

That night, it seemed as if every general officer in our food chain was there. All of the assets, including the fighter support, were involved, and it was our last chance to nail it down before deploying for the mission. We launched the mock raid against another scale model of the embassy and its environs, flying under NVGs, and everything had to be super tight. Cliff roared in and took out his targets, while I attacked the "Iraqi" barracks buildings and let loose with ten pairs of HE rockets. The customers had landed so close that they were only fifty meters from my targets and there was no room for error. But the whole thing came off about as perfectly as it could, with only minor wrinkles to iron out before we deployed.

When I walked into the debrief a couple of folks asked me if I was the guy who had rocketed those barracks buildings. I admitted to it, but I wasn't sure if maybe I had screwed the pooch somehow and a very public ass-chewing was in the offing. But then General Carl Stiner, the commander in chief of Special Operations Command, got up and addressed the assembly of officers from every branch of the services.

"I don't know who took out those barracks buildings," he said. "But I wouldn't want to be in there when that pilot shows up in Kuwait."

It was probably the proudest moment of my professional career at that point, but my enjoyment of it was short-lived. The next night, Saddam Hussein agreed to the release of all American personnel from the embassy and the operation was canceled. Yet I don't remember hearing a single sigh of relief, even though intelligence estimates had predicted a possible 30 percent casualties. Clay Hutmacher had been slated to fly the SAR bird, and with so many predicted casualties he knew that the odds of his coming back alive were low, but he only cursed the cancellation. Plenty of pilots, crews, and special operators had known that this might be their last mission, but just like Clay, Cliff, and myself, they all kicked the ground in disappointment. I'll never forget how, after being briefed on the risks involved, I had looked around the room and noted that not a single pilot, crew chief, or customer had backed away from the table and said they couldn't go. I knew right then and there that if I had to, these were the kind of people I wanted to go to war with and God have mercy on the poor souls we decided to take on.

There was disappointment in the fact that we would not be able to execute our plan. It was very good to know, however, that we could in fact pull off such an "impossible" mission. We told ourselves that sometime, somewhere, in this world of low-intensity conflict, wild dictators, and terrorists, we pilots would fly this mission for keeps. As our commander Herb Rodriguez said during his assumption of command ceremony in the summer of 1993, "It is not a matter of if we will go to war. It is a matter of when."

I DID NOT HAVE long to drink beer, watch TV, and brood. As the SCUDs kept on launching, our beepers went off and we were on our way to the war after all. We deployed with our helos aboard C-5As and made our way to Dahran on January 31, then waited while our crew chiefs and maintenance men "built up" our birds, then fueled and armed them. We spent one long night in a hangar in Dahran, while the sirens went off and television reporters tried to decide whether to take pictures or take cover. The drill was to don your gas mask and leave it on until someone sounded an "all clear." Those masks are far from comfortable, but when you've been flying aboard a C-5A for sixteen hours, all keyed up for impending combat, nature eventually takes its course. Still wearing my mask, I lay down on a cot and fell into a dead sleep, and I didn't wake up until a crew chief shook me to announce that our birds were ready to go.

The next day we received our orders to deploy to Arar, so we piled into our helos and started out on the first leg to KKMC, the Coalition airstrip at King Khalid Military City. During the flight an enormous sandstorm suddenly kicked up, its howling winds so powerful and its twisters of grit so impenetrable that we had no choice but to climb out of it. Our engines were designed to discharge any sand so we were in no danger of flaming out, but we just couldn't see a damn thing. I contacted the air controller at KKMC and told him we'd "punched into the sand," while we climbed up to ten thousand feet. It was not a good spot to be in, that slice of the sky where Iraqi surface-to-air missiles could lock on and kill you. But by that time we had Global Positioning Systems in our helo, which certainly made it easier to shoot an instrument approach into the airfield. We landed and waited for the *hamsin* to clear before continuing on to Arar.

Now that sandstorm was a distant memory because we'd already engaged our first targets, and although I suffered frustration and near humiliation over my weapon system problems, those first bursts from my miniguns and my wingman's follow-up had paid off. Together we had disabled that SCUD, and even better, we had it on tape.

Major General Wayne Downing, the commander of the Joint Special Operations Task Force, recovered the tapes from us and personally flew them down to General Norman Schwarzkopf's headquarters in Riyadh. The SCUD launches were throwing wrenches into all of Schwarzkopf's plans, and his mood was particularly foul. He was infuriated by the Coalition's inability to stop them, and he hadn't believed Downing's telephoned report that 160th DAPs had nailed a SCUD.

It was the crowning moment for Cliff Wolcott's concept. Some years before, Schwarzkopf had taken Downing to task for pushing the idea of mounting rockets, miniguns, and "whatever else" on Night Stalker Blackhawks. But while Schwarzkopf was a "ground-pounder" and inherently suspicious of all special operations types, Downing believed in Cliff's innovation and had approved the DAP program anyway. Now, as Schwarzkopf skeptically viewed the tapes from our gun cameras, his infamous scowl broke into a wide grin and he actually danced around his war room. The tapes were immediately copied and couriered to Washington. The 160th SOAR had scored the first

helicopter kill against a SCUD. In fact, Schwarzkopf paid us a personal visit during his victory tour prior to our redeployment back to
the States.

But our safari continued, even as the volume of SCUD launches
began to drop off. Saddam was rapidly depleting his inventory, and
with so many Coalition air and ground assets assigned to the search-
and-destroy mission, only the bravest or most foolhardy Iraqis were
still attempting to launch. We took out a few more of the missiles,
and probably some decoys as well, but they were getting harder to
find as H-hour for the ground campaign approached.

Meanwhile, we were hardly the only element of the 160th operating in-theater. Night Stalker MH-47 pilots flew countless missions
behind enemy lines, maneuvering their huge twin-rotor Chinooks to
deposit Special Forces teams along with their heavily armed, desert
dune buggies. The big birds were very vulnerable to ground fire, but
those pilots never quit.

And Night Stalker Blackhawk pilots pulled off some incredible
deeds of daring that would never make the nightly news. Shortly before the ground war was to begin, a three-man Special Forces reconnaissance team was discovered in its "hide site" by Bedouin
villagers, nearly two hundred miles behind Iraqi lines. Soon the Special Forces men were engaged in a firefight with armed militia, while
members of an Iraqi infantry division bore down on them. They took
cover in a ditch next to a highway and called for emergency extraction, but they were running out of ammo and facing the end. Then
one of our 3rd Battalion pilots showed up, screaming down the highway in his Blackhawk, six feet off the deck. The SF men popped
smoke, but there was a 120-foot power line between them and the
bird. The crew yanked the helo into a climb, rolled over the line, and
landed, picking up the team while the crew chiefs held off hundreds
of Iraqis with their miniguns. When they returned to base, the helo
was so shot up that it was out of commission for a week.

On the night of February 21, we took off on another armed re-

connaissance mission. I was flying with Lance Hill again, with another Blackhawk as our lead. The SCUD hunt was intensifying as the
targets became more elusive—all of the DAPs would be in the air
that night. Wolcott and Wood, Hutmacher and Mull had already
launched two hours earlier. In addition to that, a contact had come
into the JOC from a team of customers deep inside Iraqi territory. A
special operator had been seriously injured downrange, and two of
our Blackhawks were dispatched on an evacuation mission, carrying
medics and emergency supplies. The lead bird was being piloted by
two more of my friends, CW3 Mike Anderson and his platoon leader,
Captain Chuck Cooper. It was going to be a very busy evening.

Conditions that night were zero-illum, no moon and no stars, and
a thick quilt of clouds that made for a flat, ominous ceiling stretch-
ing to all points of the compass. As we followed our designated pattern through our kill box, lines of Triple-A fire crawled up to the
clouds from distant Iraqi batteries, but that was no longer of much
concern. The ground appeared to be the only enemy this night, as
we spotted no SCUDs or any other targets of value.

We were four hours into the mission when we began to pick up
some precipitation on the windshield. I checked the outside air temperature, and sure enough we were hovering close to thirty-two degrees, so I knew that the spatter was freezing rain. We turned on all
of our anti-icing equipment and pressed on, but as we approached
some higher terrain and had to gain altitude, the droplets turned into
sticky snow and started coming down hard. The lead bird called us
on the internal net.

"Zulu Three-Two, you'd better tighten it up."

"Roger that," I answered.

We pulled our helo in to about one rotor disk separation, maybe
fifty feet, closing formation so we wouldn't lose sight of each other
in the growing storm. The snow was starting to pelt even harder now,
and we made the decision to go for some altitude and avoid any
unanticipated obstacles on the ground, but that just made the desert

harder to see in the darkness and obscuration. Yet we really had no choice but to press on. If we climbed high enough to execute an instrument recovery back into Arar, we'd be vulnerable to the Iraqi mid- and high-altitude air defense systems. If we landed to wait out the storm, we could be overrun by ground troops before our blades stopped turning. But soon we had reached the "bingo" point of our fuel consumption, and we slipped into the return route back toward Saudi Arabia.

The temperature rose as we flew south and the precipitation stopped, but the visibility was still deteriorating, and as we tuned up the combat controller frequency at the airfield, a dense fog had begun to roll into Arar.

"Zulu Three-Two, it's getting pretty thick down here," the controller warned me. "Visibility's down to one mile."

Well, that wasn't great, but it was good enough to come in without using a GPS instrument approach. We spotted the runway, its black strip barely discernible beneath a blanket of shifting steam, and as we settled onto the tarmac a dense cloud of fog enveloped the helo like the hand of a giant ghost. We had made it home just in time.

We tied up the bird and made our way back to the terminal, which had become sort of a Night Stalker "mall" with everything in a single large space: the barracks, chow hall, entertainment area, and the JOC. True to our new tradition, we beat each other up over the smallest mistakes we had made, then wound down a bit and hit our racks.

I lay there in my bunk, looking over at Mike Anderson's empty sleeping bag. He should have been in it by then, but having just flown through that midnight soup out there, I reasoned that his medevac mission might take longer than expected. As I closed my eyes and drifted off to sleep, I knew that he and Cooper would have a significant challenge getting back through the fog. Fortunately, they had plenty of fuel and could divert, if necessary, to an A-10

Warthog base located south of Arar. It looked like, worst case, they'd simply have to spend the night there and recover to Arar the next day.

Mike's bunk was still empty when I woke up in the morning. I could see out the terminal windows that it was a fine day. The sun was shining and most of the fog had burned off. Yet there was an air of gloom in the huge room, something not quite right, and I grunted a "good morning" to a passing crew chief.

"Not really," he replied. "We lost a bird last night. Anderson's bird. There were no survivors."

The price of conflict and war hit me in the face like a round-house punch. I looked over at Anderson's empty bunk, and at Cooper's. What was it that Mike Anderson and I had been laughing about the day before? Oh yeah, Chuck Cooper had gotten himself a buzz cut. And now all those small details of their lives were suddenly so insignificant, just ancient history.

Now the lives of so many people would be changed forever. Anderson's and Cooper's crew chiefs, Mario Vega-Velazques and Chris Chapman, had also been killed in the crash, along with the recovery team and special operator they had tried so valiantly to rescue. More innocent children would grow up without fathers, the kind of men who would have made such fine role models. The kind of patriots we needed more of in America. Instead, we had less.

I had little time to grieve, as I was assigned to the accident investigation team. Every accident team had to have an instructor pilot aboard, and it was my turn to go. Later that day, we drove out to the crash site.

Anderson and Cooper had made it back to within a few miles of the airfield, then had slammed into the ground in the middle of what appeared to have been a right-hand turn. I was amazed at the conclusions that were so quickly drawn by the Safety Center experts on our team. The blade tips had touched the ground, then the nose had hit and the bird had flipped end over end, crushing the cockpit and killing everyone aboard. But we would never know exactly what had happened in those final seconds. We would never know if a critical component had suddenly failed, or perhaps why the crew's attention had been diverted long enough for those hundred feet of altitude to suddenly evaporate. All that was left were Anderson's and Cooper's final radio transmissions, and the emotional devastation that would spread from their crash, like the waves from a heavy rock thrown into a placid pond.

I stood there in the desert, looking at the twisted black hulk of the helicopter, while the sun warmed the sand and the sky above turned so clear and blue. And I thought of how the earth could be such a jealous mistress.

She would allow you to leave her, over and over again. And then one day when you returned, she would crush you to death in one last embrace.

Chapter 13

WELCOME THREATS

October 13, 1993

I LONGED FOR THE SOUNDS of Night Stalker helicopters, but there was nothing in the air.

The days of my captivity had begun to run together. Two more of them had passed, but now the significance of each day's small events had begun to diminish. There were fewer notations in my blank Bible pages, fewer meaningful details to recall. I had kept up the ruse, writing my secret codes whenever I could, but I'd started to wonder about the value of it all. Would the Army really want to know at which hour I'd eaten? If my prison had been cleaned up or not? When my captors had seemed hostile, or why Firimbi had laughed? I had noted the appearance of my visitors and their apparent motives, while beginning to wonder if I'd ever get the chance to go home and translate my encoded journal. With the help of the radio, I was painfully aware of the days of the calendar and had marked each blank page with a date. Yet now those days had started to blur into slow-motion orbits of waiting, changed only by darkness and light.

I did not note my emotions. No combat pilot includes them in his after-action reports.

The atmosphere in the compound had become strangely calm. Gunfire was rarer and my guards seemed more relaxed, yet that lifting of tension seemed only to increase my sense of irritation. I felt less threatened, yet more frustrated. Being a problem-solver by nature, I'd always had a powerful drive to fix things rather than bitch about them. But here I was, stuck in a situation over which I had no control, my fate completely in the hands of others.

The Somalis hadn't deemed it necessary to move me again, and at least that was a good thing. But the pain in my leg was horrendous, probably because the broken bones had now overlapped by more than two inches, the muscles atrophying and nerves twitching to compensate for the damage. My spine was locked stiff and I'd discovered more shrapnel buried in my leg, the shards of metal cocooned inside knots of swollen flesh. But I still prayed that my buds would show up. They could haul me out of there any way they wanted, and I would welcome the agony.

It was Wednesday, the eleventh day of my captivity, and ever since Sunday and the roaring flyover of the Task Force I'd been racking my brain to come up with some sort of plan that might help them locate me. I had searched that room a hundred times, scanning each corner of it and every object from where I lay, looking for something I could use as a signal. One night while Firimbi was sleeping, I stared at his flickering oil lamp for quite a while, wondering if I could quietly crawl over and retrieve it. When the helos showed up again, maybe I could set fire to the room! Then I remembered that the floor was embedded with kerosene. Firimbi would flee, and the flies with him, while I immolated myself and got sent home in a box—a very *small* box.

Then I considered the possibility of grabbing the lamp, somehow pulling myself out the window, and crawling up onto the roof. If there were "eyes in the sky" or an overflying helo, maybe they would spot me waving the lantern.

Who are you kidding, Durant? I said to myself as I scratched that idea. *You can't even sit up or take a crap without help, and you're gonna climb up on the roof?*

I could just imagine all the guards standing out there in the courtyard, watching me struggle as they laughed their heads off. "Should we shoot his ass now? Or wait till he almost makes it up there?"

The only decent solution I came up with involved my army T-shirt. The Somalis had taken it away sometime after my video interrogation, and now I thought that maybe I could get them to wash it. They would have to hang it up somewhere to dry, hopefully outside in the courtyard. The chances of my comrades seeing it from the air were slim to none, but on the other hand, who knew? Maybe some slick Intel kid back in the JOC would spot it on a surveillance monitor and go nuts: "Sir! I've got Durant's T-shirt hanging from an olive tree!" I tried to make Firimbi understand what I wanted.

"My T-shirt," I said to him on Monday morning, as I pointed to my bare chest and then sketched the shape of the shirt in the air.

"Tee shoot?"

"*Camisa*," I said in Spanish. Then I gestured at the sliver of soap sitting in my dog bowl and mimed a whole scene of scrubbing, rinsing, and hanging.

"Ahh, *camisa!*" He nodded enthusiastically. "Yes, yes!"

I never did see that T-shirt again.

The musical dedications on the radio continued, but they ebbed and flowed, causing me to speculate. When the requests dropped off altogether, I had some uncomfortable hours, wondering if maybe someone out there was pissed off at me for the comments I'd made to the reporters. When the songs started up again, I imagined my comrades gearing up for a rescue mission and listened closely for any kind of signal. My wife's statement was broadcast again and again, and while it boosted my spirits, I wondered if the Army should have put a stop to it. Had I still been facing interrogations, the sound of her voice might have weakened my resistance.

My mood was affected mostly by things I heard: a song on the radio or a piece of news. But on Monday morning, it had been another sort of sound that had lifted my spirits. The compound started to vibrate, and then the screaming engines of jet aircraft roared over the city at rooftop level. I could tell they were fast-movers—a Navy F-18 and an A-6, as I'd find out later—which meant that an aircraft carrier had anchored off the coast. I made a notation in my Bible.

"Upping the ante."

That night, my friend Dan's wife "sang" me a lullaby. A dedication for me came into the Armed Forces Network from the 9th Battalion of the 101st. Jane Jollota was a company commander in the 9th and she knew that one of my favorite songs was "Paradise by the Dashboard Light." I went to sleep with a smile, serenaded by the gravelly voice of Meat Loaf.

On Tuesday I had taken myself to task, deciding that for a thirty-two-year-old helo pilot, I was already getting lazy in my old age. I was lying there like a slug, not doing enough to ensure my own survival, and had to get my butt in gear. First, I started drinking as much water as Firimbi could deliver. He complied without complaint, even though it would mean doubling my piss calls. Then I decided to get down to some serious exercise. I couldn't sit up, but I could reach the ledge of the window, so I grabbed it with my left hand and flexed my muscles over and over, trying to lift my weight just an inch off the bed. I switched arms and repeated the exercise until I could feel that my heart rate was up, then cupped my fingers into each other and pulled isometrically until I finally had to lie back down again, sweating as if I'd run five kilometers.

Firimbi decided that I needed a bath. It had become sort of a daily ritual now, so I took no notice of it until he insisted on washing my hair. He had done that only once before, prior to my Red

Cross visit, but I squashed my speculations about any twist of fate. While he rinsed me off in my dog bowl, I turned on the radio and heard a report from the BBC that the Somali Clan Elders had met and were discussing my unconditional release. But by that point I had learned to ignore all such "rumors." The Somali National Alliance was turning out to have similarities to every other army; everyone talked about Christmas, but you couldn't believe it unless Santa showed up.

Instead of St. Nick, I got Dr. Kediye. He looked me over and changed all my dressings, then talked about putting a full plaster cast on my leg.

"Roger that, Doc," I responded.

But by my tone of voice and the way my arms were crossed over my chest, he must have known that his chances of getting a cast on me were about the same as taking a steak bone away from a pit bull.

Yet I was stunned and very thankful when the doc rummaged in his tackle box and handed me two photographs. Somehow, one snapshot of Lorrie and one of Joey had made it to the Red Cross. I waited until Kediye left, and then I stared at my family for an hour, slowly caressing their images with my fingers, like a blind man touching velvet.

The doc had also left me with a new MRE and a box of milk, the kind that allegedly requires no refrigeration. I made the mistake of eating the army rations and downing the entire milk carton, reasoning that with bone damage even a meager dose of calcium would be helpful. By evening, I was sick as a dog. My stomach churned, I was racked with chills, and Firimbi had earned another combat medic decoration. When I finally fell asleep, my rumbling intestines must have sounded like helo rotors to my brain, because the nightmares came in full force.

For some reason, in my dream I was not a Blackhawk pilot.

I was a young Ranger, a "straight-leg" infantryman, and I had the distinct feeling of being the new guy, not fully aware of or in tune with what was happening around me. My chalk was deep inside enemy territory and we'd just been in combat, but now the firefight was over and we were into the consolidation phase. The helos were coming back in for us.

The Blackhawks were roaring in low and fast, appearing out of the night sky. I was supposed to be on the last helo, Chalk Four, and I was trying to find my chalk leader and get to the aircraft. But my legs just wouldn't move me along. It was like my feet were stuck in molasses, my gear so heavy that each step was an impossible effort. Everything around me was happening so fast and I knew that I wasn't doing what I was supposed to, trying so hard to get it done and feeling so helpless and frustrated by failure.

And then I was moving *backward*. With every attempted step, the image of the helos and my comrades scrambling aboard moved farther and farther away into a slowly shrinking black tunnel. I was yelling for them to wait, but no sound emerged from my mouth. Everyone else was getting on the helos, but no matter how I tried, I just couldn't get any closer.

And then the lead bird took off. And then the second bird. And then the *third*. I was running now, trying frantically to reach the fourth Blackhawk, and it felt like my helmet and gear and ammo and grenades were all doubling in weight, dragging me down. And the ground just rolled beneath my feet like a treadmill, and I watched in horror as that last helo lifted off and disappeared into the night. . . .

It was as silent as a graveyard. Utter darkness. I looked desperately around as a cold chill rippled through my body and a wave of terror choked my throat. My heart was hammering, and I was hyperventilating, gripping my weapon in my sweat-soaked palms.

I had been left behind in enemy territory. All by myself.

I woke up gasping for air, my ears wide open like radar dishes, listening for the beating of helo blades. But those heavy thumps were all from my heart. There were no sounds other than the steady snores of Firimbi.

I did not want to dream again, and I did my best to resist sleep that night.

BY MIDMORNING on Wednesday, I sensed another shift in the atmosphere.

I had finally drifted off close to dawn, holding the photos of my family in one hand, my Bible clutched in the other. The visceral fears brought up by that nightmare had receded as I assured myself that no such thing could happen to me, nor to any other member of Task Force Ranger. Dan Jollota's promise from the sky was not hollow, but backed up by the determination of the team and my country. It was simply not acceptable in our special ops culture to leave a man behind, dead or alive, under any circumstances. That was part of what made it possible to do the job. You might be wounded, cut off from your comrades, surrounded by the enemy, but someone would be coming to get you. You might be killed in action, but you were going to be buried at home. To an outsider it might appear foolish to risk more lives for the sake of one, but that was the core of our creed, the essence of honor.

For some reason on that morning, the requests for me were pouring into the radio station. That immediately lifted my mood, but I also took note that Firimbi and his men seemed somehow more animated. I could hear a change in the tone of their Somali exchanges throughout the crumbling hacienda, more movement out in the courtyard. I was already feeling better after my intestinal storm of the previous day, drinking lots of water to counter the dehydration, when the chatter suddenly died. I turned off the radio as Minister Abdi arrived, in broad daylight.

The entire compound fell into silence as he entered my room. I had slipped my pen beneath my leg and tucked my Bible under my blanket—Abdi was sharp, and I didn't want to give him even a hint of what I was doing. He stood just inside the doorway, his fingers laced behind his back. He inspected the room and then focused on me with a deep frown, as if I were the catalyst of so much trouble that he didn't know how to begin without losing his cool.

"Morning, Mr. Minister." I tried to break the ice.

"Mr. Durant." He nodded as he thought for a moment, then asked almost reluctantly, "Any requests?"

His tone was almost ominous, like something you'd ask a prisoner just before execution. So I just shook my head politely and offered him a thumbs-up. He squinted at me and left the room, followed by his bodyguards and Firimbi. I could hear the Minister snapping at them as he strode into the courtyard, and then a gate opened and a car moved away.

I had no idea what had fouled up the Minister's morning, but I took out my Bible and made a quick notation.

Abdi—↓

I was still wondering what that was all about when Firimbi hurried back into the room, flicking his fingers at my radio with one hand and pointing at his ear with the other.

"BBC," he said excitedly. "BBC *now*."

I tuned to the British broadcast while Firimbi paced back and forth, watching me.

"The former American ambassador to Somalia, Robert Oakley," the announcer said in his clipped British accent, "has arrived in the Somali capital of Mogadishu to engage in talks on behalf of the U.S. government. Ambassador Oakley was apparently dispatched at the behest of President Clinton in order to maintain the tenuous cease-fire presently in effect between Somali militias and U.N. forces. And perhaps to secure the release of a U.S. helicopter pilot who was shot down and captured on October the third . . ."

Well, that was certainly good news. I was no great fan of the present administration, but I'd certainly be grateful for anything they tried to do to get me out of there. Yet I didn't understand why Firimbi seemed so happy about it. He was grinning and pointing at the radio.

"Oak-a-lee good! Oak-a-lee good!" he kept saying.

Two of the other guards had also come into the room, joining Firimbi in his apparent optimism.

"Yes, Oak-a-lee good!" one of them said. "Howe, very baadddd."

He was referring to the present commander of U.N. forces in the Mog, Admiral Jonathan Howe. The admiral had retired from the Navy and served as a national security adviser to President Bush, and had subsequently been sent to Somalia to oversee U.N. relief and military operations. He was widely known as a Mohamed Aidid detractor, and the Somalis hated him in turn. They called him "*Animal* Howe."

"Oak-a-lee good," Firimbi said again as his guards grinned and stuck their thumbs up.

"Oak-a-lee shoot straighter," one of the younger guards said, and I couldn't help laughing at the reversal of "straight shooter."

"Animal Howe, baaad." They all nodded at each other and turned their thumbs down, looking like some African version of the Three Stooges. And I just smiled at them and nodded, not really understanding the significance of what was happening.

In fact, Ambassador Robert Oakley had already been in Mogadishu for some days. Back in March, his term as ambassador to Somalia had ended as the Clinton administration replaced President Bush's people with their own diplomats. Yet by October 5, the Clinton White House was in a panic and had summoned Oakley to a meeting, asking him to go back into the fray. Clinton and his national security team had already decided that Operation Gothic Serpent would stand down, and Oakley was to personally relay the message to the Somalis that the hunt for Aidid was over. In addition, he was to make every effort to have me released, unconditionally.

It would be some months until I learned exactly what had happened that morning in Mogadishu. But I would hear it directly from the ambassador himself, in the quiet, self-deprecating manner that is his style.

Mohamed Aidid was in hiding. He would not come out to meet with Oakley, so the ambassador had gone into Mogadishu to meet instead with the ranking members of the Habr Gidr clan. The tall, gracious diplomat had very little security with him, just a few courageous agents from the State Department's Diplomatic Security Service. They could all have been taken hostage or killed without much effort.

Oakley made his position very clear. There would be no deals. There would be no exchanges of prisoners. Either Mohamed Aidid would release me, immediately and unconditionally, or a rescue attempt would be made. He framed the rest of his message as a speculation rather than a threat.

"I imagine that such a raid will come sooner rather than later," he said. "And with massive U.S. forces gathering here each day, fighter aircraft and tanks and so forth, it will certainly be a tragedy. A large portion of your city will no doubt be destroyed, and perhaps Mr. Durant along with it. But the U.S. is not going to sit idly by and let the clock tick any longer."

Yet being a seasoned and veteran diplomat, Ambassador Oakley also knew how to follow a thinly veiled threat with a face-saving suggestion.

"On the other hand, if General Aidid releases Mr. Durant unconditionally," he added, "it will place the general in a positive light on the world stage. You have my word that the efforts to capture him will cease, and such a gesture may erase some of the damage done to his image as a result of the recent battle."

His meaning was clear: Do something good and maybe the world will stop thinking of all of you as savages.

I suspect now that that's why Minister Abdi was in such a foul mood that Wednesday morning. He had attended the meeting at which Ambassador Oakley had virtually threatened his leader and his clan with extinction, and it was a bitter pill to swallow. As I had lain there listening to the radio and reading Exodus, Oakley had been playing Moses to Aidid's Pharaoh. Maybe he hadn't exactly turned Aidid's walking stick into a snake, but when he said, "Let my pilot go," and threatened them with a plague of air strikes and armor, I'm pretty sure they felt the earth shake.

Yet at the time, to me the ambassador's arrival was just one more strange occurrence, another act in the three-ring circus that had become my captivity. I couldn't wholly ignore it, but I couldn't count on it, either. Yet I wondered if in the course of history any prisoner of war had ever experienced anything quite like this, and I doubted it. My captors had tortured, killed, and mutilated my comrades, then summoned medical attention to keep me alive. I had been tormented and interrogated, then taped for international television and had my interview comments splashed across headlines. My Task Force mates called out to me from the air, dedicated songs to keep my spirits up, and my wife spoke to me over the airwaves. Enemy dignitaries and officers came to visit me, couriers from the Red Cross delivered my mail. The might of America strained at its leash just outside my prison, while these Third World "primitives" who were holding me were as savvy as a New York PR firm, knowing exactly how to manipulate the media and use me for their own ends. It was more than bizarre, almost like a high-stakes game of international poker, with me lying there as the "pot" while everyone held their cards close, blustering and bluffing and tossing in an ace on occasion.

But it was the kind of celebrity only a fool would covet. If a genie had walked into my prison, I would have asked for only one wish: to be magically back in the States, sitting on a lake in a boat, with my son in my lap.

As the sun set that evening, the guns appeared again. The guards distributed the weapons and ammunition and moved on out to the courtyard, so there was no reason for me to assume that the situation had really changed. Colonel Kalif made a brief appearance, questioning me about my condition, but when he left I had the distinct feeling that he hadn't gone very far away. There was no way for me to know that with a resolution to my situation so close at hand, the SNA had become increasingly edgy, calling in reinforcements and surrounding the compound. If anything happened to me now, heads would roll.

It was very quiet that night. There were no machines of any kind in the air. The pretty house girl passed the open doorway, her tin jewelry ringing softly like a wind chime, her smile still shy. There were no children playing anywhere and no car horns honking, just the buzzing of my pet flies as they bounced off the scarred walls. I ate half a packet of beef from an MRE and was careful to drink plenty of bottled water. Firimbi bowed toward Mecca and prayed, then accepted my offer of a shot of hot sauce and smiled. He sat cross-legged on his mat while I lay on my bed, both of us reading our respective interpretations of the word of God. The oil lamp flickered ghostly patterns across the ceiling and walls. It seemed as if the entire city was holding its breath.

It was late when Minister Abdi returned. I had been reading the Bible rather than writing in it, so I placed it open against my chest. I gripped the edges of the bed frame and slid my body up a bit, making the pillow bunch up so I could raise my head.

Two visits in one day? I thought that might mean something good, but then I warned myself, *Don't jump the gun. He might be here to announce that you're being tried as a war criminal.*

But his demeanor was much different from what it had been that morning. He was as calm and relaxed as he had always seemed before. He murmured something in Somali, and Firimbi nodded and slipped behind him, out the door. Abdi's bodyguards faded away as well, leaving the two of us alone.

"I have some news for you, Mr. Durant," he said.

"I'm all ears, Mr. Minister," I said.

He smiled slightly at that. But actually, I was all nerve endings. I could feel them twitching just under my skin.

"The elders of the Somali National Alliance have convened." He folded his hands behind his back. "They have made a decision."

I did not say anything. I just watched him, waiting.

"You will go home tomorrow, Mr. Durant," he said. And then he added, "Unconditionally."

I could almost feel the walls of my defenses cracking, like thin fissures appearing in the face of a dam. I was trying like hell not to succumb to the incredible weight of his words, but suddenly all the images came tumbling forth, no matter what I told myself to keep them at bay. It was like what people always said about those last seconds before death, when your entire life flashes before your eyes. But I had already been "killed" in a Blackhawk crash and no such thing had happened on my way into the ground. Instead, it happened now.

I could smell the summer grass of New Hampshire again. I could feel the bite of the winter snow. I was inhaling cold clean air without a speck of desert dust in it or the stench of refuse and death. I saw my parents, my wife, my uncles, my cousins, and my childhood friends. I heard Christmas sleigh bells and the cheers of my comrades, and felt their fingers gripping my shoulders and slapping my back. I touched Joey's hair. I watched him raise his arms up for me, laughing. . . .

It all passed in an instant. And then I was there again, in that room, looking at Abdi. I wanted to believe him, but I couldn't, not completely. And not knowing how to respond, I repeated back to him the same Muslim phrase that he had used so often.

"*Insh' Allah*," I said. "If God wills it."

"It is no longer in the hands of God," he answered. "It is in the hands of General Mohamed Farrah Aidid."

Chapter 14

FREEDOM

October 14, 1993

"TODAY'S THE DAY."

That was the entry I made in my Bible that morning.

I had woken up to bright sunlight lancing through the window shutters and the sounds of birds chirping in the courtyard. The chill of dawn was still in the air and the flies had dwindled to just a few. Firimbi was not in the room, and remembering Abdi's promise of the night before, I had tuned in to the Armed Forces Network, hoping to hear some sort of formal announcement about my release. But before the news began, the DJ had something else to say.

"Good morning, Mogadishu . . . And here's a song dedicated to Mike Durant, from Donovan Briley."

I closed my eyes, laid my head back, and smiled. It was a perfect way to start an important day, and even as a melancholy country fiddle began the strains of "Seminole Wind," I set aside the song's sad theme and let Donovan's dedication take me away. Just that summer we had all been training out west, conducting live fire gunnery exercises with Delta and the Rangers, flying our helicopters from one end of the country to the other and back. John Anderson's tune about the loss of Native American lands had become a big hit. All of us liked it, and of course Donovan had played it over and over again, and hearing it now made me think of how maybe we'd all get a chance to go on another training mission like that one.

"So blow, blow Seminole wind,
Blow like you're never gonna blow again;
I'm calling to you like a long-lost friend,
But I don't know who you are . . ."

It was going to be an incredible reunion. Cliff and Donovan would be there, along with Dan and Stan and all the other guys who'd come through this mission okay. But it also wouldn't be easy, because we had lost some of our best men, and I knew that now for certain. Over the past few days, the radio had announced the gradual return of the remains of our comrades who'd been listed as missing in action. The numbers matched up, a total of five. Ray, Tommy, Bill, and those two Delta operators would at last be going home as well. Yet they would be making that final journey in flag-draped coffins, carried by solemn honor guards of our brothers-in-arms. No, it wouldn't be easy at all.

Yet as I listened to that song, I knew that Donovan would be the one to raise our spirits, even as we mourned our lost comrades. He would help us remember the lightest moments of the darkest hours, and the details of each man's life that we could hold in our memories. I nodded and thanked him silently, realizing how close we had all become over the years. We were truly like brothers, yet we'd been through things together that most siblings never shared. We had laughed hard, fought hard, and no one and nothing could come between us. I would have done anything for them, and they would have done the same for me. I thought about the day that summer when the whole group had come over to the construction site to help me with the house I was building. We were pouring concrete and had to carry a good bit of it to some hard to reach places in five-gallon plastic pails. Donovan showed up wearing small, black nylon running shorts, no shirt and sandals on. What a character. I guess that's how they dress on the construction sites out there in Oklahoma. We hit the beer pretty early that day.

Once I heard that dedication, I just had the feeling that it was all true, that I was going to be released. And just afterward, the news announcer confirmed it. He didn't specify a time or venue, but he said that the Somalis had agreed to release me unconditionally. So I took up my Bible and wrote number fourteen for the date and "Today's the Day" on a blank page. And still, since I had never been the type to count my winnings before the game was over, I decided to let the dice roll and get some rest, and I dozed off.

When I woke up, Firimbi and the guards were escorting a stranger into the room. He was a young African man, but I could tell by his features that he wasn't a Somali. The indigenous population had somewhat aquiline features and skin tones diluted by European conquerors. This man's nose was broad and flat, his face nearly ink-black. He was wearing a T-shirt, baggy trousers, and flip-flops and he looked absolutely ecstatic, grinning from ear to ear. Firimbi "introduced" him.

"This man prisoner," he said. "Nigerian."

For a moment I thought that instead of being released, I was being saddled with another cell mate. But then the Nigerian opened his arms wide and beamed at me.

"Free!"

As it would turn out, he was a U.N. soldier who had been captured by the Somalis a month before. Suzanne Hofstetter had told me that she had visited this man in captivity as well, but apparently his treatment had been less hospitable than mine. He had been interrogated, tortured, and hung by his arms from a ceiling somewhere. At the moment, though, he looked pretty happy to me. I soon forgot about him, because that's when the circus came to town.

Four African dignitaries shuffled into the room. I blinked at them, because the scene was absolutely surreal. They were wearing very fancy, traditional ethnic outfits. They had flat-sided caps on their heads, like fezzes with geometric patterns, and colorful robes of silk were braided across their shoulders and around their torsos. They looked like Nubian kings from some biblical tale. Each of them appeared to hail from a different country, and they seemed thrilled at having been invited to this momentous occasion. They waved their arms and babbled in foreign tongues while the Somalis suddenly brought in trays holding teapots and ornate cups. And it all became like some weird cocktail party in an African embassy, with me as the ice sculpture, as these dignitaries encircled me and joked and chatted while Firimbi passed out crackers and snacks from a wooden tray. One of them sat himself down on the edge of the bed and smiled at me as he sipped his tea.

"Mr. Doorant," he said. "Where are you from in the United States?"

I laughed. I couldn't believe I'd heard him right.

"New England," I said. "A small state, I doubt you've heard of it— New Hampshire."

"Ahhh. Very *nice*."

As this bizarre party went on, Firimbi and the guards dressed me carefully in a thin blue hospital robe. Someone handed me a stick of gum, as if my breath had to be fresh for my coming debut. I could hear many voices outside in the courtyard, and the room was filling with more people. Minister Abdi came in with his bodyguards, but he busied himself with the African dignitaries, as if I was no longer the focus of his tasks and that was just fine with him.

A Red Cross doctor arrived. He was European, wearing a safari vest and carrying a large, professional-looking medical kit. I looked past his shoulder, expecting to see my "regular" doc, but Kediye was nowhere in sight. He handed me a packet of letters from home, but I hardly had time to focus on them as he took out a Red Cross form.

"I am going to administer some morphine, Mr. Durant," he said. "But you'll have to fill out this release form first."

Morphine? Did he say morphine??

This all looked very real, yet still, one part of me remained cautious. The form required personal facts, but there were spaces for military details as well. For all I knew, the Somalis might be trying to get one last piece of information out of me, or unlikely but possible, this could all be some elaborate ruse. So where the form said "Unit" I wrote what I'd been instructed to write back at SERE School: "USASOC." It would take the Somalis some days to figure out the acronym for "United States Army Special Operations Command," and I wouldn't be around for further questioning. The rest seemed benign enough.

The doctor checked my heart and lungs and took my pulse, then asked me some general questions about my condition. But I could only focus on the glass vial of golden liquid in his hand and the syringe sucking up that morphine. I had hardly moved over the last couple of days and the pain was manageable, but I knew that when they hauled me up and rocked my world again it was going to come back like thunder and lightning. He shot me up in the right shoulder and within a few minutes my entire body began to finally let go. The torn muscles and tendons in my back seemed to exhale a long sigh, and the throb from my broken bones receded. The morphine didn't give me a "high and happy" sensation, but my nerves were certainly numbed. It was like taking that first sip of cool, clear water after crawling across a broiling desert for eleven days.

The Somalis brought in a standard-issue, military-type litter and laid it out on the floor. It had wooden poles and a canvas bed. Now there were plenty of people to lift me onto it, hands supporting every part of my body, yet in spite of the morphine the move still hurt like hell and I chewed that gum furiously, like I was biting on a bullet. They covered my legs with the flowered bedsheet, raised the stretcher, and we moved to the doorway, with the African dignitaries gleefully joining Firimbi and the guards. But they had a problem. The corridor outside was very narrow and they couldn't make the left-hand turn into it. They argued and babbled at each other, then decided to tip the stretcher up and squeeze me through. I was at a forty-five-degree angle, gripping the litter and trying to hold on to my Bible, praying that I'd survive this Keystone Kops comedy.

I'm almost out of here, and now they're gonna dump me onto this cement floor and bust me up some more? I thought as I held my breath and hung on. *I wouldn't let you guys move my goddamn couch!*

But somehow, with a lot of arguing and tilting, they managed to make the turn, and then we were suddenly outside in the courtyard. The sun was blazing, people were shouting, there were television cameras all around. My guards were gripping their AK-47s, looking around nervously, scanning the surroundings like Secret Service agents. A three-vehicle convoy of panel vans was waiting in the street with their engines rumbling and coughing, but all I could think of was that this was no damn way to run a prisoner release in a war zone. There were still plenty of people in Mogadishu who would have loved to kill me right then and there, and my captors were making a public spectacle of it all.

Get me the hell out of the open, people! Let's move!

Someone opened the rear doors of the center van in the convoy. Firimbi jumped inside, and they slid my litter into the bed and the Red Cross doctor crawled in after me. But the stretcher was too long for the vehicle, so the ends of the poles and my bare feet were hanging out over the rear bumper. Suddenly, the convoy started to move out, and as our van lurched forward, my litter torpedoed halfway out the back.

Jesus!

I closed my eyes and braced for impact, but Firimbi and the doctor snatched at the stretcher and just barely saved me from being hurled into the street and turned into roadkill by the trailing van. Their panicky scramble would have been almost funny if we hadn't come so close to disaster. They squatted on both sides of me now, trying to keep me inside and hold the flapping doors partially closed as we careened through the city. I could see the follow van just beyond my bare toes, with *mooryan* gunmen on the running boards. Our vehicle suddenly cornered hard as the driver and horn cussed in unison, but Firimbi took my hand in a "brother" grip and locked his biceps. The litter, the doctor, and everything else in the back might go sailing out those doors, but he wasn't going to let me go.

I looked up at him. He was wearing a T-shirt with big, bold print splashed across the chest in English: VIVA AIDID! SOMALI NATIONAL ALLIANCE! The van was bucking, and he snapped something at the driver and we slowed down a bit. Then he looked back down at me. He was smiling only slightly, but there was genuine relief in his eyes. His task was complete and I really was going to get that plane ticket home I'd been asking for.

I actually wanted to thank him, but there was no opportunity to do that. Everything seemed to be happening so fast now. We had spent hours and hours in the same barren rooms. We had begun as enemies who would have killed each other in combat without thinking twice, and had both learned to respect each other. Behind Firimbi's head in the wall of the van was a large glass window, and outside a flatbed "people mover" rolled past, the truck overflowing with clinging Somalis. They looked down at us with a mix of curiosity and confusion until someone realized who I was and some of them began to wave, as if bidding farewell to a departing cruise ship. The van braked sharply as it encountered a traffic snarl, then jolted forward again. I heard the doctor curse and felt the litter start to slide, but Firimbi didn't let me budge. He looked at me and grinned very broadly, as if he was truly happy to see that I was going to be released.

"Allah has willed it," he said.

I grinned back at him, but I still wasn't allowing myself to take it all in. I had kept my hope in check for too long to let it all just flow that easily. The whole scene was like some bizarre dream, and I had woken up recently from plenty of nightmares, only to face the harsher realities of truth. The morphine had somewhat numbed my pain, but I also wondered if it wasn't playing tricks on my mind. And then I saw the gates.

The van had stopped again and I could see towering steel gates on both sides of the vehicle, topped by concertina wire. Uniformed soldiers hefting assault rifles were crowding around the van. They were wearing light blue helmets. We were at the United Nations compound in the western sector of the city.

The driver showed some sort of ID card to the gate guard, who then walked around to the back of the van. He pulled the doors open and looked inside cautiously. The Red Cross doctor offered up his organization's special pass. And then, to my utter amazement, Firimbi pulled a chain from around his neck and flashed a bona fide set of United Nations credentials.

Holy shit! I was stunned for a moment, and then almost laughed at the surrealism of it. *Firimbi's wearing a "Viva Aidid" T-shirt, which is like waving a sign that says, "I'm the Enemy." But he's got U.N. credentials!?* It was the final bit of absurdity in a totally screwed-up world, and I shook my head. *You're just a babe in the woods out here, Durant. A goddamn babe in the woods. . . .*

The guards opened the gate and waved us through, as we rolled across the smooth asphalt and stopped. I heard excited voices, people running. The van doors suddenly opened again, and standing there with his mouth gaping was a *lawyer.* He was an American major, the Task Force Ranger JAG officer, and I recognized him instantly. He'd been involved in that stolen goggle recovery effort. The Somalis hadn't notified our people of the time of my release, or exactly where it would occur, and he just happened to be at the U.N. compound that morning. But when I lifted my head and saw him, a fellow American soldier, I knew right then and there that it was all true. It was over. I was going home. And I would never be so happy to see a lawyer again.

He stood there for a moment in shock, and then he yelled.

"Holy Mother of God! It's Mike Durant! *Medic!*"

And then all hell broke loose. There was an American Army field hospital right there at the U.N. compound, and medics and nurses and doctors charged across the tarmac as the U.N. soldiers pulled me out of the van. A gurney appeared and they set my litter onto it as faces crowded around me, everyone shouting and barking orders at once. People were yelling for instruments and medical equipment and it was like a scene out of *ER* as they rushed me toward the large green tents of the hospital.

I looked around, but Firimbi was nowhere in sight. He had faded away into the crowd, and I left his world much in the way I'd come into it, carried aloft and engulfed by a mob.

SOMEONE GAVE ME a more serious dose of painkillers, and the rest of that day became a hazy blur.

The team of American doctors and nurses went to work right away, wheeling me into an operating theater. My bandages were cut away as people asked me about my condition, but other than pointing out my various injuries, there was nothing much I could tell them. The first thing they did was to "debride" my leg wound, cutting away flesh that had died and begun to rot. I was X-rayed from head to toe, wounds were cleaned, and the worst bandaged up. The only serious infection appeared to be from the fractures in my face, from the blow I'd taken at the crash site, so they hooked me up to an antibiotic drip to try to get it under control. There was nothing much they could do for my back, so they put me under anesthesia and went to work on my leg.

I came to that evening, slowly, and I was reminded of the moments right after my crash as my eyes and my mind gradually focused. I was lying in a quiet recovery section of the field hospital. My lower right leg had steel bolts in it, screwed right through the bone. The bolts were hooked up to a pulley system mounted overhead, with a counterweight hanging from it. A nurse came by to check on me. She explained that the ends of my broken femur had overlapped so far that the muscles had atrophied and shrunken tight, so nothing further could be done until the leg was stretched out. I tried to talk, but my mouth was desert dry. The lights in the recovery tent were hazy and soft. People around me seemed to be speaking in long, slow drawls, but I knew that I had plenty of painkillers in me. Someone gave me water. Cool, clean, bottled, American water.

I lay there for a while, just trying to take it all in. I thought about how many days had elapsed since that long-ago Sunday, but I didn't know what day it was anymore. Yet to me, much more than a lifetime had been crushed into less than two weeks. And then, for a moment, I felt a surge of panic and I grasped for the rails of the gurney. I felt cold steel. Cold *American* steel.

It's all right. It's real. It's over. You're here. . . .

The U.N. compound was not located near the airfield and Task Force Ranger, so I hadn't expected my comrades to come rushing right over. Besides, I figured that they were plenty busy and would show up soon enough. When they did, I knew that my healing process would really begin. I had no doubt that American Army doctors would be able to patch me up physically, but it would take the strength of my friendships and family to start mending my soul. For the moment, I just held all of my swirling emotions in check. I was a free man. I'd be going home soon. It would all be fine. There was time.

The first men who arrived from the Task Force were three Delta operators. They were glad to see me back and alive, but as is their way, they were all business. Another one of us might be shot down or captured at any moment and they needed as much information as possible that might help if a rescue attempt became necessary. They wanted to know mostly about the physical details of my various prison rooms. What were the walls made of? What kinds of locks were on the doors? What sorts of weapons had I seen? Their debriefing was brief, but thorough, then they thanked me, welcomed me back, and left me alone.

I was lying there, sort of fading in and out, when I heard boots on concrete. I lifted my head. The medical staff around me seemed to drift away as Dan Jollota, Stan Wood, and Herb Rodriguez, our company commander, headed toward me along a canvas corridor. I thought I spotted Lieutenant Colonel Tom Matthews, Mark Bergamo, Trey Williams, and Gerry Izzo walking just behind them. They were all wearing their "ninja gear" and carrying weapons, so I knew they had flown over to the U.N. compound in one of our birds.

I grinned at them as they approached. Dan and Stan smiled back, but their expressions seemed somehow frozen. All of them looked extremely tired. Herb Rodriguez was a large and powerful man, but for a special ops major and company commander, he had a very soft heart. His black hair was tousled from his helo helmet and the cheeks of his tanned face seemed to be twitching. The men surrounded my gurney and laid their hands on me. No one spoke.

Something was very wrong. My smile faded as I looked at all of them.

"Where the hell's Cliff and Donovan?" I asked.

Tears began to roll down Herb's face as he slowly shook his head, looking down at his boots. His big shoulders trembled.

"They didn't make it, Mike," he whispered. "They didn't make it."

I stopped breathing.

No.

It couldn't be true.

This isn't real.

Just that morning Donovan had dedicated a song to me over the radio. I'd heard it with my own *ears*. I'd heard them say his *name*.

This wasn't possible. It didn't make sense. How could Donovan Briley be dead? No. And Cliff? He couldn't die. There was nothing and nobody in this world that could kill Cliff Wolcott. No. No way. Their smiling faces flashed in front of my burning eyes, and then their wives and their kids and their homes and everything else that I knew they loved. No. Oh please, God, no, not them too. It just couldn't be that they were both gone.

But the tortured faces around me said everything in silence. The hands gripping my forearms and shoulders told me it was true. Everything that had happened was already so bad, but this was too much, and it felt like my heart was just exploding from agony as the anguish overcame me.

It wasn't a reunion at all. It was a funeral.

I don't know how long I lay there, my chest heaving, tears running down my cheeks, but Matthews stepped up to my bedside. He was holding a telephone handset.

"It's the President, Mike," he said. "He wants to talk to you."

Somehow, I pulled myself together. Everything around me was swimming in a black whirlpool of torment, but I choked it all down and took the phone.

"Mr. President," I said. My voice sounded like a liquid whisper to me.

"Mike, we're all very glad you've been released."

I didn't know what to say. I felt the anger and loss welling up like a flood of fire. I wanted to tell him that if maybe his administration hadn't refused to augment the Task Force with tanks and AC-130s, it's likely none of this would have happened. I wanted to say, all right, we might have lost one bird, but an armored convoy like that could have punched right through to the crash site and so many lives might have been saved. But none of it mattered now. None of it. Cliff Wolcott, Donovan Briley, my crew and those two courageous Delta operators were all dead. *The blood is on your hands*, I thought, but I avoided the temptation to say it. After all, he was the commander in chief. *You will show respect*. And resentfully, I played the good military officer.

"Thank you, Sir," I said.

"We're all very proud of you, Mike. Can't wait to get you home."

"I'm just proud to be an American, Sir," I managed.

Matthews retrieved the phone. A nurse appeared and added something to my IV drip, and soon I was fading, struggling just to keep my eyes open. I welcomed it, longed for it, I wanted to be deep in a dreamless void and far away from this world of pain. I wanted to know no more, to hear no more. The phone was passed to me again and I spoke to Lorrie, and then to my parents, but I would remember nothing that was said. The army surgeon came in to tell my comrades that visiting hours were over. I was out for the rest of the night. I escaped to the sanctuary of unconsciousness.

When I awoke the next morning, I was being wheeled out of the hospital to a medevac helicopter. I was still surfing on a gentle swell of painkillers, and the only throb was from my heart. The helo was an Army Huey, just like the kind I'd flown in Korea. Now it was my turn to ride in the back on a stretcher. I was glad it wasn't snowing. We lifted off and skirted the city, but I had no trepidation about flying again, no sense of vulnerability being in that bird. I was, after all, born to fly helicopters.

When we landed at the Task Force Ranger compound, there was a C-141 waiting to take me to Germany. But between the landing pad and that jet, all four hundred men of Task Force Ranger had come out to form two long rows, a corridor of sunburned faces and desert uniforms. Someone handed me a borrowed maroon beret, and Dan Jollota and Stan Wood, Mark Bergamo and Trey Williams lifted my litter and we walked toward the ramp of the waiting transport.

Every man in the Task Force was holding some kind of a cup. Every cup had a shot of whiskey in it. The men spoke to me in murmurs as I passed. They wished me well and offered me thumbs-up.

When we reached the cargo ramp of the jet, my friends held me there so I could look out over this honor guard of my brothers, this company of heroes.

General Garrison stepped up onto the ramp. He handed me a shot glass of whiskey, while he raised his own and all the men raised theirs to the ice-blue African sky.

"To our fallen comrades," his voice echoed. "We shall never forget them."

"To our fallen comrades," four hundred said in unison.

We downed our shots, as from a speaker somewhere came a recording of "God Bless America." When the men joined in to sing it, their voices were like thunder and I could feel the earth tremble.

They carried me into the plane. At last, I was really going home. Soon, I would inhale the sweet scents of America. Soon, I would be holding my son. Yet so much had happened. So many of the best pieces of my life had been torn away that I felt empty and hollow. As the cargo ramp closed, I looked at my hands.

The only things I had left were that coveted Night Stalker beret and the Bible.

And something I had always taken for granted before—my freedom.

AFTERMATH

Not a day goes by that I don't think about the men we lost in Mogadishu.

I remember them all so clearly, as if no time has passed since then. Yet perhaps of all my fallen comrades, the one who returns to me most often is Donovan Briley.

He's been dead almost ten years now, but he still lives on in my memory as that thirty-three-year-old special operations pilot, the ultimate warrior professional, with his jokester side so thinly disguised. He loved all of it so much: the nonmilitary haircuts and the ninja gear and the nonregulation boots, the challenges of secret missions and the brotherhood of our exclusive fraternity. I see him still, in his black nylon running shorts and sandals, riding his bike at midnight up and down the runways of Fort Campbell, as if our regular duties didn't provide him enough exercise. I hear his Oklahoma twang, telling tall tales about his Native American upbringing. And sometimes still, when I'm alone in my car and the strains of that old song "Seminole Wind" whisper from the radio, my silent tears appear, and I think back to a simpler time, when it was clear which team I was on.

They were all fine men, the best our country had to offer, and I miss them every one. And as my friend Dan once put it so well, "Their memories are engraved on our hearts."

On that bright October day in Somalia, I was flown into Ramstein Air Force Base, Germany, and the chill of a cool autumn rain. As soon as the cargo ramp of the C-141 dropped, a phenomenon began that would continue for many months, something that I would never wholly understand. There were people everywhere: well-wishers hanging on the perimeter fence of the airport, reporters and photographers trying to break through lines of military police, and enough medical personnel to service the needs of an entire platoon of wounded. On a small scale, it reminded me of those black-and-white films of the Beatles first arriving in New York City. But I was not a rock star. I was just an Army helicopter pilot who had been shot down, captured, and released.

Almost immediately, my ability to perceive sincerity in those around me seemed to become very acute. I thought I'd always been a fairly good judge of people's true motivations, but now it was as if I'd suddenly developed an extrasensory awareness. There were folks who really cared about my well-being, and those who simply wanted to be part of the action and have their pictures taken. I called this the "touching the stone" phenomenon. The differences were so apparent to me that it was almost like they had it stamped on their foreheads: "For Real" or "Phony."

Inside a huge gothic U.S. military hospital that looked like a medieval castle, I was checked over again from head to foot by the local doctors and nurses. Then I was left alone in a spacious room, wondering why everyone was treating me like a fragile eggshell. When the first familiar face showed up, the unit psychologist from Fort Campbell, it was clear that some folks thought I should be on the verge of mental collapse. He was there to "prepare" me for the arrival of my wife, thinking that the reunion might trigger a break-down. But even he did not understand that after the trauma of the past two weeks, nothing in the world would be a shock to my system.

Lorrie walked in and we spent some time alone together. But for me, the reunion was not overly emotional. My well of tears was temporarily empty, for I had spent them all in Somalia. For the first time I began to understand what had been happening at home during my captivity. The phone at our house had been ringing incessantly. Journalists from every major television network and magazine had called her, followed her, cornered her at the funerals of our friends. On the commercial flight to Germany, she had discovered that the person sitting next to her was a television producer and had managed to purchase that seat in order to offer her a "deal." But I was really only interested in hearing about Joey, and was disappointed that he hadn't been able to make the trip.

Colonel Bryan Brown arrived next. He was the Regimental Commander of the 160th and had not been in Somalia, because Gothic Serpent was only a battalion mission. He was there to make sure that I got what I needed, and what I wanted. Clay Hutmacher came in and I was very happy to see my best friend, and relieved that a quirk of military fate had kept him out of harm's way on this one. When they all saw that I was functioning quite normally, the surgeons came in and a discussion began about my physical care.

The doctors in Germany wanted to keep me there for several days and perform a full regimen of surgeries and treatments. I'm sure they were concerned about my condition, but I also had the distinct feeling that they were also motivated by ego. Yet I wasn't about to hang around so they could bathe in the glow of media attention. Perhaps my feelings were unjustified, but there was no doubt, I wanted to get home.

"Time out," I said as they assaulted me with all sorts of medical lingo. "I'm going to discuss this with my commander, my wife, and my comrades."

The doctors reluctantly left, while Brown, Lorrie, and Clay came back in.

"Here's the deal," I said. "I don't want to do any more surgeries here than I need to. If there's something life-threatening that they need to take care of, let's do it. Otherwise, I want to get back to Campbell. Joey's there, my parents are there, and I don't want to spend a long time here. So let's just knock out what we have to and get the hell out of here."

"That's what you want to do?" Colonel Brown asked.

"Yes, Sir."

"Then that's what we're going to do." He had plenty of clout, and I knew that no one was going to stand in his way.

The only procedure that the surgeons insisted upon involved my face. I still had an infection and the bones were all busted up, so they performed an operation that night. They went in via my mouth, sliced my right cheek muscles away, and slid a steel pallet up inside to rearrange the shattered cheekbone and eye socket. When we flew back to the States the next day, my face was as swollen as a beach ball, I couldn't breathe through my nose, and nurses kept feeding me ice chips.

This is nothing, I said to myself. *Wait till they start on your leg.* But in truth, I couldn't wait. I was already thinking about flying again.

We landed at Andrews Air Force Base in Washington and switched to a brand-new C-9 Nightingale, the Air Force's new medevac airplane. I'm told there were hundreds of journalists and reporters surging in the terminal, but I never saw them because they never got near the plane and only an Army photographer was allowed to do his duty. Before the Nightingale took off again for Fort Campbell, Secretary of State Warren Christopher and National Security Adviser Anthony Lake came on board to have their pictures taken as they greeted me. But the only thing that impressed me was the arrival of

General Gordon Sullivan, the Army Chief of Staff. He bent over my litter and, with genuine compassion in his eyes and his voice, pinned the Purple Heart on me. The man cared an awful lot about *his* troops and that was obvious.

It was late at night when we finally arrived at Fort Campbell. As the door to the C-9 swung open and the medevac ramp was lowered, I could already see that again there were hundreds of people waiting for me. But this time it was different. This time they were all people I knew, they were family.

There were troops in formation on the tarmac and the Army band was playing. There were bleachers set up, jammed with cheering soldiers and families. As I was coming down the ramp, Major General Jack Keane, the commanding general of the 101st, spoke to me from a podium.

"Welcome home, Mike," his voice boomed from a speaker. "We're going to get you back on flight status and get you back in the cockpit!" The crowd applauded, and I smiled and filed that promise away for later use.

My entire family was there: my parents, uncles, aunts, and cousins. Some of them were wearing "Welcome Home" T-shirts with my name and the American flag stenciled on them. My dad lifted Joey up for me, and I hugged him to my chest. I felt the hands that I had dreamed of on me, I saw the faces I had longed to see just once more, right there before me. The band played and the troops and families sang as they wheeled me on my gurney across the tarmac toward a VIP room, where a catered welcome feast had been ordered up by the Night Stalkers.

Then, for a moment, time seemed to stand still and all the faces around me disappeared as someone stepped out of the crowd. It was Christine Wolcott, Cliff's wife. She had only just buried him two days before. She walked up to my gurney with a smile, touched my forehead, and laid a bottle of champagne on the litter.

AT BLANCHFIELD ARMY Community Hospital, the surgeons went to work right away, first checking every wound and injury as if no medical personnel had laid hands on me before. They didn't really ask me about my preferences, but they realized they were working on a piece of government property in which the Army had invested large sums and years of training. There are only limited ways you can treat a broken back. You can fuse the spine, immobilizing the crushed vertebrae, but I had told them that I had every intention of flying again and such a procedure would limit my future mobility. So they placed me into a "turtle shell" and made a plaster cast of my back in the preferred posture. The back brace that resulted would stay on me, night and day, for many months.

My right leg was opened up at the hip to give the orthopedic surgeons easy access to the top of the femur bone. A long hole was drilled down through the center of both femur sections and a steel rod was hammered into it and bolted, top and bottom. It would take some time before it would stop feeling like I'd broken it all over again, but their methods and medications were slightly more sophisticated than the wonders of Dr. Kediye's blue tackle box.

But I had been lying flat on my back for so long that I couldn't even sit up without passing out. My cardiovascular system had atrophied and my heart wasn't yet up to the task of pumping enough blood to my brain. They put me on a tilt table every day and gradually increased the upward angle until I could stay upright for ten minutes without my eyes rolling back and my head lolling. After a few days, they helped me out of bed and I stood up shakily. The leg held.

Outstanding! I thought. *I am definitely going to fly again.*

I suppose I'm fortunate, in that I'm the type who heals quickly, from both physical and emotional injuries. I grab joy when I see it and get over anger fast. I like to move on. But this wasn't going to be so easy.

I didn't think that I had post-traumatic stress disorder. I was progressing rapidly, relating to people, talking and planning for the future. But I was wrong. A soldier just doesn't go through an intense combat experience without some sort of residual mental effects. Soon after my leg surgery, I was sitting in the hospital in a wheelchair. It was a beautiful autumn day, and someone wheeled me outside into the hospital courtyard. I looked at the trees, those good old American trees. They were so beautiful, and I thought about the contrast of our magnificent country to places like Somalia, and I remembered thinking while in captivity that I might never see such things again, and the tears came again. In fact, I probably cried every day, at least for a brief period, for the next eighteen months. It was usually when I was alone, my mind given a brief opportunity to wander, when it would just come out of nowhere. Something would bring back a memory, I'd have a wave of emotion, and then it would go away. But I realized it was probably healthy, just a part of my healing process and no one was the wiser.

The Army psychologists, however, were more than a bit concerned about my mental state. My debriefings at Blanchfield began with them, and I got the impression they were waiting for me to wig out. Yet after some time they seemed satisfied that I could hold it together and the longer sessions began.

A number of officers appeared one day in my room. There was a psychologist from Fort Bragg, some survival experts, and a 160th intelligence officer. Then, much to my surprise, Don Landrum, The Bearded One from SERE School, entered. Hundreds of men and women had passed through his course and he did not remember me, but I certainly remembered him. Yet his demeanor was much different from what it had been during my "captivity" in those freezing North Carolina woods. He was clearly a compassionate man and his sole purpose was to be there to help me, and to learn what he could from my experience, so that other men and women might benefit from the bitter fruits of my captivity someday.

The debriefing sessions lasted for two straight days, from morning till night with a few breaks in between. My Bible was more than helpful. Everything was tape-recorded for the preparation of a classified report. At first, it was very difficult for me to speak. I'd begin talking about Somalia, and then after about ten seconds I would just shut down. But my debriefers were patient and compassionate. It was not an interrogation. No one criticized any of my actions. When we discussed certain elements of my capture and the methods that might have been used in a rescue attempt, I had to be cautious. I did not know some of these men, and they hailed from other branches of the service.

"Are you cleared for this, Sir?" I asked one officer politely before beginning to elaborate on specific sources and methods.

"He's cleared, Mike," the Intel officer said, and I figured if it was all right by him, then it was all right by me.

"Okay," I said, "but I'm not sharing any secrets about my sex life."

"No problem. We'll ask your wife about that."

I laughed, but I wasn't sure if he was kidding or not.

I was still in the hospital when the Night Stalkers returned from Somalia, and they brought me out to the airfield for the welcome home. Once again the band played, the troops stood in formation, and the families were all there. Lee Greenwood made an appearance and sang "Proud to Be an American." By that time I had begun to hear bits and pieces about the events that had occurred in Mogadishu during and after I was shot down. I now knew a little more about the two Delta men who had given their lives for me and my crew. And I had begun to really understand how much my comrades resented the actions of the Clinton administration, and their anger and bitterness over the refusal to provide us with the armor and air support we needed. So I was very surprised when Anthony Lake showed up and told me that President Clinton wanted me to come up to Washington as soon as I was released from Blanchfield. I did not respond. I wasn't going to stand on the White House lawn and make it appear that all was forgotten and forgiven, while my comrades were barely cold in their graves.

It was also then that I began to realize the role that Ross Perot had

played in all of this. When my parents had first told me how the bil-
lionaire businessman was personally involved in the events of my
captivity and release, it sounded too strange to be true. But it was all
true. A man named Brian Ages, who had worked for Mr. Perot's pres-
idential campaign, had seen the CNN clip of my interrogation and
had gone right into action. He somehow tracked down my uncle
Wayne through the police department in Berlin, New Hampshire,
and put him in touch with Ross Perot's office.

Very few people in this country know that Ross Perot has been quietly operating on behalf of U.S. Special Operations soldiers and other
veterans for years. He does not talk about it and does not seek credit
for his actions. When these men or their families are in need, and
U.S. government support for them is limited, Ross Perot steps in.
After the war in Vietnam, he hired scores of Vietnam vets and former POWs and saw to it that they'd be retrained in computer and
technical professions so they could work for his company. He took
care of the complex surgeries and prosthetic devices required for a
Delta operator who lost his leg in Somalia. He did the same for one
of our 160th pilots who lost a leg in a motorcycle accident. When
Brian Ages was manning a campaign table for Mr. Perot's election,
many wives and brothers of veterans came up to tell him stories
about what Mr. Perot had done for their families.

Throughout my captivity, Mr. Perot personally called my wife and
my parents on many occasions, asking what he could do. He set up
a special fund so that members of my family who couldn't afford the
airfares would be able to attend every celebration for me. He became decisively engaged in my release from Mogadishu, in ways
that to this day he modestly demurs from sharing with me. Later on,
when it was time for me to return to New Hampshire for a hometown
welcoming event, my mother called Mr. Perot and invited him. He
politely declined, saying that he did not want to upstage my home-
coming in any way. But when he arrived in New Hampshire on a
campaign stop, he asked my parents to come and spend some time

with him, which they did. It was a private meeting and there were no cameras present, except for my mom's.

Ross Perot receives no medals or commendations for his work. He asks for nothing in return and there is no real way for me to thank him, except for here and now. And there aren't enough words to really express how many of us feel about Mr. Perot.

After three weeks at Blanchfield, I was getting close to being released. I had my back brace and a cane, and I could get around all right for short periods of time. But the media folks had gotten wind of my imminent release and the phone calls to my home and the hospital were relentless. All of the major television networks were calling, sending us flowers and fruit baskets. I wasn't remotely interested in publicity or in appearing on television, but I wasn't sure how to handle it, so I consulted the Public Affairs Officer from the U.S. Army Special Operations Command at Fort Bragg who'd been my constant companion since I'd returned. His name was Ken McGraw and he'd dealt with the media enough to know when to befriend them, when to bark, and when to bite. He thought about it for a minute, then offered a fine piece of wisdom.

"Listen, Mike," he said. "If you say no to all of them, it'll look like you've got something to hide. When a man sticks his head in the sand, the only thing showing is his ass." It made perfect sense.

He recommended that I prepare a statement, do one major news show, such as Larry King, and pick just one of the other major networks who were interested in a "human interest" piece featuring both me and my wife. On the day of my release, I made a brief appearance before a throng of reporters outside the hospital and read the statement he helped me prepare.

Let me begin my statement by saying that I am proud to have served with some of the most professional soldiers in the world — the members of Task Force Ranger. We successfully completed a very difficult mission, but we also paid a heavy price.

The valor of the members of the Ranger Task Force served as an inspiration to me while I was detained, and will continue to serve as an inspiration to me in the future. While uncommon courage was the standard of the day for all, there are some who deserve special recognition.

Master Sergeant Gary Gordon and Sergeant First Class Randy Shughart performed one of the bravest acts I have ever witnessed, when they were inserted by helicopter into the crash site to assist our crew and secure our downed aircraft. Without a doubt, I owe my life to these two men and their bravery.

I also owe my life to my fellow crew members—Ray Frank, Bill Cleveland, and Tommy Fields. It took a team effort to get our damaged aircraft on the ground, and we were successful. My deepest sympathies go out to the families of these men, and the families of my friends Donovan Briley and Cliff Wolcott, and all of those families who have lost loved ones in Somalia. I can only assure them that their losses are a deep personal loss for me as well.

I also want everyone to remember that we still have men and women serving in Somalia, as well as around the world. The yellow ribbons that are still hanging should serve as a tribute to these soldiers and their service.

To not only the American people, but to the people from all over the world, who have shown so much compassion and concern for me and my family, your prayers have been answered and I thank you. As I said when I returned to Fort Campbell, it is your support, the strength of my wife and my family and friends, that keeps me going.

Despite the fact that I received the best care in the hospital, like all patients, I am anxious to get back home, complete the reunion with my family and friends, finish recuperating, and try to return to a normal life. It is great to be home.

Thank you.

That night, I appeared on Larry King's program on CNN, along with a number of other participants from Operation Gothic Serpent. All of us were careful about not sharing any classified details of the mission, and I was somehow able to hold it all together and speak freely about the experience. I felt I owed that to my fallen comrades. The next morning, Lorrie and I appeared on Connie Chung's show and fulfilled our commitment to do one "human interest" piece. Thankfully, after that the media telephone calls stopped. We were old news.

On November 10, the day before Veterans Day, I flew up to Fort Bragg for a memorial service. Several of the Night Stalkers were there, along with the Delta Operators, some of the Air Force folks, and some SEALs. The Rangers were not in attendance, because they were holding their own solemn ceremonies at Fort Benning, and it was that distance and disconnection that would play a part in the confusion, for some years, about what had really happened in Somalia. After the mission of October 3, a formal debrief had been scheduled at the airfield on the next day, but the Somalis had launched a mortar attack on the compound. The Delta Commander, Colonel Gary Harrel, had been wounded in the attack and one of his operators had been killed. From that day forth, no formal debriefing with all of us present ever occurred. It would not be until 1999 and the publication of Mark Bowden's book *Black Hawk Down* that many of us would finally discover just exactly what had happened that day in Somalia. For that reason, Bowden's effort would become much more than a nonfiction historical work. To many of us, it would become a treasured diary.

The memorial service was a difficult experience for all. It was held inside an auditorium at the Delta compound and attended only by the men who had fought and the friends and families of those who had died. Prayers were offered and posthumous awards were given to the loved ones of the fallen. It was a mixture of bitterness, sadness, and anguish, and it was not the forum for a postmortem evaluation of Operation Gothic Serpent despite the presence of Secretary of Defense Les Aspin, who accepted responsibility for the lack of critical mission assets. The only regrets that were quietly expressed were the dismay that we had not been allowed to stay in Somalia and complete our mission. It is difficult enough to bury a fallen comrade, but even harder to look into the eyes of his family, knowing that the objective for which he died has been deemed unobtainable by the very men who sent him to his death.

That evening, when two young women approached and hugged me, I did not know who they were. They introduced themselves as Carmen Gordon and Stephanie Shughart, the wives of the two Delta operators who had fought to the death at my crash site. I did not know what to say to them, how to express the overwhelming admiration and gratitude I felt for their husbands. Their poise and grace was simply stunning, yet I suppose I should have expected nothing less from the spouses of such men.

Truthfully, I had not experienced a classic case of what is termed "survivor's guilt." I did not feel that I should have died along with my comrades, or that I was responsible for their deaths. We had all fought hard, and I had truly expected to die right along with them. There were times when I did wonder why God had chosen me to survive, and soon after that memorial service, the answer arrived in the form of a letter from Stephanie Shughart. I wept when I read it, and she has graciously allowed me to share it here, for its power speaks for itself.

12 November 1993

Dear Mike,

I know that Wednesday evening was as difficult for you as it was for each of us. You will never know how much it meant to me to see you face to face and give you a hug. There are so many things I would like to tell you and ask you but I don't want to cause you any more pain or suffering.

When I thanked you for giving Randy's death a purpose I meant it. It is not meant to detract from the bravery or heroism of the others that died, however, I can look at you and talk to you and see that his efforts were not in vain. Perhaps your wife can explain to you what I'm sure she too experienced during those days. When you are a wife in this situation the global and political picture pales and you concentrate only on the one you love and what his immediate isolated situation is. Many people may not understand my feelings and indeed it is difficult to express them accurately. But I am going to try to express them to you.

I want you to know that because of your bravery and refusal to give up while captured I can sleep at night. Your refusal to be defeated and give up was as brave an act as Randy's. Had you given up I would have never known for sure exactly what happened to him. I can live with the fact of knowing he died to save another man rather than had he died from a random bullet shot from a hidden source. If you knew Randy you would know that he was a very quiet and unselfish man. He always put others first and therefore it is fitting and appropriate that he died the way he did. Randy truly loved what he did and had God given him the choice of how to die I know in my heart he would have chosen to go down just as he did. I also know that had Randy been injured in a helicopter you would have piloted a helicopter in to save him no matter how dangerous the situation was.

I don't ever want you to question why you lived and Randy and the others with you did not. You lived to come back and give me some peace of mind to what would have been an otherwise unexplainable situation. You are a living reminder and testament of what the Delta soldiers and those that work with them are all about. The squadron can look to you and know that the beliefs they have and the oath they swear to are valid. Randy and Gordy were not alone when they tried to rescue you. They carried a lot of insight, knowledge and strength from each mate they had ever worked with inside of them.

I want you to enjoy your life and be happy. Look back with pride not sorrow. Just as Randy fought to save you, you fought and did not give up, perhaps not knowing you were fighting to save me . . . from a tortured mind and heart.

Sincerely,
Stephanie Shughart

Perhaps until that moment, I had not been absolutely certain about my ability to recover fully and return to the 160th as a pilot. Now, nothing was going to stop me. I felt that the only genuine way to honor my fallen comrades, and to be true to myself, was to become what I had been before Somalia.

I was out of the hospital and at home now on convalescent leave. I enjoyed every minute with Joey, but my recovery wasn't progressing fast enough for me. Early on, I bagged the physical therapy program at Blanchfield and took it upon myself to work out. One of the private gyms outside Fort Campbell offered me a guest membership and I joined to use their facilities. By December I ran my first eight-minute mile on a treadmill.

At home, I did not exhibit the classic sort of postcombat behavior you might see in the movies. I didn't wake up screaming, have fits of temper, or throw plates at the wall. I was in contact with the families of my fallen friends, but I didn't feel that rehashing the events over and over again would be healthy for any of us. I realized that I was a living reminder of their losses and avoided showing up at their doors to "check in," because I knew I'd be arriving along with the ghosts of their loved ones. I think that for some of the people around me, the return to a normal existence was more difficult. All of the attention had faded away and it was rather like a funeral after all the mourners have gone home. As for me, I bathed in the glory of silence.

When I wasn't sure if I had handled all the media attention properly, I thought about one of the profound things that Clay Hutmacher had told me months before.

"When this is all over," he said to me, "you'll be able to judge how well you handled it, if you can say you have the same friends now that you had before any of this happened."

I kept that in my mind and made sure to focus on the people I had always cared about, rather than those new folks in my life who were clearly trying to "touch the stone." Today, I can proudly say that all of the people who were my friends before Somalia are still my friends today.

During this period, our house in Clarksville was overflowing with mailbags and packages. People from all over the country, and the world, had sent me letters and gifts. Because I had mentioned pizza in my Red Cross letter, and Lorrie had repeated that in her televised statement to me, the place was jammed with pizza boxes and coupons. I literally received thousands of letters from well-wishers, and while I read each and every one of them, I couldn't possibly respond to them all. But God bless every person out there who took the time to write to me.

I will never forget one particular letter. It was from a woman who had cancer and had been a member of a cancer patient support group. She was the only one of all her friends who had been cured and survived, and she told me that initially she had experienced terrible guilt for enjoying her life after her friends were gone. She offered one piece of very simple and profound advice, and I took it to heart.

"Look back, but don't stare."

There were, however, strangers out there who not only looked back at Somalia and stared, but who had the arrogance to criticize the performance of Task Force Ranger. Without exception, they were people who hadn't been there but thought they knew everything about the events, and deemed us all foolish for having been a part of it. They could not have been further off the mark.

I was stunned and infuriated when self-described military hero Colonel David Hackworth attacked me in the press. He accused me not only of "ersatz" heroism but of having spilled my guts to the enemy while in captivity—without any substantiating information to back up his claim. I didn't mind people speaking their piece, but Hackworth had sent letters to the editors of my hometown newspapers in both Clarksville, Tennessee, and Berlin, New Hampshire.

I had no idea what had spurred this very personal attack, but I was infuriated. At the time, had I run into him, I would have choked him. I responded to his rantings with my own letter to the editor, wondering why a man who considered himself a fine example of military leadership would chastise a fellow soldier in public, and challenged him to debate the issue. Shortly afterward, I received a postcard from Hackworth, claiming that he "didn't have the time" to discuss it with me. I was furious. He clearly had the time to rip me apart in public, but not to face me man-to-man.

Yet when things like this happened, I could only assume that some men could only bolster their self-worth by diminishing the deeds of others. I did not consider myself a hero, just a soldier who had done his best under difficult circumstances. Most of the true heroes I had ever known were dead. The rest of us were just survivors with medals.

The Night Stalkers were exemplary in their support for me. I could have just stayed home and mowed the lawn for six months and that would have been fine with them. But I don't like wasting time, and I didn't think such a prolonged leave would be good for me or for the government. There was a man at Fort Campbell who ran a center for Embry-Riddle Aeronautical University, one of the country's finest institutions for aviation studies. One day he showed up at my door, with an application for degree completion already filled out. All I had to do was to sign my name, so I got out my pen. Fifteen months later, I would have my bachelor's degree, and after going back to work, my master's.

And still, my main focus of interest was to get back on flight status. It wasn't going to be easy. Due to my back injury, it didn't look good. The deformity in my spine had permanently disqualified me from flying helicopters, so the first thing I'd have to accomplish would be to obtain a medical waiver. The only way to do that would be to prove to the Army leadership that I was physically up to the task.

That January, I began a serious regimen of running. I was visiting my folks up in New Hampshire when I went out for my first long-distance effort, still wearing my back brace. There was two feet of snow on the ground and ice on the roads, and the steel rod in my leg felt like a lightning rod, but I loved inhaling that pure frigid air and pumping that steam from my lungs.

From then on, I ran every day. Running can become sort of like meditation. It offers you a lot of time to contemplate life, which can be uplifting or painful, but I found it to be more than just part of my physical healing process. The activity became my therapy, a time to sort things out, and as I loped through the countryside I began to see the beauty of my surroundings again. Perhaps one part of me knew that if I ran fast enough, far enough, I would leave Somalia behind.

The world began to look different to me. Things that I'd long since taken for granted jumped out at me. The trees, the birds, the smells of things. One day that spring, when I was flying in a commercial jet over Florida, I looked down at the coast from 30,000 feet and was suddenly in awe of the beauty of it all. It made me realize that all of this could not just have happened. I accepted the truth, that I had been bitter and angry up until that moment. I acknowledged the fact that I had blamed God for what all of us had endured in Somalia, rejecting the notion that a loving God could inflict that kind of pain on his children. But as I looked at the world once again, I knew that He was responsible for all of its majesty, and I renewed my commitment to set an example for my children and to live my life the way I think He intended.

In early February, I received a telephone call out of the blue from a man named Mohamoud Iman. He was a Somali, calling from New Jersey, and claimed to be a personal representative of Mohamed Farrah Aidid. I was surprised, to say the least. For some reason, he addressed me as "Major." They never did seem to work out that issue of my rank.

"How can I help you?" I asked him cautiously.

"Well, Major Durant," he said. "General Aidid has asked me to deliver some things to you."

"All right. I'll give you a post office address and you can send them."

"No. He would like me to *personally* deliver these things."

My curiosity was piqued, but I wanted to mull it over.

"Call me back in two days," I said. I wasn't about to take his number and start making phone calls to some Somali intelligence operative.

I went over to Fort Campbell and spoke to some of the Intel folks at 1st Battalion.

"What do you guys think?" I asked them. "Is there any reason why I shouldn't do this?"

"Well, you do have to be careful," they responded. "You have no idea what this person wants and your physical security could be at risk. It's your call, Mike, but don't give them any personal information at all."

So I thought it over some more, but my curiosity got the best of me. I figured that I could take some security precautions on my own, so when Iman called back, I laid out my conditions; on a day of my choosing, we would meet in Nashville in the lobby of the Marriott Hotel at precisely 11:00 A.M. We would stay in the lobby, I'd give him one hour of my time, and he would remain there while I left. He agreed to my terms.

On February 17, I parked my car some distance from the Marriott so that no one could get a make on my vehicle. At 10:30, I set myself up in the lobby and just watched the flow of human traffic. Somalis aren't too difficult to spot in Tennessee, and there were none in sight. But at precisely 11:00 A.M., Mohamoud Iman walked in. He was dressed much like all the other men in Aidid's inner coterie, wearing a Miami-style shirt and loose trousers and carrying a large package. I waited a few minutes to see if he made eye contact with anyone else in the room and then when it appeared to be safe, I approached him, and we sat down to talk.

He had letters for me from Firimbi, Dr. Kediye, and Mohamed Aidid himself. The letters from Firimbi and Kediye were of a personal nature, primarily wishing me well and hoping for good things for me in the future. The letter from Aidid was pure propaganda, an attempt to enlist me somehow in forming a Somali-American "alliance." Mohamoud Iman then pulled out a T-shirt from his parcel and held it up in front of me. It had the American and Somali flags stenciled next to each other and a "Somali-American Friendship Association" logo. I was disappointed that it wasn't my army T-shirt.

"We believe that you could do very much to improve the relationship between our countries," Iman said. "We believe that only you can represent us to the Americans and say that the Somalis are good people."

Well, I had already long ago come to the conclusion that not all Somalis were bad people. As with all countries, there were some bad ones and some good ones, and I had encountered both. But I told him straight.

"I can't do that," I said. "The American people aren't going to forget what happened any time soon and I can't change that. They're justified in their bitterness, and I'm not going to do it."

But I quickly realized that I could turn the tables on Aidid and perhaps force the Somalis to make some meaningful gestures of their own.

"But maybe you can do something for me," I said. "There were a lot of personal effects that were taken from me and my comrades in Mogadishu." I was thinking in particular of Randy Shughart's wedding ring. Stephanie had asked me if I had any idea where it had ended up. "If your people can locate some of these things and return them, it would be a show of good faith."

I didn't really believe that any of us would ever see those personal effects again, but I thought that throwing the ball back in their court was a good idea. Iman said he would do his best, and then he handed me the entire parcel he was carrying. All of the small "comfort items" from my Red Cross box were in it: the crosses, the playing cards, the paperback books, and even my dog bowl. I took down his mailing address, thanked him, and left. My ride back to Clarksville was inhabited by fresh ghosts.

I decided to write back to Firimbi and Dr. Kediye. I felt that both of them had done more for me than they had to. In my letter to Dr. Kediye, I included a copy of the X ray of my back, thinking that he'd be pleased to at last have his curiosity satisfied about that injury. I made copies of both letters, gave them to the Intel folks at Campbell, and sent them on to Mohamoud Iman. He called me some time later to tell me that my letters had been received, but I never heard from the Somalis again.

I did not write back to Mohamed Farrah Aidid. I didn't need any warlords as pen pals. In 1996, he would be assassinated by one of his own people, a victim of his own twisted concepts about national reunification.

And so I ran, throughout that year and on into the next. I set my sights on the Marine Corps Marathon of 1995, determined to achieve five goals: 1. finish the race; 2. beat Oprah's time (she ran it in 1994); 3. beat my 1992 time; 4. beat my battalion commander's time; and 5. qualify for the Boston Marathon. I figured that if I could reach four out of five of those goals, it would be difficult for the Army to claim that I was no longer fit to fly helicopters. Eventually, I had to undergo another round of surgeries to remove the steel rod from my leg. The operation set me back, but not for long, and I was out running on the roads again within a month.

Yet even while I was healing, there were other "veterans" of Somalia who would never fully recover. The scars of combat, both physical and mental, remain with soldiers forever, but their families also suffer the traumas of warfare. One of those casualties was my marriage. My wife and I had another baby, a beautiful girl named Taylor, but we were never able to be together as we had once been before Somalia. And even though I was firmly committed to the sanctity of marriage, we would eventually divorce.

In March of 1996, one of our Night Stalkers, a fine Chinook pilot named Pierre desRoches, was killed in a training accident along with the entire crew of his MH-47E. Ironically, he wasn't flying the bird at the time, but sitting in the jump seat while a Night Stalker candidate was going through his check ride. Pierre was married at the time to a woman named Lisa.

Lisa desRoches had herself been an army helicopter pilot. Like Jane Jollota, she had been a company commander in the 101st and had hundreds of hours flying Hueys. She had also gone through jump school at Fort Benning and was airborne qualified. But she and Pierre had decided that having one full-time helo pilot in the family was enough. After nearly ten years of service, Lisa had left the army in order to care for her sons Joey and Christopher, and she was nine months pregnant with their daughter, Dena, when Pierre's Chinook crashed one stormy night in a wheat field in Kentucky. Suddenly she was a widow, a member of the Gold Star Wives Club, a single mother with three children. At the time, I did not know her, but Pierre and I had been discussing some training issues over at Fort Campbell. After his funeral, when his personal effects were delivered to Lisa at home, among the family photographs and manuals from his desk there was a Post-it note to Pierre inside that said, "Call Mike Durant."

By the spring of 2000, I was a full-time chief warrant officer again, and I also had full custody of my two children. It wasn't easy, but my kids were and are the most important people in my life. When I wasn't working or flying, I was a soccer coach, and Lisa was a soccer mom. Her son Christopher and my son Joey both ended up on my team roster. We met at one of the games. She was a beautiful young woman with sandy hair, sparkling green eyes, a warm laugh, and a demeanor that hinted at nothing she had been through. After some time, she told me about the note from me that had appeared at her door along with Pierre's effects. By that time, I had become a man who believes in omens.

We were married in the spring of 2001, and I retired from the Army after twenty-one and a half years of service. We have a house full of children and memories. And while we do look back, we never stare.

I no longer fly helicopters for a living, but I do get behind the controls whenever someone offers me the opportunity, which is often, but not nearly enough for me. I am now an employee of NLX Corporation, a technology company that specializes in flight simulators and aviation training. I am often asked to speak about my experiences in Somalia to all sorts of groups, both military and civilian. Some of the military conferences are classified, and that's where I share my opinions about both the good and bad aspects of our efforts in Operation Gothic Serpent, and how we might improve things on a tactical level. In general, my emphasis is never to underestimate the enemy's capability or willingness to fight.

When speaking to military helicopter pilots, I invariably encourage them to make sure to carry all the ammunition and water they can, including grenades and whatever else they can get their hands on. I remind them that in the space of thirty minutes, I ran out of ammunition *twice* in the middle of a firefight. As an aviator, if you need your weapon, odds are you aren't flying anymore, so you ought to take along whatever your customer has in his basic combat load.

He's looked at the threat and knows what he needs to counter it, and it's wise to emulate him.

Having lost many friends in combat and training, and seen their families suffer, I emphasize to military organizations the superb notification and support model of the 160th SOAR(A). Some military branches tend to support the wives and families of the fallen for a while, and then just fade away. But the Night Stalkers are always there for the Gold Star Families, no matter how many years pass. They're there to worry about the kids, the medical bills, and the leaky pipes in the basement. Bereaved families, no matter how much they have healed or how far away they've moved, are included and invited to every memorial ceremony, every picnic, every Night Stalker event. Long after taps have been played, the Night Stalkers will be there.

I am often asked to speak at leadership conferences, and I have distilled my thoughts to just a few key points on that subject:

Trust and empower your people to do their jobs, then stand behind them. Unless they are absolute lowlifes, always, even when they screw up, go to bat for them. However, also call a spade a spade. Supporting your people doesn't mean carrying the deadweight. If there are stellar performers and nonperformers, make it obvious that you know the difference and reflect that in mission taskings and performance evaluations. In a military situation, be dedicated to your people, the mission, and the customer first and foremost, and only then to yourself and your career. And then I always emphasize a quote from Colin Powell that I think summarizes the leadership failure with regard to Somalia: "The Commander in the field is always right and the rear echelon is always wrong, unless proven otherwise." In other words, if you are going to overrule decisions or requests from the field, you damn well better have done your homework.

I try to say "yes" to as many of these invitations as I can, because if my experiences can help just one man, woman, or child, then I feel that it's well worth my time and effort. With young people in particular, I try to emphasize the fact that we must never give up, regardless of what happens to us. My point is that life is ten percent circumstance and ninety percent how we deal with it. In other words, it's all about attitude. If we make positive decisions on the parts of our lives that we can influence, then the rest will fall into place. I use my personal experience as an example, and of course, these appearances give me the opportunity to honor my fallen comrades.

In honoring these men, I always remind my listeners that I probably would not have survived if not for a soldier named Gary Gordon and his friend Randy Shughart, who were both posthumously awarded the Congressional Medal of Honor for their heroic actions in Mogadishu. In 1994, I myself was reminded that such men are not just born with these qualities of courage but are at times inspired to emulate them. I had been invited to Gary Gordon's hometown of Lincoln, Maine, to participate in honoring his memory with a ceremony and monument to his courage and professionalism. In order to prepare some remarks for my statement, I got a book on the Medal of Honor from the local library. The book was full of interesting historical facts, and its record of heroic deeds was quite overwhelming. But when I got to the back of the book, what I found truly astounded me. There, located in a small pocket, was the library checkout card. Apparently, the book had been checked out only a few times since its publication, and the last reader had taken it home almost twenty years before. The last person to sign out that book on the Congressional Medal of Honor would in fact become the next recipient of our nation's highest military award, a young teenager named Gary Gordon.

And any time I'm ever near Fort Campbell, I make a personal stop at the wall. There is a memorial wall on the Night Stalker compound, filled with many names. Far too many names. As of this writing, the 160th alone has lost another thirteen soldiers in the war on terrorism. It serves as a silent reminder of the price we pay for living at the point of the spear and as a place to gather to remember our fallen comrades.

Some of us from Somalia and Panama and Iraq can still attend our memorial ceremonies. Some of us cannot. To add to the tragic losses suffered in combat operations, Lance Hill was killed in the crash of an Army C-12 aircraft in Germany. Mike Goffena died in a light plane crash in Florida. Herb Rodriguez eventually retired from the Army, and Trey Williams quietly left the service. Gerry Izzo retired and flies commercial jets for Comair, and Jim Yacone commands the helos of the FBI's Hostage Rescue Team. Many others with whom I served are still at the point of that spear.

On one of those somber days, a few years ago, with the sounds of helos in the air, each of us spoke on behalf of one of our fallen friends. And I was honored to share my personal memories of Cliff Wolcott, to remind us all of his sly smile, the signature tilt of his head, his Blackhawk *Velvet Elvis*, his love for his family, the glint in his eye, and how he could sell coolers to Eskimos.

But I am getting ahead of myself.

I did run that Marine Corps Marathon in 1995 and achieved four out of five of my goals—I didn't qualify for the Boston Marathon, but I blew past Oprah's time, beat mine and my battalion commander's personal best, and finished ahead of all my comrades but one. That accomplishment did convince the Army leadership that I was physically fit enough to fly helicopters, and eventually I became a full-time Night Stalker again. I worked in the SIMO office at Fort Campbell, which I know would have pleased Cliff, although I'd proceeded down a path that did not involve flying, in the event my plan to regain flight status did not become a reality.

But my waiver packet wasn't going to go anywhere until I proved that I could still fly. It would be just fine if I could run forever and beat half my buds in a footrace, but unless I could get myself into a Blackhawk cockpit and perform like a Night Stalker, the discussions about getting back my old job were going to end right there.

It was a beautiful June day when I geared myself up, for the first time in a long time. I was confident, but not cocky. I wasn't nervous, but I was hopeful. I hadn't been in the cockpit for nearly a year, but it was as if I had flown just the day before. My hands and feet had memories of their own, and as we lifted off, I thought about Donovan and Cliff, about Ray and Tommy and Bill, and I was going to make them proud.

We took off into a beautiful blue sky, the wind was cool and rushing through the cockpit. Sitting next to me was an instructor pilot, whose job it was to evaluate my performance. It was Dan. We hardly spoke, and we didn't have to. I looked at him and grinned, and he nodded back, and we both turned our eyes to the sun and clouds.

I was flying again, with my friend who had promised me from the skies above Mogadishu. . . .

"Mike Durant. We will not leave without you."

Among the many tributes to the members of the special operations aviation community, there is one monument that stands alone. The Night Stalker memorial wall, an arrangement of three simple stones, is inscribed with the names of all members of the 160th Special Operations Aviation Regiment (Airborne) who have given their lives in service to our nation. The memorial is located in front of the regimental headquarters on the 160th compound at Fort Campbell, Kentucky, a short distance from the flight line, and the mission that these men lived and died for.

Then I heard the voice of the Lord saying,
"Whom shall I send? And who will go for us?"
And I said, "Here am I. Send me!"

—ISAIAH 6:8

NAMES INSCRIBED ON THE
NIGHT STALKER MEMORIAL WALL

1980

CW2 *Bobby M. Crumley*
SP4 *Timothy Hensley*

1981

CW3 *John W. Williams*
LTC *Michael C. Grimm*

1982

SGT *Ricky D. Zizelman*

1983

CW4 *Ralph L. Thompson*
CW2 *Donald R. Alvey*
SGT *Claude J. Dunn*
SP4 *Jerry L. Wilder*
PFC *Gregory D. Eichner*
CW4 *Larry K. Jones*
CW3 *Thomas B. Crossan III*
CW2 *James N. Jansen*
SSG *Mark J. Rielly*
SSG *Luis A. Sanchez*

SSG Mark D. Cornwell
CPT Robert E. Brannum
WO1 Allen E. Jennings
CW2 David W. Jordan
CW3 William H. Tuttle
SP4 Richard J. Thompson
CPT Keith J. Lucas

1985

1SG Ronnie R. Orebo

1987

CPT Frederick M. Maddock II

1988

CW3 Stephen A. Hansen
CW3 Jerry H. Landgraf

1989

1LT John R. Hunter
CW2 Wilson B. Owens

1991

CPT Charles W. Cooper
CW3 Michael F. Anderson
SSG Mario Vega-Velazquez
SSG Christopher J. Chapman

1993

MAJ Robert P. Mallory
CW4 Clifton P. Wolcott
CW3 Donovan L. Briley
CW4 Raymond A. Frank
SSG Thomas J. Field
SSG William D. Cleveland, Jr.

1994

CW3 Carlos P. Guerrero

1995

SSG Edwidge Pierre
SGT Jeffrey D. Tarbox

1996

CW5 Walter M. Fox
CW3 Pierre R. desRoches

CW3 William R. Monty, Jr.
SSG Tracy A. Tidwell
SSG Bradley C. Beem

1997

SGT Edward G. Palacio

2002

MAJ Curtis D. Feistner
CPT Bartt D. Owens
CW2 Jody L. Egnor
SSG James P. Dorrity
SSG Kerry W. Frith
SSG Bruce A. Rushforth, Jr.
SGT Jeremy D. Foshee
SGT Thomas F. Allison
SGT Philip J. Svitak

2003

CW3 Mark O'Steen
CW3 Thomas Gibbons
SSG Daniel Kisling
SGT Gregory Frampton

DELTA OPERATORS KIA
OPERATION GOTHIC SERPENT

MSG Gary Gordon
MSG Timothy Martin
SFC Earl Fillmore
SFC Matthew Rierson
SFC Randy Shughart
SSG Daniel Busch

Rangers KIA Operation Gothic Serpent

SGT James Joyce
SGT Lorenzo Ruiz
SGT Dominick Pilla
CPL James Cavaco
CPL James Smith
PFC Richard Kowalewski

10th Mountain Division KIA Operation
Gothic Serpent

SGT Cornell Houston
PFC James Martin

Michael J. Durant retired from the Army as a CW4 Blackhawk helicopter master aviator in the 160th SOAR (A), the Night Stalkers. He participated in combat operations Prime Chance, Just Cause, Desert Storm, and Gothic Serpent. His awards include the Distinguished Service Medal, Distinguished Flying Cross with Oak Leaf Cluster, Bronze Star with Valor Device, Purple Heart, Meritorious Service Medal, three Air Medals, POW/MIA ribbon, and numerous others. He and his wife Lisa have five children.

Steven Hartov is an Airborne veteran and author of the international thrillers *The Heat of Ramadan, The Nylon Hand of God,* and *The Devil's Shepherd.* His non-fiction has appeared in *Special Operations Quarterly, Counterstrike,* and *The Journal of International Security.* He has two fine sons.